C-4908   CAREER EXAMINATION SERIES

This is your
PASSBOOK for...

Social Work Supervisor I, II

Test Preparation Study Guide
Questions & Answers

COPYRIGHT NOTICE

This book is SOLELY intended for, is sold ONLY to, and its use is RESTRICTED to individual, bona fide applicants or candidates who qualify by virtue of having seriously filed applications for appropriate license, certificate, professional and/or promotional advancement, higher school matriculation, scholarship, or other legitimate requirements of education and/or governmental authorities.

This book is NOT intended for use, class instruction, tutoring, training, duplication, copying, reprinting, excerption, or adaptation, etc., by:

1) Other publishers
2) Proprietors and/or Instructors of "Coaching" and/or Preparatory Courses
3) Personnel and/or Training Divisions of commercial, industrial, and governmental organizations
4) Schools, colleges, or universities and/or their departments and staffs, including teachers and other personnel
5) Testing Agencies or Bureaus
6) Study groups which seek by the purchase of a single volume to copy and/or duplicate and/or adapt this material for use by the group as a whole without having purchased individual volumes for each of the members of the group
7) Et al.

Such persons would be in violation of appropriate Federal and State statutes.

PROVISION OF LICENSING AGREEMENTS – Recognized educational, commercial, industrial, and governmental institutions and organizations, and others legitimately engaged in educational pursuits, including training, testing, and measurement activities, may address request for a licensing agreement to the copyright owners, who will determine whether, and under what conditions, including fees and charges, the materials in this book may be used them. In other words, a licensing facility exists for the legitimate use of the material in this book on other than an individual basis. However, it is asseverated and affirmed here that the material in this book CANNOT be used without the receipt of the express permission of such a licensing agreement from the Publishers. Inquiries re licensing should be addressed to the company, attention rights and permissions department.

All rights reserved, including the right of reproduction in whole or in part, in any form or by any means, electronic or mechanical, including photocopying, recording, or by any information storage and retrieval system, without permission in writing from the Publisher.

Copyright © 2025 by
National Learning Corporation

212 Michael Drive, Syosset, NY 11791
(516) 921-8888 • www.passbooks.com
E-mail: info@passbooks.com

PASSBOOK® SERIES

THE *PASSBOOK® SERIES* has been created to prepare applicants and candidates for the ultimate academic battlefield – the examination room.

At some time in our lives, each and every one of us may be required to take an examination – for validation, matriculation, admission, qualification, registration, certification, or licensure.

Based on the assumption that every applicant or candidate has met the basic formal educational standards, has taken the required number of courses, and read the necessary texts, the *PASSBOOK® SERIES* furnishes the one special preparation which may assure passing with confidence, instead of failing with insecurity. Examination questions – together with answers – are furnished as the basic vehicle for study so that the mysteries of the examination and its compounding difficulties may be eliminated or diminished by a sure method.

This book is meant to help you pass your examination provided that you qualify and are serious in your objective.

The entire field is reviewed through the huge store of content information which is succinctly presented through a provocative and challenging approach – the question-and-answer method.

A climate of success is established by furnishing the correct answers at the end of each test.

You soon learn to recognize types of questions, forms of questions, and patterns of questioning. You may even begin to anticipate expected outcomes.

You perceive that many questions are repeated or adapted so that you can gain acute insights, which may enable you to score many sure points.

You learn how to confront new questions, or types of questions, and to attack them confidently and work out the correct answers.

You note objectives and emphases, and recognize pitfalls and dangers, so that you may make positive educational adjustments.

Moreover, you are kept fully informed in relation to new concepts, methods, practices, and directions in the field.

You discover that you are actually taking the examination all the time: you are preparing for the examination by "taking" an examination, not by reading extraneous and/or supererogatory textbooks.

In short, this PASSBOOK®, used directedly, should be an important factor in helping you to pass your test.

SOCIAL WORK SUPERVISOR I, II

DUTIES:

As a Social Work Supervisor I (Licensed Clinical Social Worker), you would be responsible for administrative and clinical supervision of professional and paraprofessional social work staff. In addition, you may oversee a social work department's administrative and reporting functions, including fiscal, human resources, program statistical, reports and other support services.

As a Social Work Supervisor II (Licensed Clinical Social Worker), you would direct a social work program or department. In addition, you may perform all the duties and activities of a Social Work Supervisor I (Licensed Clinical Social Worker).

SUBJECT OF EXAMINATION:

The written test is designed to test for knowledge, skills, and/or abilities in such areas as:

1. **Developing & implementing treatment in a social work program** - These questions test for knowledge, understanding, and ability to apply social work concepts, theories, standards, principles, and practices in various settings. Questions may cover such topics as assessment, development, implementation, monitoring and evaluation of treatment for individuals and families; coordination of services; advocacy and counseling for individuals and families of all backgrounds; and crisis intervention.
2. **Educating and interacting with the public** - These questions test for knowledge of techniques used to interact effectively with individuals and/or community groups, to educate or inform them about topics of concern, to publicize or clarify agency programs or policies, to negotiate conflicts or resolve complaints, and to represent one's agency or program in a manner in keeping with good public relations practices. Questions may also cover interacting with others in cooperative efforts of public outreach or service.
3. **Preparing reports and official documents** - These questions test for the ability to prepare reports and other official documents for use within and among governmental agencies, in legal or regulatory settings, or for dissemination to the public. Some questions test for a knowledge of grammar, usage, punctuation, and sentence structure. Others test for the ability to present information clearly and accurately, to use the proper tone, and to organize paragraphs logically and comprehensibly.
4. **Social work program oversight** - These questions test for knowledge and ability required to manage and direct a social services program in a variety of settings. Questions may include planning, implementing, monitoring and evaluating programs and services; case consultation and training; interpreting and applying various laws, regulations and standards; developing and implementing relevant policies and procedures; and maintaining organizational effectiveness and efficiency.
5. **Supervision** - These questions test for knowledge of the principles and practices employed in planning, organizing, and controlling the activities of a work unit toward predetermined objectives. The concepts covered, usually in a situational question format, include such topics as assigning and reviewing work; evaluating performance; maintaining work standards; motivating and developing subordinates; implementing procedural change; increasing efficiency; and dealing with problems of absenteeism, morale, and discipline.
6. **Administrative supervision** - These questions test for knowledge of the principles and practices involved in directing the activities of a large subordinate staff, including subordinate supervisors. Questions relate to the personal interactions between an upper level supervisor and his/her subordinate supervisors in the accomplishment of objectives. These questions cover such areas as assigning work to and coordinating the activities of several units, establishing and guiding staff development programs, evaluating the performance of subordinate supervisors, and maintaining relationships with other organizational sections.

HOW TO TAKE A TEST

I. YOU MUST PASS AN EXAMINATION

A. WHAT EVERY CANDIDATE SHOULD KNOW

Examination applicants often ask us for help in preparing for the written test. What can I study in advance? What kinds of questions will be asked? How will the test be given? How will the papers be graded?

As an applicant for a civil service examination, you may be wondering about some of these things. Our purpose here is to suggest effective methods of advance study and to describe civil service examinations.

Your chances for success on this examination can be increased if you know how to prepare. Those "pre-examination jitters" can be reduced if you know what to expect. You can even experience an adventure in good citizenship if you know why civil service exams are given.

B. WHY ARE CIVIL SERVICE EXAMINATIONS GIVEN?

Civil service examinations are important to you in two ways. As a citizen, you want public jobs filled by employees who know how to do their work. As a job seeker, you want a fair chance to compete for that job on an equal footing with other candidates. The best-known means of accomplishing this two-fold goal is the competitive examination.

Exams are widely publicized throughout the nation. They may be administered for jobs in federal, state, city, municipal, town or village governments or agencies.

Any citizen may apply, with some limitations, such as the age or residence of applicants. Your experience and education may be reviewed to see whether you meet the requirements for the particular examination. When these requirements exist, they are reasonable and applied consistently to all applicants. Thus, a competitive examination may cause you some uneasiness now, but it is your privilege and safeguard.

C. HOW ARE CIVIL SERVICE EXAMS DEVELOPED?

Examinations are carefully written by trained technicians who are specialists in the field known as "psychological measurement," in consultation with recognized authorities in the field of work that the test will cover. These experts recommend the subject matter areas or skills to be tested; only those knowledges or skills important to your success on the job are included. The most reliable books and source materials available are used as references. Together, the experts and technicians judge the difficulty level of the questions.

Test technicians know how to phrase questions so that the problem is clearly stated. Their ethics do not permit "trick" or "catch" questions. Questions may have been tried out on sample groups, or subjected to statistical analysis, to determine their usefulness.

Written tests are often used in combination with performance tests, ratings of training and experience, and oral interviews. All of these measures combine to form the best-known means of finding the right person for the right job.

II. HOW TO PASS THE WRITTEN TEST

A. NATURE OF THE EXAMINATION

To prepare intelligently for civil service examinations, you should know how they differ from school examinations you have taken. In school you were assigned certain definite pages to read or subjects to cover. The examination questions were quite detailed and usually emphasized memory. Civil service exams, on the other hand, try to discover your present ability to perform the duties of a position, plus your potentiality to learn these duties. In other words, a civil service exam attempts to predict how successful you will be. Questions cover such a broad area that they cannot be as minute and detailed as school exam questions.

In the public service similar kinds of work, or positions, are grouped together in one "class." This process is known as *position-classification*. All the positions in a class are paid according to the salary range for that class. One class title covers all of these positions, and they are all tested by the same examination.

B. FOUR BASIC STEPS

1) Study the announcement

How, then, can you know what subjects to study? Our best answer is: "Learn as much as possible about the class of positions for which you've applied." The exam will test the knowledge, skills and abilities needed to do the work.

Your most valuable source of information about the position you want is the official exam announcement. This announcement lists the training and experience qualifications. Check these standards and apply only if you come reasonably close to meeting them.

The brief description of the position in the examination announcement offers some clues to the subjects which will be tested. Think about the job itself. Review the duties in your mind. Can you perform them, or are there some in which you are rusty? Fill in the blank spots in your preparation.

Many jurisdictions preview the written test in the exam announcement by including a section called "Knowledge and Abilities Required," "Scope of the Examination," or some similar heading. Here you will find out specifically what fields will be tested.

2) Review your own background

Once you learn in general what the position is all about, and what you need to know to do the work, ask yourself which subjects you already know fairly well and which need improvement. You may wonder whether to concentrate on improving your strong areas or on building some background in your fields of weakness. When the announcement has specified "some knowledge" or "considerable knowledge," or has used adjectives like "beginning principles of…" or "advanced … methods," you can get a clue as to the number and difficulty of questions to be asked in any given field. More questions, and hence broader coverage, would be included for those subjects which are more important in the work. Now weigh your strengths and weaknesses against the job requirements and prepare accordingly.

3) Determine the level of the position

Another way to tell how intensively you should prepare is to understand the level of the job for which you are applying. Is it the entering level? In other words, is this the position in which beginners in a field of work are hired? Or is it an intermediate or advanced level? Sometimes this is indicated by such words as "Junior" or "Senior" in the class title. Other jurisdictions use Roman numerals to designate the level – Clerk I, Clerk II, for example. The word "Supervisor" sometimes appears in the title. If the level is not indicated by the title, check the description of duties. Will you be working under very close supervision, or will you have responsibility for independent decisions in this work?

4) Choose appropriate study materials

Now that you know the subjects to be examined and the relative amount of each subject to be covered, you can choose suitable study materials. For beginning level jobs, or even advanced ones, if you have a pronounced weakness in some aspect of your training, read a modern, standard textbook in that field. Be sure it is up to date and has general coverage. Such books are normally available at your library, and the librarian will be glad to help you locate one. For entry-level positions, questions of appropriate difficulty are chosen – neither highly advanced questions, nor those too simple. Such questions require careful thought but not advanced training.

If the position for which you are applying is technical or advanced, you will read more advanced, specialized material. If you are already familiar with the basic principles of your field, elementary textbooks would waste your time. Concentrate on advanced textbooks and technical periodicals. Think through the concepts and review difficult problems in your field.

These are all general sources. You can get more ideas on your own initiative, following these leads. For example, training manuals and publications of the government agency which employs workers in your field can be useful, particularly for technical and professional positions. A letter or visit to the government department involved may result in more specific study suggestions, and certainly will provide you with a more definite idea of the exact nature of the position you are seeking.

III. KINDS OF TESTS

Tests are used for purposes other than measuring knowledge and ability to perform specified duties. For some positions, it is equally important to test ability to make adjustments to new situations or to profit from training. In others, basic mental abilities not dependent on information are essential. Questions which test these things may not appear as pertinent to the duties of the position as those which test for knowledge and information. Yet they are often highly important parts of a fair examination. For very general questions, it is almost impossible to help you direct your study efforts. What we can do is to point out some of the more common of these general abilities needed in public service positions and describe some typical questions.

1) General information

Broad, general information has been found useful for predicting job success in some kinds of work. This is tested in a variety of ways, from vocabulary lists to questions about current events. Basic background in some field of work, such as sociology or economics, may be sampled in a group of questions. Often these are principles which have become familiar to most persons through exposure rather than through formal training. It is difficult to advise you how to study for these questions; being alert to the world around you is our best suggestion.

2) Verbal ability

An example of an ability needed in many positions is verbal or language ability. Verbal ability is, in brief, the ability to use and understand words. Vocabulary and grammar tests are typical measures of this ability. Reading comprehension or paragraph interpretation questions are common in many kinds of civil service tests. You are given a paragraph of written material and asked to find its central meaning.

3) Numerical ability

Number skills can be tested by the familiar arithmetic problem, by checking paired lists of numbers to see which are alike and which are different, or by interpreting charts and graphs. In the latter test, a graph may be printed in the test booklet which you are asked to use as the basis for answering questions.

4) Observation

A popular test for law-enforcement positions is the observation test. A picture is shown to you for several minutes, then taken away. Questions about the picture test your ability to observe both details and larger elements.

5) Following directions

In many positions in the public service, the employee must be able to carry out written instructions dependably and accurately. You may be given a chart with several columns, each column listing a variety of information. The questions require you to carry out directions involving the information given in the chart.

6) Skills and aptitudes

Performance tests effectively measure some manual skills and aptitudes. When the skill is one in which you are trained, such as typing or shorthand, you can practice. These tests are often very much like those given in business school or high school courses. For many of the other skills and aptitudes, however, no short-time preparation can be made. Skills and abilities natural to you or that you have developed throughout your lifetime are being tested.

Many of the general questions just described provide all the data needed to answer the questions and ask you to use your reasoning ability to find the answers. Your best preparation for these tests, as well as for tests of facts and ideas, is to be at your physical and mental best. You, no doubt, have your own methods of getting into an exam-taking mood and keeping "in shape." The next section lists some ideas on this subject.

IV. KINDS OF QUESTIONS

Only rarely is the "essay" question, which you answer in narrative form, used in civil service tests. Civil service tests are usually of the short-answer type. Full instructions for answering these questions will be given to you at the examination. But in case this is your first experience with short-answer questions and separate answer sheets, here is what you need to know:

1) Multiple-choice Questions

Most popular of the short-answer questions is the "multiple choice" or "best answer" question. It can be used, for example, to test for factual knowledge, ability to solve problems or judgment in meeting situations found at work.

A multiple-choice question is normally one of three types—

- It can begin with an incomplete statement followed by several possible endings. You are to find the one ending which *best* completes the statement, although some of the others may not be entirely wrong.
- It can also be a complete statement in the form of a question which is answered by choosing one of the statements listed.

- It can be in the form of a problem – again you select the best answer.

Here is an example of a multiple-choice question with a discussion which should give you some clues as to the method for choosing the right answer:

When an employee has a complaint about his assignment, the action which will *best* help him overcome his difficulty is to
   A. discuss his difficulty with his coworkers
   B. take the problem to the head of the organization
   C. take the problem to the person who gave him the assignment
   D. say nothing to anyone about his complaint

In answering this question, you should study each of the choices to find which is best. Consider choice "A" – Certainly an employee may discuss his complaint with fellow employees, but no change or improvement can result, and the complaint remains unresolved. Choice "B" is a poor choice since the head of the organization probably does not know what assignment you have been given, and taking your problem to him is known as "going over the head" of the supervisor. The supervisor, or person who made the assignment, is the person who can clarify it or correct any injustice. Choice "C" is, therefore, correct. To say nothing, as in choice "D," is unwise. Supervisors have and interest in knowing the problems employees are facing, and the employee is seeking a solution to his problem.

2) True/False Questions

The "true/false" or "right/wrong" form of question is sometimes used. Here a complete statement is given. Your job is to decide whether the statement is right or wrong.

SAMPLE: A roaming cell-phone call to a nearby city costs less than a non-roaming call to a distant city.

This statement is wrong, or false, since roaming calls are more expensive.

This is not a complete list of all possible question forms, although most of the others are variations of these common types. You will always get complete directions for answering questions. Be sure you understand *how* to mark your answers – ask questions until you do.

V. RECORDING YOUR ANSWERS

Computer terminals are used more and more today for many different kinds of exams.
For an examination with very few applicants, you may be told to record your answers in the test booklet itself. Separate answer sheets are much more common. If this separate answer sheet is to be scored by machine – and this is often the case – it is highly important that you mark your answers correctly in order to get credit.
An electronic scoring machine is often used in civil service offices because of the speed with which papers can be scored. Machine-scored answer sheets must be marked with a pencil, which will be given to you. This pencil has a high graphite content which responds to the electronic scoring machine. As a matter of fact, stray dots may register as answers, so do not let your pencil rest on the answer sheet while you are pondering the correct answer. Also, if your pencil lead breaks or is otherwise defective, ask for another.

Since the answer sheet will be dropped in a slot in the scoring machine, be careful not to bend the corners or get the paper crumpled.

The answer sheet normally has five vertical columns of numbers, with 30 numbers to a column. These numbers correspond to the question numbers in your test booklet. After each number, going across the page are four or five pairs of dotted lines. These short dotted lines have small letters or numbers above them. The first two pairs may also have a "T" or "F" above the letters. This indicates that the first two pairs only are to be used if the questions are of the true-false type. If the questions are multiple choice, disregard the "T" and "F" and pay attention only to the small letters or numbers.

Answer your questions in the manner of the sample that follows:

32. The largest city in the United States is
    A. Washington, D.C.
    B. New York City
    C. Chicago
    D. Detroit
    E. San Francisco

1) Choose the answer you think is best. (New York City is the largest, so "B" is correct.)
2) Find the row of dotted lines numbered the same as the question you are answering. (Find row number 32)
3) Find the pair of dotted lines corresponding to the answer. (Find the pair of lines under the mark "B.")
4) Make a solid black mark between the dotted lines.

VI. BEFORE THE TEST

Common sense will help you find procedures to follow to get ready for an examination. Too many of us, however, overlook these sensible measures. Indeed, nervousness and fatigue have been found to be the most serious reasons why applicants fail to do their best on civil service tests. Here is a list of reminders:

- Begin your preparation early – Don't wait until the last minute to go scurrying around for books and materials or to find out what the position is all about.
- Prepare continuously – An hour a night for a week is better than an all-night cram session. This has been definitely established. What is more, a night a week for a month will return better dividends than crowding your study into a shorter period of time.
- Locate the place of the exam – You have been sent a notice telling you when and where to report for the examination. If the location is in a different town or otherwise unfamiliar to you, it would be well to inquire the best route and learn something about the building.
- Relax the night before the test – Allow your mind to rest. Do not study at all that night. Plan some mild recreation or diversion; then go to bed early and get a good night's sleep.
- Get up early enough to make a leisurely trip to the place for the test – This way unforeseen events, traffic snarls, unfamiliar buildings, etc. will not upset you.
- Dress comfortably – A written test is not a fashion show. You will be known by number and not by name, so wear something comfortable.

- Leave excess paraphernalia at home – Shopping bags and odd bundles will get in your way. You need bring only the items mentioned in the official notice you received; usually everything you need is provided. Do not bring reference books to the exam. They will only confuse those last minutes and be taken away from you when in the test room.
- Arrive somewhat ahead of time – If because of transportation schedules you must get there very early, bring a newspaper or magazine to take your mind off yourself while waiting.
- Locate the examination room – When you have found the proper room, you will be directed to the seat or part of the room where you will sit. Sometimes you are given a sheet of instructions to read while you are waiting. Do not fill out any forms until you are told to do so; just read them and be prepared.
- Relax and prepare to listen to the instructions
- If you have any physical problem that may keep you from doing your best, be sure to tell the test administrator. If you are sick or in poor health, you really cannot do your best on the exam. You can come back and take the test some other time.

VII. AT THE TEST

The day of the test is here and you have the test booklet in your hand. The temptation to get going is very strong. Caution! There is more to success than knowing the right answers. You must know how to identify your papers and understand variations in the type of short-answer question used in this particular examination. Follow these suggestions for maximum results from your efforts:

1) Cooperate with the monitor

The test administrator has a duty to create a situation in which you can be as much at ease as possible. He will give instructions, tell you when to begin, check to see that you are marking your answer sheet correctly, and so on. He is not there to guard you, although he will see that your competitors do not take unfair advantage. He wants to help you do your best.

2) Listen to all instructions

Don't jump the gun! Wait until you understand all directions. In most civil service tests you get more time than you need to answer the questions. So don't be in a hurry. Read each word of instructions until you clearly understand the meaning. Study the examples, listen to all announcements and follow directions. Ask questions if you do not understand what to do.

3) Identify your papers

Civil service exams are usually identified by number only. You will be assigned a number; you must not put your name on your test papers. Be sure to copy your number correctly. Since more than one exam may be given, copy your exact examination title.

4) Plan your time

Unless you are told that a test is a "speed" or "rate of work" test, speed itself is usually not important. Time enough to answer all the questions will be provided, but this does not mean that you have all day. An overall time limit has been set. Divide the total time (in minutes) by the number of questions to determine the approximate time you have for each question.

5) Do not linger over difficult questions

If you come across a difficult question, mark it with a paper clip (useful to have along) and come back to it when you have been through the booklet. One caution if you do this – be sure to skip a number on your answer sheet as well. Check often to be sure that you have not lost your place and that you are marking in the row numbered the same as the question you are answering.

6) Read the questions

Be sure you know what the question asks! Many capable people are unsuccessful because they failed to *read* the questions correctly.

7) Answer all questions

Unless you have been instructed that a penalty will be deducted for incorrect answers, it is better to guess than to omit a question.

8) Speed tests

It is often better NOT to guess on speed tests. It has been found that on timed tests people are tempted to spend the last few seconds before time is called in marking answers at random – without even reading them – in the hope of picking up a few extra points. To discourage this practice, the instructions may warn you that your score will be "corrected" for guessing. That is, a penalty will be applied. The incorrect answers will be deducted from the correct ones, or some other penalty formula will be used.

9) Review your answers

If you finish before time is called, go back to the questions you guessed or omitted to give them further thought. Review other answers if you have time.

10) Return your test materials

If you are ready to leave before others have finished or time is called, take ALL your materials to the monitor and leave quietly. Never take any test material with you. The monitor can discover whose papers are not complete, and taking a test booklet may be grounds for disqualification.

VIII. EXAMINATION TECHNIQUES

1) Read the general instructions carefully. These are usually printed on the first page of the exam booklet. As a rule, these instructions refer to the timing of the examination; the fact that you should not start work until the signal and must stop work at a signal, etc. If there are any *special* instructions, such as a choice of questions to be answered, make sure that you note this instruction carefully.

2) When you are ready to start work on the examination, that is as soon as the signal has been given, read the instructions to each question booklet, underline any key words or phrases, such as *least, best, outline, describe* and the like. In this way you will tend to answer as requested rather than discover on reviewing your paper that you *listed without describing*, that you selected the *worst* choice rather than the *best* choice, etc.

3) If the examination is of the objective or multiple-choice type – that is, each question will also give a series of possible answers: A, B, C or D, and you are called upon to select the best answer and write the letter next to that answer on your answer paper – it is advisable to start answering each question in turn. There may be anywhere from 50 to 100 such questions in the three or four hours allotted and you can see how much time would be taken if you read through all the questions before beginning to answer any. Furthermore, if you come across a question or group of questions which you know would be difficult to answer, it would undoubtedly affect your handling of all the other questions.

4) If the examination is of the essay type and contains but a few questions, it is a moot point as to whether you should read all the questions before starting to answer any one. Of course, if you are given a choice – say five out of seven and the like – then it is essential to read all the questions so you can eliminate the two that are most difficult. If, however, you are asked to answer all the questions, there may be danger in trying to answer the easiest one first because you may find that you will spend too much time on it. The best technique is to answer the first question, then proceed to the second, etc.

5) Time your answers. Before the exam begins, write down the time it started, then add the time allowed for the examination and write down the time it must be completed, then divide the time available somewhat as follows:
    - If 3-1/2 hours are allowed, that would be 210 minutes. If you have 80 objective-type questions, that would be an average of 2-1/2 minutes per question. Allow yourself no more than 2 minutes per question, or a total of 160 minutes, which will permit about 50 minutes to review.
    - If for the time allotment of 210 minutes there are 7 essay questions to answer, that would average about 30 minutes a question. Give yourself only 25 minutes per question so that you have about 35 minutes to review.

6) The most important instruction is to *read each question* and make sure you know what is wanted. The second most important instruction is to *time yourself properly* so that you answer every question. The third most important instruction is to *answer every question*. Guess if you have to but include something for each question. Remember that you will receive no credit for a blank and will probably receive some credit if you write something in answer to an essay question. If you guess a letter – say "B" for a multiple-choice question – you may have guessed right. If you leave a blank as an answer to a multiple-choice question, the examiners may respect your feelings but it will not add a point to your score. Some exams may penalize you for wrong answers, so in such cases *only*, you may not want to guess unless you have some basis for your answer.

7) Suggestions
    a. Objective-type questions
        1. Examine the question booklet for proper sequence of pages and questions
        2. Read all instructions carefully
        3. Skip any question which seems too difficult; return to it after all other questions have been answered
        4. Apportion your time properly; do not spend too much time on any single question or group of questions

5. Note and underline key words – *all, most, fewest, least, best, worst, same, opposite*, etc.
6. Pay particular attention to negatives
7. Note unusual option, e.g., unduly long, short, complex, different or similar in content to the body of the question
8. Observe the use of "hedging" words – *probably, may, most likely,* etc.
9. Make sure that your answer is put next to the same number as the question
10. Do not second-guess unless you have good reason to believe the second answer is definitely more correct
11. Cross out original answer if you decide another answer is more accurate; do not erase until you are ready to hand your paper in
12. Answer all questions; guess unless instructed otherwise
13. Leave time for review

b. Essay questions
1. Read each question carefully
2. Determine exactly what is wanted. Underline key words or phrases.
3. Decide on outline or paragraph answer
4. Include many different points and elements unless asked to develop any one or two points or elements
5. Show impartiality by giving pros and cons unless directed to select one side only
6. Make and write down any assumptions you find necessary to answer the questions
7. Watch your English, grammar, punctuation and choice of words
8. Time your answers; don't crowd material

8) Answering the essay question

Most essay questions can be answered by framing the specific response around several key words or ideas. Here are a few such key words or ideas:

M's: manpower, materials, methods, money, management
P's: purpose, program, policy, plan, procedure, practice, problems, pitfalls, personnel, public relations

a. Six basic steps in handling problems:
1. Preliminary plan and background development
2. Collect information, data and facts
3. Analyze and interpret information, data and facts
4. Analyze and develop solutions as well as make recommendations
5. Prepare report and sell recommendations
6. Install recommendations and follow up effectiveness

b. Pitfalls to avoid
1. *Taking things for granted* – A statement of the situation does not necessarily imply that each of the elements is necessarily true; for example, a complaint may be invalid and biased so that all that can be taken for granted is that a complaint has been registered

2. *Considering only one side of a situation* – Wherever possible, indicate several alternatives and then point out the reasons you selected the best one
3. *Failing to indicate follow up* – Whenever your answer indicates action on your part, make certain that you will take proper follow-up action to see how successful your recommendations, procedures or actions turn out to be
4. *Taking too long in answering any single question* – Remember to time your answers properly

IX. AFTER THE TEST

Scoring procedures differ in detail among civil service jurisdictions although the general principles are the same. Whether the papers are hand-scored or graded by machine we have described, they are nearly always graded by number. That is, the person who marks the paper knows only the number – never the name – of the applicant. Not until all the papers have been graded will they be matched with names. If other tests, such as training and experience or oral interview ratings have been given, scores will be combined. Different parts of the examination usually have different weights. For example, the written test might count 60 percent of the final grade, and a rating of training and experience 40 percent. In many jurisdictions, veterans will have a certain number of points added to their grades.

After the final grade has been determined, the names are placed in grade order and an eligible list is established. There are various methods for resolving ties between those who get the same final grade – probably the most common is to place first the name of the person whose application was received first. Job offers are made from the eligible list in the order the names appear on it. You will be notified of your grade and your rank as soon as all these computations have been made. This will be done as rapidly as possible.

People who are found to meet the requirements in the announcement are called "eligibles." Their names are put on a list of eligible candidates. An eligible's chances of getting a job depend on how high he stands on this list and how fast agencies are filling jobs from the list.

When a job is to be filled from a list of eligibles, the agency asks for the names of people on the list of eligibles for that job. When the civil service commission receives this request, it sends to the agency the names of the three people highest on this list. Or, if the job to be filled has specialized requirements, the office sends the agency the names of the top three persons who meet these requirements from the general list.

The appointing officer makes a choice from among the three people whose names were sent to him. If the selected person accepts the appointment, the names of the others are put back on the list to be considered for future openings.

That is the rule in hiring from all kinds of eligible lists, whether they are for typist, carpenter, chemist, or something else. For every vacancy, the appointing officer has his choice of any one of the top three eligibles on the list. This explains why the person whose name is on top of the list sometimes does not get an appointment when some of the persons lower on the list do. If the appointing officer chooses the second or third eligible, the No. 1 eligible does not get a job at once, but stays on the list until he is appointed or the list is terminated.

X. HOW TO PASS THE INTERVIEW TEST

The examination for which you applied requires an oral interview test. You have already taken the written test and you are now being called for the interview test – the final part of the formal examination.

You may think that it is not possible to prepare for an interview test and that there are no procedures to follow during an interview. Our purpose is to point out some things you can do in advance that will help you and some good rules to follow and pitfalls to avoid while you are being interviewed.

What is an interview supposed to test?

The written examination is designed to test the technical knowledge and competence of the candidate; the oral is designed to evaluate intangible qualities, not readily measured otherwise, and to establish a list showing the relative fitness of each candidate – as measured against his competitors – for the position sought. Scoring is not on the basis of "right" and "wrong," but on a sliding scale of values ranging from "not passable" to "outstanding." As a matter of fact, it is possible to achieve a relatively low score without a single "incorrect" answer because of evident weakness in the qualities being measured.

Occasionally, an examination may consist entirely of an oral test – either an individual or a group oral. In such cases, information is sought concerning the technical knowledges and abilities of the candidate, since there has been no written examination for this purpose. More commonly, however, an oral test is used to supplement a written examination.

Who conducts interviews?

The composition of oral boards varies among different jurisdictions. In nearly all, a representative of the personnel department serves as chairman. One of the members of the board may be a representative of the department in which the candidate would work. In some cases, "outside experts" are used, and, frequently, a businessman or some other representative of the general public is asked to serve. Labor and management or other special groups may be represented. The aim is to secure the services of experts in the appropriate field.

However the board is composed, it is a good idea (and not at all improper or unethical) to ascertain in advance of the interview who the members are and what groups they represent. When you are introduced to them, you will have some idea of their backgrounds and interests, and at least you will not stutter and stammer over their names.

What should be done before the interview?

While knowledge about the board members is useful and takes some of the surprise element out of the interview, there is other preparation which is more substantive. It *is* possible to prepare for an oral interview – in several ways:

1) Keep a copy of your application and review it carefully before the interview

This may be the only document before the oral board, and the starting point of the interview. Know what education and experience you have listed there, and the sequence and dates of all of it. Sometimes the board will ask you to review the highlights of your experience for them; you should not have to hem and haw doing it.

2) Study the class specification and the examination announcement

Usually, the oral board has one or both of these to guide them. The qualities, characteristics or knowledges required by the position sought are stated in these documents. They offer valuable clues as to the nature of the oral interview. For example, if the job involves supervisory responsibilities, the announcement will usually indicate that knowledge of modern supervisory methods and the qualifications of the candidate as a supervisor will be tested. If so, you can expect such questions, frequently in the form of a hypothetical situation which you are expected to solve. NEVER go into an oral without knowledge of the duties and responsibilities of the job you seek.

3) Think through each qualification required

Try to visualize the kind of questions you would ask if you were a board member. How well could you answer them? Try especially to appraise your own knowledge and background in each area, *measured against the job sought*, and identify any areas in which you are weak. Be critical and realistic – do not flatter yourself.

4) Do some general reading in areas in which you feel you may be weak

For example, if the job involves supervision and your past experience has NOT, some general reading in supervisory methods and practices, particularly in the field of human relations, might be useful. Do NOT study agency procedures or detailed manuals. The oral board will be testing your understanding and capacity, not your memory.

5) Get a good night's sleep and watch your general health and mental attitude

You will want a clear head at the interview. Take care of a cold or any other minor ailment, and of course, no hangovers.

What should be done on the day of the interview?

Now comes the day of the interview itself. Give yourself plenty of time to get there. Plan to arrive somewhat ahead of the scheduled time, particularly if your appointment is in the fore part of the day. If a previous candidate fails to appear, the board might be ready for you a bit early. By early afternoon an oral board is almost invariably behind schedule if there are many candidates, and you may have to wait. Take along a book or magazine to read, or your application to review, but leave any extraneous material in the waiting room when you go in for your interview. In any event, relax and compose yourself.

The matter of dress is important. The board is forming impressions about you – from your experience, your manners, your attitude, and your appearance. Give your personal appearance careful attention. Dress your best, but not your flashiest. Choose conservative, appropriate clothing, and be sure it is immaculate. This is a business interview, and your appearance should indicate that you regard it as such. Besides, being well groomed and properly dressed will help boost your confidence.

Sooner or later, someone will call your name and escort you into the interview room. *This is it.* From here on you are on your own. It is too late for any more preparation. But remember, you asked for this opportunity to prove your fitness, and you are here because your request was granted.

What happens when you go in?

The usual sequence of events will be as follows: The clerk (who is often the board stenographer) will introduce you to the chairman of the oral board, who will introduce you to the other members of the board. Acknowledge the introductions before you sit down. Do not be surprised if you find a microphone facing you or a stenotypist sitting by. Oral interviews are usually recorded in the event of an appeal or other review.

Usually the chairman of the board will open the interview by reviewing the highlights of your education and work experience from your application – primarily for the benefit of the other members of the board, as well as to get the material into the record. Do not interrupt or comment unless there is an error or significant misinterpretation; if that is the case, do not hesitate. But do not quibble about insignificant matters. Also, he will usually ask you some question about your education, experience or your present job – partly to get you to start talking and to establish the interviewing "rapport." He may start the actual questioning, or turn it over to one of the other members. Frequently, each member undertakes the questioning on a particular area, one in which he is perhaps most competent, so you can expect each member to participate in the examination. Because time is limited, you may also expect some rather abrupt switches in the direction the questioning takes, so do not be upset by it. Normally, a board member will not pursue a single line of questioning unless he discovers a particular strength or weakness.

After each member has participated, the chairman will usually ask whether any member has any further questions, then will ask you if you have anything you wish to add. Unless you are expecting this question, it may floor you. Worse, it may start you off on an extended, extemporaneous speech. The board is not usually seeking more information. The question is principally to offer you a last opportunity to present further qualifications or to indicate that you have nothing to add. So, if you feel that a significant qualification or characteristic has been overlooked, it is proper to point it out in a sentence or so. Do not compliment the board on the thoroughness of their examination – they have been sketchy, and you know it. If you wish, merely say, "No thank you, I have nothing further to add." This is a point where you can "talk yourself out" of a good impression or fail to present an important bit of information. Remember, *you close the interview yourself*.

The chairman will then say, "That is all, Mr. _____, thank you." Do not be startled; the interview is over, and quicker than you think. Thank him, gather your belongings and take your leave. Save your sigh of relief for the other side of the door.

How to put your best foot forward
Throughout this entire process, you may feel that the board individually and collectively is trying to pierce your defenses, seek out your hidden weaknesses and embarrass and confuse you. Actually, this is not true. They are obliged to make an appraisal of your qualifications for the job you are seeking, and they want to see you in your best light. Remember, they must interview all candidates and a non-cooperative candidate may become a failure in spite of their best efforts to bring out his qualifications. Here are 15 suggestions that will help you:

1) Be natural – Keep your attitude confident, not cocky
If you are not confident that you can do the job, do not expect the board to be. Do not apologize for your weaknesses, try to bring out your strong points. The board is interested in a positive, not negative, presentation. Cockiness will antagonize any board member and make him wonder if you are covering up a weakness by a false show of strength.

2) Get comfortable, but don't lounge or sprawl
Sit erectly but not stiffly. A careless posture may lead the board to conclude that you are careless in other things, or at least that you are not impressed by the importance of the occasion. Either conclusion is natural, even if incorrect. Do not fuss with your clothing, a pencil or an ashtray. Your hands may occasionally be useful to emphasize a point; do not let them become a point of distraction.

3) Do not wisecrack or make small talk
This is a serious situation, and your attitude should show that you consider it as such. Further, the time of the board is limited – they do not want to waste it, and neither should you.

4) Do not exaggerate your experience or abilities
In the first place, from information in the application or other interviews and sources, the board may know more about you than you think. Secondly, you probably will not get away with it. An experienced board is rather adept at spotting such a situation, so do not take the chance.

5) If you know a board member, do not make a point of it, yet do not hide it
Certainly you are not fooling him, and probably not the other members of the board. Do not try to take advantage of your acquaintanceship – it will probably do you little good.

6) Do not dominate the interview
Let the board do that. They will give you the clues – do not assume that you have to do all the talking. Realize that the board has a number of questions to ask you, and do not try to take up all the interview time by showing off your extensive knowledge of the answer to the first one.

7) Be attentive
You only have 20 minutes or so, and you should keep your attention at its sharpest throughout. When a member is addressing a problem or question to you, give him your undivided attention. Address your reply principally to him, but do not exclude the other board members.

8) Do not interrupt
A board member may be stating a problem for you to analyze. He will ask you a question when the time comes. Let him state the problem, and wait for the question.

9) Make sure you understand the question
Do not try to answer until you are sure what the question is. If it is not clear, restate it in your own words or ask the board member to clarify it for you. However, do not haggle about minor elements.

10) Reply promptly but not hastily
A common entry on oral board rating sheets is "candidate responded readily," or "candidate hesitated in replies." Respond as promptly and quickly as you can, but do not jump to a hasty, ill-considered answer.

11) Do not be peremptory in your answers
A brief answer is proper – but do not fire your answer back. That is a losing game from your point of view. The board member can probably ask questions much faster than you can answer them.

12) Do not try to create the answer you think the board member wants
He is interested in what kind of mind you have and how it works – not in playing games. Furthermore, he can usually spot this practice and will actually grade you down on it.

13) Do not switch sides in your reply merely to agree with a board member
Frequently, a member will take a contrary position merely to draw you out and to see if you are willing and able to defend your point of view. Do not start a debate, yet do not surrender a good position. If a position is worth taking, it is worth defending.

14) Do not be afraid to admit an error in judgment if you are shown to be wrong

The board knows that you are forced to reply without any opportunity for careful consideration. Your answer may be demonstrably wrong. If so, admit it and get on with the interview.

15) Do not dwell at length on your present job

The opening question may relate to your present assignment. Answer the question but do not go into an extended discussion. You are being examined for a *new* job, not your present one. As a matter of fact, try to phrase ALL your answers in terms of the job for which you are being examined.

Basis of Rating

Probably you will forget most of these "do's" and "don'ts" when you walk into the oral interview room. Even remembering them all will not ensure you a passing grade. Perhaps you did not have the qualifications in the first place. But remembering them will help you to put your best foot forward, without treading on the toes of the board members.

Rumor and popular opinion to the contrary notwithstanding, an oral board wants you to make the best appearance possible. They know you are under pressure – but they also want to see how you respond to it as a guide to what your reaction would be under the pressures of the job you seek. They will be influenced by the degree of poise you display, the personal traits you show and the manner in which you respond.

ABOUT THIS BOOK

This book contains tests divided into Examination Sections. Go through each test, answering every question in the margin. We have also attached a sample answer sheet at the back of the book that can be removed and used. At the end of each test look at the answer key and check your answers. On the ones you got wrong, look at the right answer choice and learn. Do not fill in the answers first. Do not memorize the questions and answers, but understand the answer and principles involved. On your test, the questions will likely be different from the samples. Questions are changed and new ones added. If you understand these past questions you should have success with any changes that arise. Tests may consist of several types of questions. We have additional books on each subject should more study be advisable or necessary for you. Finally, the more you study, the better prepared you will be. This book is intended to be the last thing you study before you walk into the examination room. Prior study of relevant texts is also recommended. NLC publishes some of these in our Fundamental Series. Knowledge and good sense are important factors in passing your exam. Good luck also helps. So now study this Passbook, absorb the material contained within and take that knowledge into the examination. Then do your best to pass that exam.

EXAMINATION SECTION

EXAMINATION SECTION
TEST 1

DIRECTIONS: Each question or incomplete statement is followed by several suggested answers or completions. Select the one the BEST answers the question or completes the statement. *PRINT THE LETTER OF THE CORRECT ANSWER IN THE SPACE AT THE RIGHT.*

1. During an assessment interview, a social worker and a client try to clarify and analyze the client's sense of self. If the worker wants to discover something about the client's spirituality, which of the following questions is MOST appropriate?

    A. Do you have regrets or guilt about the past?
    B. How do you explain or make sense out of the suffering and pain you and others experience in life?
    C. How do you want to be remembered after you die?
    D. Are you comfortable with your membership in your family?

1.____

2. In general, Americans with strong Asian cultural traditions are LEAST likely to be receptive to _____ support services.

    A. psychological
    B. financial
    C. educational
    D. material

2.____

3. A client comes to a social worker with multiple problems related to his poor health, unemployment, and low income. In developing an intervention plan, the social worker should FIRST

    A. have the client identify and list what he sees as problems or concerns
    B. have the client identify the significant others who are affected by the problems
    C. offer recommendations for what problems need to be addressed
    D. identify the two or three most significant problems that need to be addressed

3.____

4. A social history report includes the statement "X completed three years at the University of Kansas and then transferred to Stanford University, where he is currently a senior in education." This should be included under the heading

    A. Family Background and Situation
    B. Use of Community Resources
    C. Intellectual Functioning
    D. Such a statement shouldn't appear at all in a social history report

4.____

5. When a social system adapts to environmental conditions, _____ has occurred.

    A. Assimilation
    B. Accommodation
    C. Acculturation
    D. Adaptation

5.____

6. Of the statements below, which BEST states the purpose of staff development in a social services agency?

6.____

A. advance one's career through study
B. improve performance through enhanced skills
C. acquire and apply new knowledge
D. orient oneself to an organization

7. The primary criticism leveled against the use of self-anchored scales for practice evaluation is mat they

   A. focus on the practitioner rather than the client
   B. do not measure internal states
   C. require training in order to implement
   D. are too subjective

8. Classification skills that emerge in middle childhood involve a mental ability known as

   A. object permanence
   B. decentering
   C. scripting
   D. detachment

9. "Mezzo" social work practice refers to practice with

   A. groups
   B. families
   C. communities
   D. an individual

10. When considering who is a member of a family system, the _____ is the point that divides those who are continually interacting around family concerns and those who have little or no input into family functioning.

    A. boundary
    B. period
    C. margin
    D. focal system

11. The functions of coping mechanisms include
    I. protecting an individual against anxiety
    II. solving problems
    III. reducing the emotional discomfort caused by stressors

    A. I and II
    B. I and III
    C. II and III
    D. I, II and III

12. The most universally held perspective among social workers is the _____ perspective.

    A. ecosystems
    B. generalist
    C. task-centered
    D. psychodynamic

13. Adult protective service programs supported by state statutes protect elderly people from abuse and neglect under the doctrine of

   A. parens patriae
   B. habeas corpus
   C. in loco parentis
   D. volenti non fit iniuria

14. Which of the following generally does the LEAST to contribute to an adolescent's process of individuation?

   A. Maintaining consistent peer relations
   B. Achieving a sexual identity
   C. Working a part-time job
   D. Completing a high-school education

15. During an interview with a client, the client's response to a practitioner's statement suggests that the client has heard exactly the opposite of what was said. This is an example of

   A. projection
   B. reaction formation
   C. displacement
   D. repression

16. During an interview, a client expresses feelings of being different or deviant Which of the following techniques would be MOST appropriate for counteracting these feelings?

   A. Encouragement
   B. Reassurance
   C. Negative reinforcement
   D. Universalization

17. Which of the following statements about suicide is FALSE?

   A. Suicide occurs most frequently as a result of severe depression.
   B. People who talk about suicide rarely follow through with the act
   C. Among adolescents, boys are more likely to succeed in a suicide attempt than girls
   D. People commit suicide at almost every stage of the life cycle.

18. Which of the following elements can be drawn into a one-page ecomap?
   I. Informal resources and natural helpers
   II. Social activities and interests
   III. Job situation, employment, and responsibilities
   IV. Age, sex, and marital status

   A. I and IV
   B. I, II, and IV
   C. IV only
   D. I, II, III, and IV

19. In order to be functional and appropriate for the situation, a professional social worker/client relationship must

A. be established in the initial stages by the worker's statement of purpose
B. be determined by the client's willingness to accept the worker's intervention
C. establish itself early, with an empathetic response to a client's statement of need
D. develop from the worker's joint problem-solving work with clients

20. Which of the following assessment instruments is used to graphically depict barriers and supports that affect a person's interactions with his or her social environment?

    A. Life cycle matrix
    B. Social network grid
    C. The dual perspective
    D. Self-anchored rating scale

21. The phenomenon of "groupthink" is promoted by a number of factors. Which of the following is NOT typically one of them?

    A. Members have an illusion of vulnerability that compels them to avoid risk.
    B. Members have an unquestioning belief in the group's moral lightness.
    C. Social measures of disapproval are applied to dissenters.
    D. Members keep quiet about misgivings and internally minimize their importance.

22. Which of me following is NOT an advantage associated with the use of written service contracts?

    A. Definitive legal status
    B. Clarity of purpose
    C. Unalterable reference point
    D. Reduced client-worker conflict

23. Which of the following is NOT typically involved in the intervention technique known as behavioral rehearsal?

    A. The worker makes suggestions for how to more effectively handle a situation.
    B. The client assumes the role of himself/herself in a role play.
    C. The worker identifies the client's appropriate behaviors after the role-play.
    D. The client describes how he or she would act in a certain situation.

24. Which of the following statements is/are TRUE?
    I. Most elderly people are residents of nursing homes
    II. There are generally more elderly women than men in the population
    III. The elderly are increasing, in numbers as well as a percentage of the population
    IV. Most elderly people move many times following retirement

    A. I only
    B. II and III
    C. III and IV
    D. I, II, III and IV

25. The most important consideration for a worker who looks to collateral information sources during a social work assessment is

    A. the possible hidden agendas of collateral sources
    B. the limited time in which most workers have to gather assessment data

C. whether the collateral sources of information genuinely want to help change the situation
D. whether the client has signed appropriate release forms

26. Which of the following approaches to social work presumes that a client will be involuntary? 26._____

    A. Reality therapy
    B. Structural
    C. Behavioral
    D. Psychodynamic

27. A social worker's "duty to warn" presents a potential conflict with the ethical principle of 27._____

    A. cultural sensitivity
    B. self-determination
    C. competence
    D. confidentiality

28. During an assessment interview, a client describes her relationship with her husband as a strong positive influence. In putting together an ecomap of this client and her environment, the social worker would depict this relationship by using 28._____

    A. a line with several vertical hashmarks (-l-l-l-l-l-l-)
    B. an arrow pointing away from the husband, toward the client
    C. a dotted line
    D. a heavy black line

29. Typically, the _____ stage of an interview is the one which is most powerful in determining the interviewee's impression of the interview as a whole. 29._____

    A. opening
    B. questioning
    C. closing
    D. discussion

30. During a client assessment, each of the following should be considered a useful question, EXCEPT 30._____

    A. Who do you think bears most of the responsibility for the current problem?
    B. Despite your current problems, what parts of your life are going fairly well?
    C. What would you not change about yourself or your life?
    D. Where did you find the energy to deal with problems like this in the past?

31. A social worker's best defense against a malpractice suit or complaint is usually 31._____

    A. a vigorous legal advocate
    B. the testimony of professional character witnesses
    C. a counterclaim against the plaintiff
    D. detailed case records

32. For social service professionals who are responsible for making decisions about the type of program or service that would be most appropriate for a particular client, the most useful assessment instrument is probably a(n) 32._____

A. social history
B. collateral data set
C. genogram
D. ecomap

33. During an interview with a family, a practitioner observes that the youngest son often exhibits overly adaptive behavior—he strenuously attempts to comfort the father when the father appears to be upset. Later, the practitioner learns that in school, the child often becomes uneasy or upset whenever another child cries or acts out. The practitioner should interpret these signs as suggestive of possible

A. repressed memories of past trauma
B. sexual abuse
C. formation of a dysfunctional triad
D. physical abuse

34. The primary purpose of a Gantt chart in agency planning is to provide a visual depiction of the relationship between

A. the resources demanded by a project and the resources that are readily available
B. the possible alternatives in a plan and their likely corresponding outcomes
C. the activities required by a project and the time frame for completion
D. the people within an agency and their specific functions

35. A social worker sits down to assess a child who is currently struggling with behavior problems at school. Which of the following assessment instruments should be considered by the worker as especially useful in shedding light on the current situation?

A. Life history grid
B. Self-anchored rating scale
C. Social network map
D. Genogram

36. Which of the following is NOT an advantage associated with the use of multiworker family assessments?

A. Creation of several consultants who may be helpful to the primary worker
B. Firmer post-assessment commitment on the part of family members
C. More open discussion of issues
D. Considerably shorter data-gathering stage

37. The idea that a social system not only adapts to an environment, but in turn has a direct influence on the environment through feedback cycles, is an element of the theory of

A. chaos
B. coevolution
C. synergy
D. autopoiesis

38. Forcing the mentally disabled to work without pay is a violation of the _____ Amendment to the Constitution.

A. Fourth
B. Ninth

C. Thirteenth
D. Sixteenth

39. School-age children are involved in mastering the skills of the _____ stage of cognitive development

    A. preoperational thought
    B. formal operations
    C. sensorimotor
    D. concrete operations

40. Which of the following communication variables is a cognitive barrier to effective transmission?

    A. Speech impediment
    B. Distractions
    C. Language competence
    D. Speech inappropriate to context and client jargon

41. Which of the following reinforcement schedules is almost always used in the beginning stages of an intervention program, because of the speed with which behaviors are learned?

    A. Random
    B. Intermittent
    C. Differential
    D. Continuous

42. A client who is a schoolteacher confesses that he is not comfortable in that role, because it requires intellectual and organizational skills that he does not possess. This is an example of

    A. inter-role conflict
    B. role incapacity
    C. role ambiguity
    D. self-role incongruence

43. Which of the following is NOT an example of a social worker fulfilling the operational purpose of a professional relationship?

    A. Lobbying for local tax reforms that will ease the burden on clients
    B. Conducting a behavioral intervention for a child with school behavior problems
    C. Referring a couple to a marriage counselor
    D. Enrolling a young mother in the federal WIC program

44. A client is having trouble managing problems caused by insufficient resources: she's experiencing difficulties in finding employment, hi finding care for her child while she looks for work, and in finding transportation to accomplish simple errands. Which of the following models of social Work would probably be MOST useful for this client?

    A. Crisis intervention
    B. Task-centered
    C. Cognitive-behavioral
    D. Structural

45. A mother's 6-year-old son is not feeling well, so the mother takes him to the local health clinic, where's she's told the boy needs to be admitted to the hospital immediately for extensive testing. The mother wants to stay with the boy, but the administrative nurse refuses her request The mother comes to a practitioner for help. The MOST appropriate first action would be to

    A. check on the child to see if he is okay
    B. tell the mother not to worry and mat the child will be looked after
    C. find out whether the hospital allows parents to stay with their children
    D. tell the mother not to worry and call the administrative nurse to complain about the situation

46. In a family, rules and social roles are examples of _____, a factor that characterizes the family as a social system.

    A. interdependence
    B. hierarchy
    C. genography
    D. patterns

47. Which of the following is an advantage associated with the use of professional organizations for providing staff with continuing education?

    A. Identification with practice value
    B. Low costs
    C. Agency control over content
    D. Accountability for performance

48. Which of the following approaches to family therapy recognizes the tendency of a family to repeat patterns established in prior generations?

    A. Family systems
    B. Structural
    C. Strategic
    D. Social learning

49. Which of the following statements about the single-system evaluation approach is FALSE?

    A. It makes use of an experimental control groups
    B. Clients or systems are observed repeatedly before, during, and after interventions.
    C. Changes in the outcome measure are noted that coincide with the intervention
    D. It is compatible with clinical practice.

50. Which of the following ego defense mechanisms is most common among physically ill persons who are experiencing much fear or pain?

    A. Displacement
    B. Reaction formation
    C. Fantasy
    D. Regression

KEY (CORRECT ANSWERS)

1. B	11. C	21. A	31. D	41. D
2. A	12. B	22. A	32. A	42. D
3. A	13. A	23. B	33. D	43. A
4. C	14. D	24. B	34. C	44. B
5. B	15. B	25. D	35. A	45. C
6. C	16. D	26. A	36. D	46. D
7. D	17. B	27. D	37. B	47. A
8. B	18. D	28. D	38. C	48. A
9. B	19. D	29. C	39. D	49. A
10. A	20. C	30. A	40. C	50. D

TEST 2

DIRECTIONS: Each question or incomplete statement is followed by several suggested answers or completions. Select the one the BEST answers the question or completes the statement. *PRINT THE LETTER OF THE CORRECT ANSWER IN THE SPACE AT THE RIGHT.*

1. A social worker who wants to use a small group as a resource for clients should keep in mind that for preadolescents, a group numbering _____ is preferred.

    A. 3 or 4
    B. 6 to 10
    C. 10 to 12
    D. 12 to 15

1.____

2. Significant disadvantages and risks involved in the teamwork approach to solving problems include each of the following, EXCEPT

    A. escalations in cost
    B. greater risk of confidentiality breach
    C. tendency for activities to center on needs of professionals rather than clients
    D. frequent exclusion of clients from meetings

2.____

3. What is the term used in systems theory to denote the unique character of a group, analogous to a person's "personality"?

    A. Morphostasis
    B. Syntropy
    C. Schema
    D. Syntality

3.____

4. In terms of societal stigma, another term for "self-fulfilling prophecy" is

    A. passing
    B. subculture development
    C. secondary deviance
    D. social rejection

4.____

5. A worker assigned to a ward for the criminally insane makes an effort to understand each individual patient's situation. Which of the following professional values or ethics is the worker implementing?

    A. Self-determination
    B. Privacy
    C. Dignity and respect
    D. Competence

5.____

6. The "problem search" method is useful for initial interviews with clients who
    I. have more than one problem that needs to be addressed
    II. have requested an agency service that shows a poor understanding of the problem
    III. are involuntary, referred by an agency or family

    A. I only

6.____

B. I and II
C. II and III
D. I, II and III

7. Which of the following is a term for a social system's efficient use of energy, as well as the addition of energy to the system from outside?

    A. Entropy
    B. Dynamism
    C. Negative entropy
    D. Synergy

8. In the ecosystems model for analyzing psychosocial factors that impact special populations, a worker first evaluates a client on Level I, the individual level, and eventually expands the analysis to Level V, the _____ level.

    A. Historical
    B. Family
    C. Cultural
    D. Environmental-structural

9. For inmates of the criminal justice system, the right to freedom from cruel and unusual punishment includes
    I. the right to be free from physical abuse and punishment
    II. the right to reasonable opportunity for physical exercise
    III. the right to receive education and training
    IV. the right to adequate medical treatment

    A. I and II
    B. I and III
    C. I, II and IV
    D. I, II, III and IV

10. During a home interview with a single mother, the mother responds to her three-year-old child's repeated interruptions in a harsh and angry manner. Finally, the child is scolded and sent to her room, crying loudly. In this situation, the MOST appropriate response on the part of the practitioner would be to

    A. say, "It must be tough to be both a father and a mother to your child."
    B. say, "I wonder if you might have handled that differently."
    C. say, "I hate to see children cry like that"
    D. ignore the mother's behavior entirely and continue with the interview

11. According to Parsons, there are four functions necessary to a system. Which of the following is NOT one of these?

    A. Differentiation
    B. Goal-directed activity
    C. Pattern maintenance
    D. Adaptation

12. Which of the following is an example of an assessment interview?

A. A vocational rehabilitation counselor interviews a client with a developmental disability to determine grant eligibility.
B. A social worker at a mental hospital seeks background information to understand the problems and social functioning of a patient
C. A worker at a nursing home compiles a social history on a new resident to obtain information on current social and personal problems.
D. A couple having marital problems is counseled on how to handle their troubles.

13. Many social workers operate under the belief that members of an oppressed group have a more immediate, subtle, and critical knowledge of their oppression than do members of the dominant culture. This is a concept known as

   A. implicit stereotyping
   B. cultural relativism
   C. teleology
   D. epistemic privilege

14. The contemporary model of the diagnostic approach to social work is usually referred to as the _____ approach.

   A. ecological
   B. milieu
   C. psychosocial
   D. medical

15. A program evaluation that focuses on the process of social work programs is described as

   A. functional
   B. systemic
   C. transactional
   D. formative

16. Piaget believes school-age children learn to master _____ at this stage of the life span.

   A. object relations
   B. irreversibility
   C. object permanence
   D. conservation

17. In formulating an intervention plan, a social worker writes the following objective: "Mrs. Talley is to obtain counseling for her grief." The MAIN problem with this objective is that it

   A. is too negative
   B. describes an input but ignores the outcome
   C. doesn't name the counselor
   D. doesn't specify when Mrs. Talley will obtain counseling

18. Which of the following principles is used by social workers to guard against abuses of power?

   A. Cultural relativism
   B. Least restrictive environment
   C. Professional competence

D. Advocacy for social justice

19. When cross-cultural social work, it is best for the worker to operate under the assumption that

    A. human personality can generally be reduced to cultural identity
    B. applicants should always interact with a worker from the same culture
    C. cultures are not homogeneous
    D. there are no cross-cultural absolutes

20. Which of the following kinds of authority is/are appropriate in a professional helping relationship?
    I. The authority of social sanction
    II. The authority of power
    III. The authority of knowledge

    A. I only
    B. I and III
    C. II and III
    D. I, II and III

21. As an advocacy technique, pressuring differs from persuasion in that it involves

    A. the invocation of legal remedies
    B. an appeal to reason
    C. forceful action
    D. understanding the opposing viewpoint

22. The developmental task of symbolic thought is most likely to be acquired by an individual between the ages of

    A. 2-4
    B. 5-7
    C. 8-12
    D. 13-17

23. The use of "soft" criteria (such as cooperativeness, adaptability, and attitude) in supervisory social work evaluations

    A. is an unfair use of unverifiable standards and should be avoided
    B. can make an evaluation sterile and of little value if overused
    C. are too difficult to articulate verbally and should be scaled in some quantifiable way in order to avoid accusations of bias or litigation
    D. should be used in conjunction with objective criteria to provide the "big picture" of how a social worker contributes to the agency or organization

24. Which of the following role problems is most likely to occur in times of rapid social change?

    A. Role ambiguity
    B. Role overload
    C. Self-role incongruence
    D. Role rejection

25. Which of the following types of social work practice would typically place the LEAST amount of emphasis on the client's social and environmental factors?

    A. Structural
    B. Generalist
    C. Psychodynamic
    D. Cognitive-behavioral

25.____

KEY (CORRECT ANSWERS)

1.	A	11.	A
2.	B	12.	A
3.	D	13.	D
4.	C	14.	C
5.	C	15.	D
6.	C	16.	D
7.	C	17.	B
8.	A	18.	B
9.	A	19.	C
10.	A	20.	B

21. C
22. A
23. D
24. A
25. C

TEST 3

DIRECTIONS: Each question or incomplete statement is followed by several suggested answers or completions. Select the one the BEST answers the question or completes the statement. *PRINT THE LETTER OF THE CORRECT ANSWER IN THE SPACE AT THE RIGHT.*

1. Which of the following is an example of a task-focused coping strategy?

    A. Seeking support
    B. Modeling behaviors after those of others
    C. Talking about an experience
    D. Withholding an emotional investment in a desired by unlikely outcome

2. During an assessment interview, a social worker and a client try to analyze problems hi the client's role performance. The worker is interested in discovering whether the problem is caused by the client's rejection of or lack of interest in the role. Which of the following questions is MOST appropriate to ask the client?

    A. Do you think you can learn the behaviors needed to perform this role?
    B. Have you ever been punished in any way for the performance of this role?
    C. What do think will happen if there is no change in performance?
    D. Why don't you like performing this role?

3. A social worker visits a family of five who admit to having multiple problems, many of them resulting from the recent death of a grandmother who had much power and control over the household. During the interview, each family members lists his or her problems and concerns, and then the social worker mentions two possible problems that were not mentioned on any family member's list The MOST appropriate next step during mis meeting would be for

    A. the worker to name the two or three problems of highest priority
    B. the family members to discuss in turn how they feel about the grandmother's death
    C. the family members to examine the list and vote on the two or three problems of highest priority
    D. the family members and worker to review and sort the problems into logical groupings

4. The greater level of physical activity among school-age children, as compared with pre-schoolers, is attributed to

    A. changes in perceptual skills
    B. increased brain development
    C. increased muscle development
    D. improved social skills

5. The purpose of metacommunication is to

    A. identify the objectives of an interview
    B. establish an environment in which barriers to communication are removed
    C. provide whatever symbolic elements are necessary for encoding or decoding the content of a message

D. provide the frame of reference within which a message's content may be interpreted

6. In the parent-child relationship, the parent is expected to provide the child with food, shelter, supervision, and guidance. This is a description of a parent's

   A. role conception
   B. role ambiguity
   C. social role
   D. role overload

7. As a profession, social work addresses the controversial issue of abortion as

   A. an issue which a social worker may refuse to discuss, based on his or her beliefs, but not without a referral to another professional willing to engage in such a discussion
   B. a legal right of every client that must sublimate personal beliefs
   C. an immoral act that must be passively discouraged by social service professionals
   D. an unfortunate by-product of a societal worldview that devalues its most powerless members

8. Which of the following behavioral techniques is/are used to increase the frequency, intensity, or duration of a target behavior?
   I. Positive reinforcement
   II. Negative reinforcement
   III. Extinction
   IV. Punishment

   A. I only
   B. I and II
   C. II and III
   D. II, III and IV

9. The psychodynamic approach to social work is useful for clients who are

   A. heavily burdened by socioeconomic problems
   B. nonverbal
   C. chemically dependent
   D. actively working for change

10. A client's mental illness or drag addiction are most likely to contribute to a problem of role

    A. misconception
    B. incapacity
    C. rejection
    D. ambiguity

11. The percentage of a community's residents over the age of 65 and under 18 is an expression of the community's

    A. dependency ratio
    B. age margin
    C. generational inversion
    D. generic demand for services

12. A client with a poor employment record confesses her anxiety about a coming job interview to a social worker. The client is nervous about the interview because of her lack of experience in such settings, and doesn't really feel as if she knows how to conduct herself properly. The MOST appropriate intervention technique the social worker can use is

    A. behavioral rehearsal
    B. self-esteem building
    C. role reversal
    D. behavioral contracting

13. For a social worker, the process of assessment ends when

    A. the last assessment interview or form has been recorded
    B. a treatment plan has been formulated
    C. the first set of behavioral and/or environmental goals are met
    D. the terminal phase of service is completed

14. Which of the following is an example of a social worker fulfilling the normative purpose of a professional relationship?

    A. Teaching parenting skills to a young mother
    B. Advocating on behalf of a client to avoid an eviction
    C. Lobbying for an increase in child-care benefits to unemployed mothers seeking work
    D. Referring a client family to a family therapist

15. Which of the following is a type of cognitive intervention?

    A. Managing self-talk
    B. Behavioral contracting
    C. Building self-esteem
    D. Role reversal

16. In response to a high number gay and lesbian runaways on the streets of a community, the director of a social services agency called together a group of prominent lesbian and gay community leaders who would help to define a solution, and to make initial contacts to confirm interest In this way, the director sought

    A. professional consultation
    B. to assess the community
    C. to legitimize the problem
    D. a redefinition of the problem

17. Time-series data are often characterized by their central tendency or location. Another term for this characteristic is

    A. level
    B. validity
    C. trend
    D. variability

18. During an interview with a father and his young daughter, the practitioner picks up signs that the father is invested to an unusual degree in whether the daughter makes the school basketball team hi the coming week of tryouts. On several occasions, the father has mentioned the daughter's past achievements with pride-but the daughter seems slightly embarrassed by his interest. During the remainder of the assessment, the practitioner should spend at least some time exploring the possibility that the relationship between these two is

   A. disengaged
   B. incestuous
   C. enmeshed
   D. closed

19. Most appropriately, a committee of co-workers at a social service agency should perform the hiring function(s) of
   I. screening applicants
   II. recommending a "short list" to hiring personnel
   III. assisting with employment interviews
   IV. voting on final hiring decisions

   A. I and II
   B. II and III
   C. II, III and IV
   D. I, II, III and IV

20. Which of the following statements about a triadic process is TRUE?

   A. It is usually characterized by inappropriate generational boundaries
   B. It refers to the formation of a three-person subsystem
   C. It is often socioeconomic in origin
   D. It introduces cultural features into the arena of boundary management

21. Which of the following statements is FALSE?

   A. Homeless people have federally guaranteed "squatters' rights."
   B. The right to adequate shelter is guaranteed by most states.
   C. Homeless people have the right to public assistance in the form of food stamps, disability benefits, and medical care.
   D. Some states have expanded how they define a "resident" of the state in order to ensure that the homeless can vote.

22. Which of the following would be classified by a social work practitioner, working in the dual perspective, as having a positive nurturing environment but a negative sustaining environment?

   A. A gay teenager who is rejected by his parents and by peers at school
   B. A minority child from a supportive home who feels marginalized in school
   C. A teenager from a supportive home who is sexually abused by an uncle
   D. A child who is abused by her parents but who has several close friends at school

23. A second-year social work student, an intern at a school, performs as a discussion-group leader for immigrant children. One of these children, a Filipino child, in response to a teacher's assignment to bring in a newspaper article, has brought in an article from a Tagalog newspaper. The teacher told the child mat he did not correctly complete his homework assignment The discussion leader's FIRST action should be to

    A. discuss the incident with a supervisor
    B. meet with the child and assure him that he did nothing wrong
    C. confront the teacher to discuss his or her cultural sensitivity
    D. plan a departmental seminar in cultural sensitivity

23.____

24. When an interviewer considers what type of nonverbal behavior will be appropriate given the interviewee's cultural background, the interviewer is making a decision about

    A. processing
    B. encoding
    C. decoding
    D. transmission

24.____

25. Which of the following is NOT a guideline to be followed in compiling a social history report?

    A. Avoid psychiatric labels and use behavioral examples instead.
    B. Numerous headings should be used to break information into topical categories.
    C. The report should be as comprehensive as possible.
    D. Label opinions and personal judgements as such.

25.____

26. In writing a social history report, the practitioner should focus as much as possible on

    A. resources and internal strengths that clients may use to address problems
    B. personal weaknesses and limitations that might impede progress
    C. environmental obstacles to change
    D. possible psychopathology

26.____

27. A client requests that a social worker help her figure out how to get money in order to purchase a car, because the client needs to get to and from a new job. The FIRST thing the worker should try to do is

    A. conduct a social history of the client
    B. help the client recognize the difference between means and ends
    C. challenge the client's motivation for buying a new car
    D. understand how expensive a car is to buy

27.____

28. During an interview, a general assistance client expresses frustration with the practitioner, and wonders aloud why he has to disclose so much information in order to get help. He makes the statement that social workers are all alike, and that all they know how to do is ask one question after another. In response to this, the MOST appropriate answer the practitioner can make is

    A. I don't like having to ask these questions any more than you like answering them.
    B. You think I ask too many questions?
    C. I'm sorry, but you'll have to provide this information if you expect any help.
    D. You're not making my job easy, either.

28.____

29. A social work supervisor sits down for an annual evaluation with a practitioner who is a counselor for sex-offenders. The greatest impediment to a fair evaluation of this person's demonstrated success is the

   A. tentative level of knowledge available to the practitioner in her work
   B. supervisor's lack of direct contacts with the counselor's clients
   C. extreme psychological strain involved in such work
   D. degree of specialization required by the field

30. The purpose of the _____ model of social work is to ensure that interventions give adequate and appropriate attention to the client's social environment, and to social change.

   A. task-centered
   B. interactional
   C. cognitive-behavioral
   D. structural

31. Which of the following is NOT an accurate description of a social worker/client relationship?

   A. Sympathetic
   B. Inherently unequal
   C. Purposeful
   D. Nonjudgemental

32. A social worker is fulfilling the role of a "broker" when he or she

   A. challenges an institution's decision not to provide services
   B. refers a physically abused wife to a shelter home
   C. helps a client to articulate his or her needs
   D. coordinates services from different agencies

33. First-order changes within a family typically affect

   A. communication patterns
   B. levels of pride or satisfaction
   C. role assignments
   D. shared worldview

34. Ethical difficulties with nonsexual dual relationships are most likely to occur in

   A. therapeutic settings
   B. community organizing
   C. mobilizing informal social support
   D. community development

35. Which of the following age groups leads the nation in percentage of suicides?

   A. 15- to 24-year-olds
   B. 25- to 40-year olds
   C. 40- to 64-year-olds
   D. 65 and older

36. In hiring preprofessional staff to work at a social services agency, administrators should consider their greatest benefit to be

A. greater flexibility in accepting difficult task assignments
B. substantial cost savings
C. improved understanding and relationships among clients
D. fresh insights and questioning mat may motivate change

37. Which of the following is NOT characteristic of a maladaptive defense to a set of stressors?

   A. reaction are generally passive
   B. patterns of behavior are stereotyped
   C. devised solutions are reality-oriented
   D. the reaction is unconscious

38. The "strength" of a particular behavior is commonly described in terms of each of the following, EXCEPT

   A. desirability
   B. intensity
   C. frequency
   D. duration

39. Which of the following is LEAST likely to be an indicator of child neglect?

   A. Poor school attendance
   B. Unsocialized eating habits
   C. Serious behavioral problems
   D. Voluntarily staying at school or in public places for extended periods

40. A social worker attempts to interview a young child who is believed to have suffered physical abuse. The worker notices that the child appears frightened, and says, "When I was your age, I was afraid to talk to people I didn't know that well." This is an example of the worker's attempt at

   A. parallelism
   B. encouragement
   C. normalization
   D. universalization

41. Which of the following is NOT a guideline to be used in writing intervention objectives?

   A. Compose two- or three-part objectives,
   B. Break down long-term objectives into ones with shorter time frames.
   C. Use positive ("will...") rather than negative ("will not...") language.
   D. Use behavioral language.

42. The NASW code states explicitly that a social worker has an ethical duty to
   I. take action against the incompetent practice of other social workers
   II. present materials at professional conferences and writing for professional journals
   III. protect the privacy of clients at all costs

   A. I and II
   B. I and III

C. II and III
D. I, II and III

43. In the helping continuum, which of the following types of support systems is most likely to occupy places on both the formal and informal ends of the spectrum?   43._____

   A. Professionals
   B. Mutual aid
   C. Self-help groups
   D. Assigned peer helpers

44. Which of the following is probably the BEST available method for a social worker to measure change's in a client's internal state?   44._____

   A. Time sampling
   B. Self-anchored rating scale
   C. Latency recording
   D. Frequency counting

45. Each of the following is a guideline for legislative advocacy at the state level of government, EXCEPT   45._____

   A. the advocate should press for open committee hearings on the bill
   B. support should be obtained from the governor and relevant state agencies, if possible
   C. the bill should be introduced toward the end of a legislative session
   D. the advocate should use the amendatory process as a strategy

46. In the ecological perspective of human behavior, the attributes of relatedness, competence, self-direction, and self-esteem can be described in each of the following ways, EXCEPT   46._____

   A. they appear to be interdependent
   B. they tend to develop at differential rates
   C. they appear to be relatively free of cultural bias
   D. they are outcomes of person/environment relationships

47. The "right to treatment" means that   47._____
   I. any person with mental illness may generally gain voluntary admission to an institution for treatment
   II. people with mental disabilities who do not live in an institution generally have rights to community-based services and treatment
   III. people who are involuntarily institutionalized for a mental illness generally have the right to a professionally acceptable treatment plan

   A. I and II
   B. II and III
   C. III only
   D. I, II and III

48. Which of the following ways of thinking about social work practice is most useful and most important during the beginning phases of the helping process? 48.____

    A. Feminist perspective
    B. Generalist perspective
    C. Task-centered model
    D. Behavioral theory

49. A worker believes that a client should change her approach toward her family, but does nothing to compel her to do so. Which of the following professional values or ethics is the worker implementing? 49.____

    A. Cultural sensitivity
    B. Self-determination
    C. Competence
    D. Dignity and respect

50. Male-dominated societies have been found by many researcher to have negative effects on men as well as women. These consequences include each of the following, EXCEPT 50.____

    A. homophobia
    B. restricted sexual behaviors
    C. restricted social mobility
    D. health care problems

KEY (CORRECT ANSWERS)

1. B	11. A	21. B	31. D	41. A
2. B	12. A	22. B	32. B	42. A
3. D	13. D	23. A	33. B	43. C
4. C	14. C	24. B	34. A	44. B
5. D	15. A	25. C	35. D	45. C
6. C	16. C	26. A	36. D	46. B
7. B	17. A	27. B	37. C	47. C
8. B	18. C	28. B	38. A	48. B
9. D	19. A	29. A	39. C	49. B
10. B	20. A	30. D	40. C	50. C

TEST 4

DIRECTIONS: Each question or incomplete statement is followed by several suggested answers or completions. Select the one the BEST answers the question or completes the statement. *PRINT THE LETTER OF THE CORRECT ANSWER IN THE SPACE AT THE RIGHT.*

Questions 51-54 refer to the genogram below.

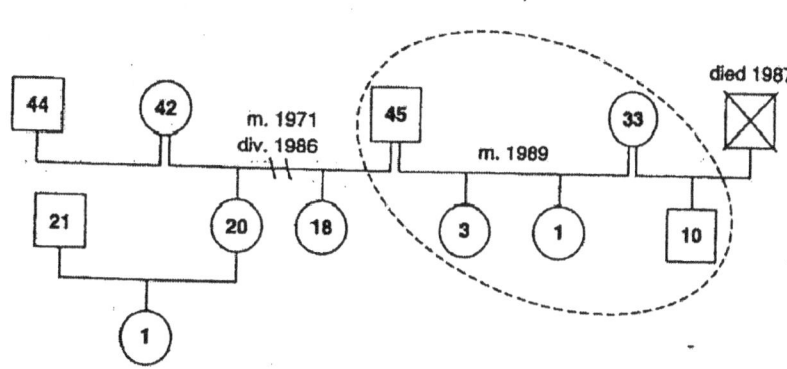

Based on the above genogram, classify each statement below as "True" or "False" in the blank next to each statement

1. The 10-year-old is from the mother's first marriage. 1.____

2. The 10-year-old lives with two stepsisters. 2.____

3. The 10-year-old's mother died in 1987. 3.____

4. The 10-year-old's stepfather is now a grandfather. 4.____

5. An aide assigned to a patient in a state mental hospital hears a complaint that the doctors and other staff have been treating him cruelly. The aide should FIRST 5.____

    A. try to persuade the doctors and staff to treat the patient better
    B. secure the patient's consent for filing a grievance
    C. find out what specific actions the patient felt were cruel
    D. determine the person to whom a grievance or complaint should be directed

6. Among the following ethnic minority groups in America, which is MOST likely to be open to help-seeking behaviors? 6.____

    A. Native Americans
    B. Latinos
    C. Jewish Americans
    D. African Americans

7. The major advantage associated with the use of commercially available data-gathering and assessment tools in social work is that they

   A. have already been field-tested
   B. are usually less costly than other measures
   C. are typically more focused and to-the-point in questioning
   D. involve broad applications

8. During an initial interview with a family of four, the social worker notices that the father and an adolescent son frequently interject with statements that are critical of the younger daughter's behavior. Each time one of them makes such a statement, the mother vigorously leaps to the daughter's defense. In her report, the social worker describes a pair of unhealthy alliances in the family system that have resulted in a split. In phrasing her assessment in this way, the worker is using the _____ approach.

   A. ecosystems
   B. functional
   C. structural
   D. psychodynamic

9. Indigenous nonprofessionals should be considered useful to a social services agency for each of the following reasons, EXCEPT

   A. willingness to undertake support functions at the agency
   B. serving as a communication channel between the organization and clients
   C. encouraging greater agency acceptance and credibility within the community
   D. helping the agency to accomplish meaningful change

10. Which of the following developmental tasks is most likely to be acquired by an individual between the ages of 13-17?

    A. Developing life-style apart from parents
    B. Abstract though processes
    C. Introspection
    D. Cooperation with others

11. According to Kadushin, the purpose of opening an initial client interview with general conversation or "small talk" is to

    A. construct an unobtrusive opportunity for making and recording initial observations
    B. ease the client's transition from a familiar mode of speaking into a new and unfamiliar role
    C. soften the client's defenses so that initial questioning will catch him/her off guard
    D. downplay the seriousness of the interview

12. The most significant difference between advocacy and other social service roles (brokerage, mediation, etc.) is that it

    A. is essentially a confrontation
    B. engages resources from different sectors of the community
    C. is directed outward
    D. cannot be accommodated by the ecosystems model

13. According to Warren, communities serve each of the following major functions, EXCEPT   13._____

    A. socialization
    B. mutual support
    C. protection from outsiders
    D. production/distribution/consumption

14. In the helping process, the social worker/client relationship may be appropriately used to   14._____
    I. convince the client of the importance of relying on others
    II. persuade a client to make necessary changes
    III. sustain clients as they work on the problem
    IV. serve as a model for other client interactions

    A. I, II and III
    B. II, III and IV
    C. III and IV
    D. I, II, III and IV

15. Which of the following stages of group development typically occurs FIRST?   15._____

    A. Power and control
    B. Differentiation
    C. Separation
    D. Intimacy

16. Each of the following is a general guideline that should be used for effective listening during the interview process, EXCEPT   16._____

    A. have a clear idea of the purpose of the interview before the session begins
    B. assume and accept a certain level of ignorance on the part of oneself
    C. develop a clear expectation about what the client will say during the interview
    D. listen for recurrent and dominant themes, rather than focus on detail

17. A child learns that her pet is called a "cat." Later, the child visits a friend's house and correctly identifies her friend's pet as a cat. According to Piaget, the child has achieved   17._____

    A. accommodation
    B. conservation
    C. assimilation
    D. object permanence

18. Which of the following statements about problem-solving planning for an agency is TRUE?   18._____

    A. Plans usually have a life span of 5 to 10 days.
    B. The need for it can be minimized with good operational or strategic planning.
    C. It is used primarily to address budget concerns.
    D. It is a proactive process.

19. A social worker wants to keep track of a client's eating behavior. Rather than have the client record the number of times he snacked between meals, the worker instructs the client to record the number of times he thought of snacking but didn't This strategy for measurement demonstrates the worker's sensitivity to _____ of a measurement.   19._____

A. reliability
B. sensitivity
C. reactivity
D. validity

20. When a family reports to a social work practitioner, each member of the family seems to focus his or her criticisms on the father, who is described in turn as uncooperative, unmotivated, and unyielding. Probably the best way for the practitioner to try to reframe this description is to say mat the father

    A. has a high regard for himself but a low regard for the opinions of others
    B. is a distraction to the others in their goal to achieve better communication
    C. has an unhealthy need to get his own way
    D. is assertive and logically resists doing things that don't make sense to him

21. The BEST description of the process involved in staff training in a social services agency is

    A. applying new knowledge to a problem situation
    B. instruction in and exposure to necessary knowledge
    C. providing knowledge that is generalizable
    D. provoking the exploration of different possible solutions

22. During an interview in which a social worker is attempting to assess a client's mental status, the worker focuses for a while on intellectual functioning-asking the client to read, write, follow simple instructions, and think abstractly. In assessing the client's intellectual functioning, it will be MOST important for the worker to consider the client's

    A. educational attainment
    B. affect
    C. cultural background
    D. recent medical history

23. Social learning theory proposes that some behaviors are learned by individuals through

    A. observation
    B. operant conditioning
    C. reinforcement
    D. classical conditioning

24. When confronted with a potential ethical conflict, a social worker following the ETHIC model of decision-making will FIRST consider

    A. how the standards of the NASW code, as well as relative laws and cases, apply to the situation
    B. the possible consequences of different decisions
    C. relevant personal, societal, agency, client and professional values
    D. who will benefit and who will be harmed by certain decisions

25. When interacting with a person who has a disability, general guidelines include 25.____
    I. Use a normal tone of voice when addressing visually impaired clients
    II. If the person is visually impaired or hard of hearing, avoid words such as "see" or "hear".
    III. If the person is deaf or hard of hearing, look directly at him or her when speaking, even if an interpreter is present.
    IV. In meeting or parting, shake whatever the person offers—hand, prosthesis, or elbow

    A. I and II
    B. I, III, and IV
    C. III and IV
    D. I, II, III and IV

KEY (CORRECT ANSWERS)

1.	True	11.	B
2.	True	12.	A
3.	False	13.	C
4.	True	14.	C
5.	C	15.	A
6.	C	16.	C
7.	A	17.	A
8.	C	18.	B
9.	A	19.	C
10.	B	20.	C

21. B
22. A
23. A
24. C
25. B

EXAMINATION SECTION
TEST 1

DIRECTIONS: Each question or incomplete statement is followed by several suggested answers or completions. Select the one the BEST answers the question or completes the statement. *PRINT THE LETTER OF THE CORRECT ANSWER IN THE SPACE AT THE RIGHT.*

1. The primary sources of data in most assessments are

   A. completed assessment forms
   B. the client's verbal statements
   C. psychological test results
   D. collateral sources

   1.____

2. A social worker is fulfilling the role of a "mediator" when he or she

   A. calls attention to the probable social consequences to a new housing development
   B. refers a jobless person to an unemployment agency
   C. evaluates the outcome of a colleague's practice
   D. helps a frustrated wife to clarify her position to a husband

   2.____

3. In the systems model of human behavior, "division of labor" is an example of

   A. autopoiesis
   B. social control
   C. differentiation
   D. hierarchy

   3.____

4. After several weeks of behavioral intervention, a child is consistently performing the desired behavior targeted by his parents and a social worker: that is, he is going to bed at the correct time without argument or delaying tactics. Now that he's reached this stage, the social worker recommends that the parents gradually withdraw the prompts and reinforcements that induced the behavior to begin with. This is an example of

   A. extinction
   B. shaping
   C. fading
   D. modeling

   4.____

5. When working with a group, a social worker encourages decision-making by consensus. Drawbacks to the use of consensus include

   A. involvement of few available group resources
   B. alienation of the minority
   C. time- and energy-intensiveness
   D. decreased likelihood of handling future controversies

   5.____

6. The primary rationale for the use of a social history for client assessment is that

   A. past behavior is the best predictor of future behavior
   B. the best source of information about a client's situation is the client her/himself
   C. the best protection against legal liability is an exhaustive data set

   6.____

D. problems exist because of an unbalanced reaction between a client system and the environment

7. Most professional codes of ethics provide that a social worker's primary ethical duty is to

   A. respect client privacy and confidentiality
   B. challenge social injustice
   C. work in the best interest of clients
   D. avoid situations that involve ethical conflicts

8. In agency planning, which of the following visual aids will be MOST useful in helping to examine the benefits and drawbacks of different alternative choices

   A. Task planning sheet
   B. Gantt chart
   C. Decision tree
   D. PERT chart

9. Which of the following questions or statements is MOST appropriate for a practitioner in initiating an interview?

   A. "I understand you have a problem."
   B. "You came in here to see me about _____."
   C. "How can I help you today?"
   D. "I'm glad you came in to see me

10. What is the term commonly used to describe children who suffer physical, mental, or emotional injuries inflicted by caretaking adults?

    A. Developmentally disabled
    B. Victims
    C. At risk
    D. Abused or neglected

11. Typically, the questioning process in a social work interview should progress

    A. chronologically
    B. from general to specific
    C. from specific to general
    D. in a series of grouped topical units

12. Assessment is a process that is considered to be the task of the

    A. agency psychiatrist or clinician
    B. social worker
    C. client
    D. social worker and client together

13. A social worker who wants to use a small group as a resource for clients should remember the general rule that the addition of new members, especially resistant ones, should be avoided during the _____ stage of group development.

    A. differentiation
    B. intimacy

C. preaffiliation
D. power and control

14. During an assessment interview with a male high school student, it becomes clear to the practitioner that the boy's behavior problems are related in some way to his frustration at the different expectations of his teachers and his peers concerning the role of a student. The boy is experiencing

    A. inter-role conflict
    B. role ambiguity
    C. intra-role conflict
    D. role incapacity

15. When considering the use of informal resources for an intervention, the social worker should

    A. view informal resources as an inexpensive alternative to formal services
    B. whenever possible, try to "professionalize" or train informal resources to lend them authority
    C. already have some knowledge of available self-help groups in the community
    D. whenever informal resources are identified, try to steer clients toward the ones that are probably most useful

16. Probably the biggest difference between the supervisory role in social work and that of other professions is the

    A. amount of psychological support that must be provided to supervisees
    B. degree of direct involvement in the work of supervisees
    C. predominant use of "soft' criteria in performance evaluations
    D. greater difficulty in matching workers to tasks

17. A social worker is interviewing a woman in a mental hospital who appears lucid but is suspected of having some mental illness. When gathering information, the worker should

    A. explain fully the reason for the interview and ask the client to give her opinion of her mental status
    B. ask short, closed-ended assessment questions up front
    C. administer a standardized assessment that may be evaluated by a psychologist
    D. work assessment questions into the ordinary flow of the conversation

18. A social worker becomes aware of a colleague's incompetent or unethical practice. According to the NASW code, the worker's FIRST obligation is to

    A. inform all of the colleague's relevant clients of the situation
    B. approach the colleague to discuss his/her incapacitation, incompetence, etc.
    C. file a complaint with the NASW
    D. file a complaint with the appropriate licensing board

19. A "communication loop" is completed when

    A. the person to whom the message is addressed begins to respond
    B. the person who initiates the message has completed the transmission
    C. the person to whom the message is addressed receives the message
    D. the person to whom the message is addressed decodes the message

20. Because many parents believe in and utilize corporal punishment as discipline, a social worker must be able to differentiate physical abuse from ordinary spanking or corporal punishment. Which of the following is NOT a useful means of making this distinction?

    A. Parent striking the child in places that are easily injured
    B. Repeated episodes of corporal punishment
    C. Child's report that punishments are severe and painful
    D. Injury to child's body tissue

21. A social worker makes an initial in-home visit to a married couple who have willingly submitted to an intervention regarding their marital problems. During the interview the couple points out that they will be leaving the area in a few weeks, because the wife has been transferred by her employer to a new location. Probably the MOST appropriate plan for dealing with this couple would involve the _____ model of social work.

    A. person-centered
    B. cognitive-behavioral
    C. solution-focused
    D. task-centered

22. The primary purpose of evaluative research in social work is to

    A. measure a client's self-satisfaction
    B. determine whether outcomes can be attributed to an intervention
    C. express the effectiveness of interventions in material terms
    D. determine whether an outcome was achieved

23. Each of the following should be used as a guideline in child placement decisions, EXCEPT

    A. efforts to protect the child should involve as little disruption as possible
    B. use of placement to compel a parent to take some action
    C. involvement of parents and child in the placement decision
    D. maintenance of child's cultural beliefs in placement

24. Which of the following is NOT a factor involved in the decoding of a message?

    A. Relationship with interviewer
    B. Social, emotional, and cognitive barriers
    C. Ethics
    D. Context of interview

25. A practitioner wants to make the parents of an adolescent aware of the behavioral manifestations of depression. Which of the following is LEAST likely to be an indicator?

    A. Sudden tearful reactions
    B. Excessive pleasure-seeking
    C. Decline in school achievement
    D. Jokes about death or dying

26. Which of the following is LEAST likely to be an area of conflict between social workers and attorneys

A. Confidentiality
B. Recording information
C. The best interests of a client
D. The definition of "client"

27. Which of the following typically occurs in the first stage of group therapy?

    A. The members are hostile toward the leader.
    B. Cliques form within the group.
    C. The members talk through the leader and seem to ignore one another.
    D. The members interact with each other tend to ignore the leader.

28. In conducting employee evaluations, a social work supervisor should use _____ as available criteria.
    I. pre-established objective measures such as timeliness
    II. "soft" criteria such as attitude
    III. the supervisor's own work experience
    IV. the performance of others in similar assignments

    A. I only
    B. I and II
    C. I and III
    D. I, II, III and IV

29. Which of the following is NOT a term that is interchangeable with "stepfamily"?

    A. Remarried family
    B. Blended family
    C. Reconstituted family
    D. Renested family

30. A worker refers a client to a colleague who specializes and is trained in law, even though the client requested the service from the worker. Which of the following professional values or ethics is the worker implementing?

    A. Self-determination
    B. Privacy
    C. Competence
    D. Confidentiality

31. Social work practice that is based on behavioral theory assumes that behaviors are determined by

    A. emotions
    B. consequences
    C. values
    D. internal thought processes

32. Which of the following is NOT a symptom associated with bipolar disorder?

    A. Increase in goal-oriented activity
    B. Distractibility
    C. Significant weight loss
    D. Decreased need for sleep

33. A 'helping relationship" between the social worker and client is BEST described as

    A. the goal of any initial contact between worker and client
    B. the medium offered to people in trouble through which they are presented with opportunities
    C. the means by which a worker gains the client's trust to solve problems
    D. a lifeline that is thrown to people in trouble in order to help them out of current problems

34. Communities often contain individuals who are categorized as "AFDC mothers" or "hard-core unemployed" or "AIDS patients," among others. This is a destructive application of the concept of

    A. service delivery
    B. niche
    C. differentiation
    D. diversity

35. The first step in any single-system practice evaluation is to

    A. record baseline data
    B. select suitable measures
    C. implement the intervention
    D. specify the goal

36. A social worker plans a behavioral intervention for a developmentally disabled adult who does not look people in the eye when speaking with them.
    Each of the following behavioral strategies may be useful to the intervention, EXCEPT

    A. overcorrection
    B. instruction
    C. prompting
    D. shaping

37. During several in-home visits with a family, the mother repeatedly refuses to acknowledge that her alcoholism is having an adverse effect on others in the household. The MOST appropriate next step for the social worker would be to initiate

    A. a challenge
    B. behavioral rehearsal
    C. self-talk management
    D. a behavioral contract

38. Working-class or low-income marriages are typically characterized by

    A. marriage late in life
    B. flexible divisions of labor
    C. troubled mother-child relationships
    D. emotional distance between partners

39. A researcher repeatedly measures the dependent variable throughout two baseline and two treatment phases of a study to assess whether variability in the dependent variable is due to the influence of the independent variable. She is using a(n) _____ design of measurement.

A. AB
B. ABAB
C. multiple baseline
D. Solomon four-group

40. What is the typical time-frame for crisis intervention?

    A. One to two weeks
    B. Six to eight weeks
    C. At least eight weeks
    D. Six months or more, depending on the nature of the crisis

41. Stigma, once it has become part of a culture, has certain predictable consequences. Which of the following is NOT one of these consequences?

    A. Discrimination
    B. Absorption
    C. Altered self-concept
    D. Development of subculture

42. A social worker is engaged in a one-on-one interview with a 10-year-old boy, in order to investigate allegations of a father's sexual abuse. The allegations were initially brought by the mother, now divorced from the father, and were later corroborated by the boy. The mother and father are engaged in a custody battle for the boy. The boy's account of events is extremely consistent over time, listing the same major events in sequence, but his affect is flat he relates his accounts of abuse in an oddly detached manner. The BEST action for the social worker at this point would be to

    A. terminate the interview and begin criminal proceedings against the father
    B. terminate the interview and refer the child for an immediate psychiatric consultation
    C. ask the mother to join in the interview and see if her account matches the boy's
    D. ask the boy to go into greater detail about the related events, out of sequence, and then repeat the request at a later time

43. When working with individuals or families of native American cultures, it is best to begin by

    A. gathering a social history
    B. using indirect approaches such as analogy or metaphor
    C. asking for open-ended descriptions of family roles
    D. direct questioning

44. In cases of elder abuse, the government may intervene if
    I. the older person requests it
    II. the older person is found at a hearing to be incompetent
    III. the abuse or neglect presents an unacceptable level of danger to the older person
    IV. the abuse is properly reported and recorded by a visiting social services worker

    A. I only
    B. I and II

C. I, II and III
D. I, II, III and IV

45. Which of the following is a guideline that should be observed in developing an assessment questionnaire for clients?

    A. Develop several focused questionnaires rather than a single all-purpose one.
    B. The most sensitive or probing questions should appear near the middle of the questionnaire.
    C. For complex ideas, form two-part questions.
    D. Include only open-ended questions.

46. During the assessment phase of an interview, checklists are most useful for identifying and selecting

    A. problems for intervention
    B. specific objectives
    C. available resources
    D. general goals

47. Which of the following is an advantage associated with the family life-cycle model?

    A. It highlights the special challenges of blended families.
    B. It identifies developmental tasks for families at specific stages.
    C. It is especially applicable to families in minority groups.
    D. It applies to those who do not have children.

48. Before making the decision to advocate on behalf of a client, it is important to consider several factors. Which of the following is NOT one of these?

    A. Client's consent for advocacy.
    B. Whether advocating is the most useful process that can be applied to the situation.
    C. Whether the complaint or decision involves a legitimate grievance
    D. Client's knowledge and feeling about human services.

49. Which of the following is an advantage associated with the use of genograms in client assessment?

    A. Targeting and identification of relevant social supports.
    B. Execution and interpretation require no instruction.
    C. Placement of an individual or family within a social context.
    D. A considerable shortening of the case record.

50. Activities involved in social casework typically include

    A. counseling those with a terminal illness
    B. supervising juvenile probation clients
    C. providing job training
    D. preparing court reports

51. In middle childhood, school-age children are generally concerned with

    A. "good" behavior in order to receive approval from others
    B. behaving appropriately because they fear punishment

C. the concordance of behaviors with an adopted moral code
D. conforming with group standards in order to be rewarded

52. When a social worker/client relationship is characterized by ineffectiveness, the most common reason is that

   A. resources are not available to meet the client's needs
   B. the client has not sufficiently specified his or her needs
   C. an incorrect solution has been identified by the worker
   D. the worker is attempting to keep the relationship on a pleasant level

53. A social history report includes the statement: "The subject claims to have completed high school." This should be included under the heading:

   A. Family Background and Situation
   B. Intellectual functioning
   C. Impressions and Assessment
   D. Such a statement shouldn't appear at all in a social history report.

54. According to Erickson, which of the following stages of psychosocial development occurs FIRST in the human life span?

   A. Initiative vs. guilt
   B. Trust vs. mistrust
   C. Identity vs. role confusion
   D. Autonomy vs. shame and doubt

55. The strategy of "reframing" is most useful for

   A. desensitizing clients to past trauma
   B. classifying client/family problems according to standard diagnostic categories
   C. helping clients to model their own behavior after others'
   D. revealing a client's strengths and opportunities for helping

56. In general, it is believed that interviewers who spend less than a minimum of _____ of an interview listening to the client are more active than they should be.

   A. one-fourth
   B. one-third
   C. one-half
   D. two thirds

57. In the _____ model of social work, the goal of the social worker is to enhance and restore the psychosocial functioning of persons, or to change noxious social conditions that impede the mutually beneficial interaction between person and their environment.

   A. structural-functional
   B. ecological
   C. medical
   D. strategic

58. In social work, "micro" practice usually focuses on

    A. resolving the problems of individuals, families, or small groups
    B. planning, administration, evaluation, and community organizing
    C. developmental activities in the social environment
    D. facilitating communication, mediation, and negotiation

59. _____ theory may prove most productive for the social work practitioner in understanding families of homosexuals, because it introduces unambiguous distinctions between stigma and homosexual behaviors and feelings.

    A. Structural
    B. Object relations
    C. Strategic
    D. Labeling

60. A client tells a practitioner that his main goal for intervention is to decide on a college major. To BEST help this client, the practitioner will assume the role of

    A. enabler
    B. mediator
    C. initiator
    D. educator

61. Which of the following is NOT a guideline for interacting with clients from a Latino culture?

    A. Efforts to foster independence and self-reliance may be interpreted by many Latinos as a lack of concern for others.
    B. Efforts to deal one-on-one with an adolescent client may serve to alienate the parents, especially the mother.
    C. A nonverbal gesture such as lowering the eyes is interpreted by many Latinos as a sign of respect and deference to authority.
    D. In much of Latino culture, the locus of control for problems tends to be much more external than internal.

62. The broadest, most general type of plan used in social work administration is the

    A. plan for meeting objectives
    B. statement of goals
    C. statement of mission
    D. guiding policies

63. In composing a social network grid with a client, which of the following steps is typically performed FIRST?

    A. Dividing acquaintances according to direction of help
    B. Dividing acquaintances according to duration of acquaintance
    C. Identifying people who can help the client in concrete ways
    D. Identifying areas of life in which people impact the client

64. An administrator notices, in several trips through the agency grounds, that a handful of the organization's support staff are often engaged in socializing or other nonproductive activities. The groups are always small and never made up of the same people, and nearly all members of the support staff have received satisfactory evaluations from their supervisor. The socializing does not occur around clients or visiting professionals. Over the past several years, the agency's efficiency record has remained about the same. The agency would probably be BEST served by the view that

   A. rigid controls should be implemented to reduce this behavior
   B. a memorandum should be circulated citing this behavior as a poor example
   C. the behavior may help to relieve boredom and should be ignored
   D. the supervisor should add an item or two to the evaluation that will address this behavior

65. Each of the following is a stage of the dying process described by Kübler-Ross, EXCEPT

   A. acknowledgement
   B. depression
   C. anger
   D. acceptance

66. For a prison inmate, "notice of rights" means the inmate
   I. receives advance notice of what conduct will result in discipline or punishment
   II. receives written notice of any charges against him
   III. is entitled to organize a group meeting for political purposes

   A. I and II
   B. I and III
   C. II and III
   D. I, II and III

67. Which of the following values is NOT generally indigenous to families of Asian heritage?

   A. Inconspicuousness
   B. Perfectionism
   C. Fatalism
   D. Shame as a behavioral influence

68. Most professionals recommend that in order to accurately evaluate the effect of an intervention, baseline data should be collected for no fewer than _____ data points.

   A. 2
   B. 3
   C. 4
   D. 5

69. During an assessment interview, a social worker and a client try to clarify and analyze the client's sense of self. If the worker wants to discover something about the client's self-acceptance, which of the following questions is MOST appropriate?

   A. To what extent do you worry about illness and physical incapacity?
   B. Is what you expect to happen mostly good or mostly bad?

C. Do you enjoy the times when you are alone?
D. Where do your other family members live?

70. Which of the following cognitive traits explains the mistaken belief held by many adolescents that they are invincible or protected from harmful consequences of their behavior?

    A. The personal fable
    B. Object delusion
    C. Egocentrism
    D. Pseudohypocrisy

71. An 18-year-old woman comes to see a social worker at a crisis center one day after being raped on a date. In the interview with this client, the social worker should FIRST:

    A. emphasize medical and legal procedures
    B. obtain factual information about the rape
    C. listen to the client and support her emotionally
    D. help the client establish contact with significant others

72. During a client assessment, each of the following should be considered a useful question, EXCEPT

    A. Can you tell me about times when you've successfully handled a problem like this in the past?
    B. When family members complain about your behavior, what to they say?
    C. How have you managed to cope up to this point?
    D. What do your friends and family seem to like most about you?

73. Norms are MOST accurately described as

    A. attitudes toward life events and processes
    B. assumptions about the world
    C. expectations of the self and others
    D. ideas about what is proper and desirable behavior

74. Generally, when a homeless person or group is removed from a condemned or abandoned property under the law, the most significant legal question to arise is whether

    A. the last owner of the property can be located for consent
    B. the property is being "rehabilitated" by the occupants
    C. the state recognizes a "right to shelter"
    D. the property has really been abandoned

75. A social worker introduces herself to a family household in which an elderly man lives. The man has been reported by neighbors on several occasions for making threats of violence to a number of adolescents in the neighborhood. The worker recognizes that she is uninvited, and the BEST way for her to describe the purpose of her relationship to the family would be as

A. helping the man to modify his behavior so that no further institutional involvement will be necessary
B. helping the man to avoid the aggravating stimulus of contact with neighborhood teens
C. protecting the neighborhood from the elderly man's threats
D. arranging for the man to get counseling in order to understand and change his behavior

KEY (CORRECT ANSWERS)

1. B	16. A	31. B	46. D	61. D
2. D	17. D	32. C	47. B	62. C
3. C	18. B	33. B	48. D	63. D
4. C	19. A	34. B	49. D	64. C
5. C	20. C	35. D	50. A	65. A
6. A	21. C	36. A	51. A	66. A
7. C	22. B	37. A	52. D	67. B
8. C	23. B	38. D	53. D	68. B
9. B	24. C	39. B	54. B	69. C
10. B	25. B	40. B	55. D	70. A
11. B	26. C	41. B	56. D	71. C
12. D	27. C	42. D	57. B	72. B
13. D	28. B	43. B	58. A	73. D
14. C	29. D	44. B	59. D	74. B
15. C	30. C	45. A	60. A	75. A

TEST 2

DIRECTIONS: Each question or incomplete statement is followed by several suggested answers or completions. Select the one that BEST answers the question or completes the statement. *PRINT THE LETTER OF THE CORRECT ANSWER IN THE SPACE AT THE RIGHT.*

1. A 24-year-old mother of four, recently widowed, tells a practitioner: "I feel like my whole life has just fallen apart. I don't think I can take care of my family on my own. My husband always made all the decisions and earned the money to support us. I haven't slept well since he died and I've started drinking more often. My parents try to help me but it's not enough."
The practitioner responds by saying: "So you're afraid about your ability to shoulder all the family responsibilities now." This response is an example of a(n)

   A. reflection
   B. clarification
   C. paraphrase
   D. summarization

   1.____

2. At the beginning of an intake interview, a social worker's tasks are to
   I. gather data and conduct an assessment
   II. establish a positive relationship with the interviewee
   III. obtain brief details that will indicate whether the situation for which the client wants help is among the problems for which the worker offers help
   IV. offer help

   A. I only
   B. I and II
   C. II and III
   D. I, II, III and IV

   2.____

3. Which of the following is NOT a basic purpose of a professional code of ethics?

   A. To provide a mechanism for professional accountability
   B. To educate professionals about sound conduct
   C. To set standards that will be understood and enforced across all cultures
   D. To serve as a tool for improving practice

   3.____

4. According to cognitive-behavioral theory, schemas represent a client's

   A. subversive attempts to persist in faulty cognitions
   B. automatic responses
   C. different response patterns
   D. core beliefs and assumptions

   4.____

5. Objective data found in a client's folder might include

   A. A neighbor's recorded statement about a previous incident
   B. Notes on an interview with his psychotherapist
   C. A work evaluation performed by a supervisor
   D. A summary of previous criminal convictions

   5.____

6. In the middle phase of a client interview, as a problem is being further explored, the practitioner should spend a considerable amount of time

   A. interpreting behavior
   B. confronting discrepancies
   C. restating or paraphrasing
   D. negotiating a service contract

7. Which of the following statements is TRUE about social work assessment?

   A. It is another term for "goal setting."
   B. It identifies a problem and its potential impact.
   C. It refers to the search for alternative solutions.
   D. It relates to the evaluation of program effectiveness.

8. An agency needs to write a proposal to a private foundation in order to request funding for renovations. It will be necessary for the agency to organize a _____ group.

   A. training
   B. task-focused
   C. recreation
   D. self-help

9. Social exchange theory is based on the idea that people

   A. often attempt to superimpose their own needs onto the desires of others
   B. aim to protect themselves from punishment in relationships
   C. aim to maximize rewards and minimize costs in relationships
   D. exchange rewards with those who are most like themselves

10. Privileged communication typically applies in cases of
    I. marital infidelity, if both spouses are participating in treatment
    II. legal proceedings in which a practitioner is asked to produce client records in court
    III. child abuse or neglect
    IV. client disclosures of personal and sensitive information

    A. I and III
    B. I, II and IV
    C. III and IV
    D. I, II, III and IV

11. During an assessment interview, a practitioner asks questions about the client's customs and traditions. The practitioner is most likely seeking information about the impact of _____ on the client's functioning.

    A. unhealthy patterns
    B. self-talk
    C. interpersonal relationships
    D. cultural diversity

12. Each of the following is true of the intervention phase of social work, EXCEPT that it

    A. is focused on problems
    B. requires interviewing, recording, letter writing, and referral skills
    C. is guided by the principles of self-determination and acceptance
    D. results naturally from a thorough assessment

13. During a client interview, a practitioner is attempting to summarize what the client has just said, but the client gives signs that he does not agree with the summary and intends to interrupt. The practitioner believes it is important for the client to hear how the summary sounds in someone else's words. In order to maintain his turn at speaking, the practitioner may want to

    A. raise an index finger
    B. raise his eyebrows
    C. speak more loudly
    D. stop all accompanying gestures and body movements

14. In Erikson's model of human development, the stage at which a child learns to meet the demands of society is

    A. identity vs. role confusion
    B. industry vs. inferiority
    C. basic trust vs. mistrust
    D. autonomy vs. shame and doubt

15. Generally, controlled experimental designs account for about _____ percent of all social work research.

    A. 5
    B. 20
    C. 35
    D. 55

16. What is the term for a social work process that brings an intervention to a close?

    A. Recognizing success
    B. Integrating gains
    C. Terminating the relationship
    D. Expanding opportunities

17. Which of the following is an example of primary prevention for mental illness?

    A. Crisis intervention
    B. Parent-child communication training
    C. Psychotherapy
    D. Teacher referrals to social workers of children targeted by bullies

18. Which of the following is an example of a closed question?

    A. How do you think you can, as you've said, 'Come more alive?'
    B. Of all the problems we've discussed, which bothers you the most?
    C. What is your relationship with your family?
    D. What kinds of things do you find yourself longing for?

19. Over time, adult personalities are likely to change in each of the following ways, EXCEPT becoming more

    A. candid
    B. dependable
    C. receptive to the company of others
    D. accepting of hardship

20. Which of the following BEST describes the mission of social work?

    A. Meeting client needs while influencing social institutions to become more responsive to people
    B. Helping clients negotiate an often complex and difficult network of services
    C. Constantly responding and adapting to social changes in micro and macro environments
    D. Identifying programs and connecting clients to needed services

21. Numerous studies have been conducted to determine which factors in a client/helping professional relationship are consistently related to positive outcomes. Which of the following is/are NOT one of these conditions?

    A. A relationship analogous to doctor/patient
    B. Empathy and positive regard
    C. A working alliance
    D. Transference and countertransference

22. A person who donates anonymously to a favorite charity is most likely driven by what Maslow called

    A. intrinsic motivation
    B. extrinsic motivation
    C. affective habituation
    D. self-actualization

23. According to the NASW code of ethics, sexual contact between practitioners and former clients is

    A. strongly discouraged under any circumstances
    B. discouraged, but considered acceptable if it occurs two years or more after the professional relationship has been terminated
    C. grounds for expulsion from the social work profession
    D. a private matter whose nature is left entirely up to the practitioner and the client

24. During an unstructured interview with a client, a practitioner generally focuses on

    A. discovering the presenting problem
    B. confronting erroneous self-talk
    C. giving reflective responses that elicit more information
    D. a prescribed list of screening questions

25. Process recording is an assessment technique that is most often used in

    A. clinical settings
    B. family sculpting

C. one-on-one interviews
D. group sessions

26. The NASW's stance on bartering with clients, rather than simply charging fees for service, includes the opinion that social workers should
    I. participate in barter in only in very limited circumstances
    II. ensure that such arrangements are an accepted practice among professionals in the local community
    III. propose bartering if it is clear the client will be unable to pay for services
    IV. never barter with clients under any circumstances

    A. I only
    B. I and II
    C. I, II and III
    D. IV only

27. Etiquette, customs, and minor regulations are examples of

    A. mores
    B. norms
    C. ethics
    D. folkways

28. A practitioner working in the Adlerian model is likely to use each of the following as an assessment instrument, EXCEPT

    A. personality inventories
    B. ecomaps
    C. lifestyle inventories
    D. early childhood recollections

29. Which of the following information would typically be solicited at the LATEST point in an intake interview?

    A. educational history
    B. family/marital/sexual history
    C. vocational history
    D. past interventions or service requests

30. According to conflict theorists, the "hidden curriculum" of schools

    A. serves to transmit different cultural values
    B. encourages social integration
    C. often results in self-fulfilling prophecy
    D. perpetuates existing social inequalities

31. The high value placed on individual freedom in American society has arguably produced each of the following, EXCEPT

    A. a cultural paradox
    B. an environmental dilemma
    C. unfair economic competition
    D. a *caveat emptor* ("let the buyer beware") approach to the market economy

32. One model of the relationship between helping professionals and clients emphasizes the social influence of professionals in counseling roles. To be effective, practitioners in the counseling role can draw on a power base that arises out of the relationship with the client. In client relationships, the power base that is typically LEAST helpful for the practitioner is known as _____ power.

    A. referent
    B. expert
    C. legitimate
    D. reward

33. In social work, experimental research designs

    A. are the most commonly conducted form of social work research
    B. obligate the researcher to offer a treatment to a control group as soon as possible after the study is terminated
    C. are usually single-system designs
    D. are generally free of ethical concerns if the research is conducted well

34. The term "social stratification" refers to social inequality that is

    A. differential
    B. structured
    C. institutionally sanctioned
    D. imperceptible

35. To a practitioner working from the behavioral perspective, the most important feature of good relationships is

    A. effective coping behaviors
    B. freedom from conflict
    C. complementary needs
    D. well-established boundaries

36. In an initial interview, it is common for clients to

    A. break down emotionally
    B. describe problems in a way that minimizes their own contributions to them
    C. disclose very personal information and emotions
    D. be someone other than the person who has arranged the interview

37. Which of the following is NOT a trend in the use of family approaches in direct social work practice?

    A. Increased attention on the family as an isolated system
    B. Increased attention to family diversity
    C. The use of a variety of social science theoretical approaches
    D. The use of multiple intervention models

38. The process whereby a client's place past feelings or attitudes toward significant people in their lives onto their social work practitioner is known as

    A. transference
    B. denial

C. countertransference
D. projection

39. Social desirability bias often causes people to

    A. make appraisals of others that are based on their social functioning rather than their effectiveness in other roles
    B. attribute their successes to skill, while blaming external factors for failures
    C. modify their responses to surveys or interviews based on what they think are desirable responses
    D. focus on the style of their interactions with others, rather than the substance

40. A social worker attends an evening anniversary party at which she has consumed some alcohol, which she rarely drinks. She doesn't think she is literally drunk, but would acknowledge feeling slightly tipsy and perhaps not in full command of herself. When she arrives at home later, she listens to a message from a client that was left on her answering machine while she was out. The client, with whom she has met several times, is feeling lonely and desperate because of the recent loss of his wife to cancer. The social worker wants to help. She should

    A. return the call immediately and try to counsel the client
    B. return the call immediately and explain that she is unable to help right now, but will call first thing tomorrow
    C. avoid contacting the client until she has recovered her ability to perform up to her usual professional standards and judgement
    D. contact a trusted colleague, give him or her the relevant information, and ask that he or she try to counsel the client over the phone

41. During an assessment interview, a practitioner asks a client: "What kinds of feelings do you have when this happens to you?" The practitioner is trying to identify the _____ associated with the problem.

    A. affect and mood states
    B. secondary gains
    C. overt behaviors or motoric responses
    D. internal dialogue

42. Hospital social workers typically engage in each of the following types of interventions or practice, EXCEPT

    A. crisis intervention
    B. discharge planning
    C. long-term counseling
    D. group work

43. For social work practitioners, symptoms of "burnout" on the job typically include each of the following, EXCEPT

    A. feeling unable to accomplish goals
    B. emotional exhaustion
    C. chronic worry
    D. a feeling of detachment from clients and work

44. When a case manager reaches the point in service coordination during which he makes a referral, he has assumed the role of

   A. evaluator
   B. broker
   C. advocate
   D. planner

45. A practitioner encounters a situation in which his own personal values conflict with a client's. In this instance, the practitioner is expected to engage in

   A. peer review
   B. value suspension
   C. legal consultation
   D. value clarification

46. Among the following American groups, the women who have the greatest risk of HIV infection are

   A. white
   B. African American
   C. Native American
   D. Hispanic

47. The trend in school social work has been a gradual shift toward an emphasis on the _____ perspective.

   A. behavioral
   B. input-based
   C. ecological
   D. psychiatric

48. The success of client-written logs as an assessment tool may depend on the client's motivation to keep a log. Which of the following is LEAST likely to help motivate a client to keep a log?

   A. Establishing a clear rationale or purpose for keeping the log
   B. Establishing negative consequences if the client fails to make log entries
   C. Adapting the log type to the client's abilities to self-monitor
   D. Involving the client in discussing and analyzing the log

49. The social work value of *empathy* is defined as a practitioner's capacity to

   A. imagine oneself in another's situation
   B. feel compassion for a person who is in distress
   C. convince a person that things will get better
   D. make a person recognize his/her own inner strength

50. Focusing on a client's positive assets and strengths during an assessment interview
    I. emphasizes the wholeness of the client system, rather than simply the problematic aspects
    II. gives a practitioner information about potential problems that might arise during an intervention
    III. helps convey to the client that they have internal resources that may prove useful
    IV. risks skewing the effectiveness of an intervention by taking the focus off the presenting problem

    A. I and III
    B. I, II and III
    C. III only
    D. I, II, III and IV

51. A hospital social worker is meeting with an 86-year-old man who suffers from Alzheimer's disease. His symptoms thus far have consisted largely of incidents of forgetfulness, and he has shown no signs of dementia or violence. The client's daughter, who has recently succeeded in having her father grant her a power of attorney over his affairs. When the social worker asks questions of the client, the daughter repeated breaks in and attempts to answer for him, though he appears to be lucid. When the social worker asks to speak to the client alone, the daughter refuses. The social worker should

    A. suspect a case of elder abuse and contact the adult protective services agency to look into it
    B. pretend to leave, and then attempt to interview the man when the daughter leaves the room
    C. suspect that the daughter may have suffered abuse at the hands of her father and adult protective services to look into it
    D. suspect a case of elder abuse and contact local law enforcement authorities

52. Which of the following is a key element of the case management paradigm?

    A. A focus on improving the quality and accessibility of resources
    B. A focus on developing vocational adjustment
    C. The selection of interventions based on empirical research
    D. Rational-emotive therapy

53. Of the following health problems, each affects the elderly to a greater extent than other age groups. The one that leads by the greatest percentage is

    A. cancer
    B. stroke
    C. heart disease
    D. Alzheimer's disease

54. Approximately _____ of all direct practice interventions are terminated because of unanticipated situational factors.

    A. an eighth
    B. a quarter
    C. half
    D. three-quarters

55. Social factors that increase the risk for suicide include each of the following, EXCEPT that the person

    A. lives alone
    B. has repeatedly rejected support
    C. has no ongoing therapeutic relationship
    D. is married

56. Practitioners are generally considered to have an ethical obligation to do each of the following, EXCEPT

    A. remain aware of their own values
    B. seek to learn about the diverse cultural backgrounds of their clients
    C. avoid imposing their values on clients
    D. refer clients whose values strongly differ from their own

57. Studies of young people who join urban gangs suggests that most often, people join gangs because of a need for a(n)

    A. peer group
    B. outlet for pent-up aggression and frustration
    C. surrogate family
    D. vehicle for criminal activity

58. After terminating a working relationship with a social worker, a client joins the local chapter of Alcoholics Anonymous. In doing so, she is attempting to

    A. form new therapeutic relationships
    B. prolong treatment
    C. maintain gains
    D. generalize gains

59. A key concept of narrative therapy is the idea tha

    A. clients often construct one-dimensional stories that don't tell the whole truth
    B. clearly naming a problem or disorder is the first step in solving it
    C. problems are inseparable from the person
    D. interventions are narrowly targeted to "revisions" of specific passages within the story

60. The creation of social service programs typically accomplishes each of the following, EXCEPT

    A. prevention
    B. enhancement
    C. retrenchment
    D. remediation

61. The most significant health problem facing Native Americans today is

    A. tuberculosis
    B. alcoholism
    C. heart disease
    D. diabetes

62. Which of the following is NOT one of the six "core values" that is cited in the preamble to the NASW's code of ethics?

    A. Service
    B. Confidentiality
    C. Integrity
    D. Importance of human relationships

63. Each of the following is a guideline for a practitioner's participation in crisis intervention procedures, EXCEPT

    A. expressing empathy by saying things such as "I understand"
    B. asking the client to describe the event
    C. letting the client talk for as long as he or she likes without interruption
    D. asking the client to describe his or her reactions and responses

64. A practitioner has begun to work with clients in one-on-one settings. He thinks perhaps self-disclosure would be a good way to establish a solid, caring relationship with his clients. He should remember that in working with clients professionally, there will always be a tension between the competing forces of self-disclosure and

    A. candor
    B. liability
    C. reciprocity
    D. privacy

65. From an ethical standpoint, practitioners may
    I. accept a referral fee
    II. refer a client to a single referral source
    III. use a place of employment, such as a social services agency, to recruit clients for their own private practice
    IV. refer clients only if their problems fall outside the practitioner's area of competence

    A. I and II
    B. II only
    C. II, III and IV
    D. I, II, III and IV

66. According to Carol H. Meyer's widely used model of social work assessment, the first step in the assessment process is

    A. evaluation
    B. inferential thinking
    C. problem definition
    D. exploration

67. What is the term for the theory that explains how people generate explanations for the behaviors of others?

    A. Attribution theory
    B. Stereotyping

C. Thematic apperception
D. Implicit personality theory

68. The most important professional risk associated with amalgamating groups under very broad headings or labels, such as "Asian American," is that

    A. these terms are considered derogatory by many people
    B. most immigrants to this country proudly insist on being referred to as simply "American"
    C. many people resent being folded in to a larger group for the purpose of classification
    D. the label may obscure significant differences in the culture and experiences of individuals or subgroups within the larger category

69. Before entering a social work field placement program, prospective students are ethically entitled to know
    I. dismissal policies and procedures
    II. employment prospects for graduates
    III. the basis for performance evaluation
    IV. names and theoretical perspectives of prospective supervisors

    A. I only
    B. I, II, and III
    C. III only
    D. I, II, III and IV

70. Of the steps involved in recruitment and training at human services organizations, the FIRST typically involves

    A. reference and background checks
    B. posting position announcements
    C. screening interviews
    D. developing a job description

71. During an intake interview, a client generally avoids making eye contact with the practitioner. Averting the eyes in this way is an example of the _____ function of eye contact.

    A. monitoring
    B. expressive
    C. regulatory
    D. cognitive

72. The educational success of American children and youth is highly correlated to

    A. home schooling
    B. regional employment patterns
    C. family values
    D. race and ethnicity

73. Which of the following techniques is a client-centered practitioner MOST likely to use?

    A. Response shaping
    B. Reflection

C. Giving advice
D. Analysis

74. During a meeting with a client who has just ended his marriage after twelve years, the client insists repeatedly that everything is fine. No matter what the practitioner asks or tries to suggest, the response is the same. The client is engaging in the facial management technique known as

   A. neutralizing
   B. masking
   C. intensifying
   D. deintensifying

75. A practitioner is considering a dual relationship with a client. Before forming such a relationship, the practitioner should consider
   I. divergent responsibilities
   II. incompatible expectations
   III. the power differential
   IV. referring the client to another practitioner

   A. I and II
   B. I, II and III
   C. II, III and IV
   D. I, II, III and IV

KEY (CORRECT ANSWERS)

1. A	16. B	31. A	46. B	61. B
2. C	17. B	32. D	47. C	62. B
3. C	18. B	33. B	48. B	63. A
4. D	19. C	34. B	49. A	64. D
5. D	20. A	35. A	50. B	65. B
6. C	21. A	36. B	51. A	66. D
7. B	22. A	37. A	52. A	67. A
8. B	23. A	38. A	53. C	68. D
9. C	24. C	39. C	54. C	69. B
10. B	25. C	40. C	55. D	70. D
11. D	26. B	41. A	56. D	71. C
12. A	27. D	42. C	57. C	72. D
13. C	28. A	43. C	58. C	73. B
14. B	29. B	44. B	59. A	74. A
15. A	30. D	45. B	60. C	75. B

EXAMINATION SECTION
TEST 1

DIRECTIONS: Each question or incomplete statement is followed by several suggested answers or completions. Select the one that BEST answers the question or completes the statement. *PRINT THE LETTER OF THE CORRECT ANSWER IN THE SPACE AT THE RIGHT.*

1. For children, divorce has been identified as a risk factor for
    I. being abused
    II. substance abuse
    III. lower academic achievement
    IV. criminal involvement

    A. I and II
    B. II and III
    C. II, III and IV
    D. I, II, III and IV

2. In formulating useful goals with clients, a social worker is guided by several principles. Which of the following is NOT one of these principles?

    A. Goal formulation is often delimited by the purpose of the agency, and may necessitate referral.
    B. It is necessary to designate a target person whose condition is to be changed or maintained.
    C. Goals should always be stated positively in terms of *doing* something, rather than simply *not doing* something.
    D. The establishment of a time frame for achievement is counterproductive in the formulation of goals.

3. In selecting members for group social work, homogeneity will prove most important regarding

    A. intelligence
    B. ethnicity
    C. age, especially for young children
    D. common interests

4. A practitioner will probably NOT work well with diverse populations if he

    A. believes he is free from any racist attitudes, beliefs, or feelings
    B. is comfortable with the differences between himself and clients
    C. is flexible in applying theories to specific situations
    D. is open to being challenged and teste

5. "Non-verbal" messages of practitioners and clients refer to

    A. statements that nobody should be permitted to make in an interpersonal relationship
    B. ideas and thoughts that are left unrevealed

C. written or otherwise documented statements about problems, recommendations, and solutions
D. the entire range of facial and body expressions that communicate feelings

6. During an assessment interview, a social worker should usually avoid asking _____ questions.

   A. "why"
   B. probing
   C. open-ended
   D. closed-ended

7. Common goals of foster parent organizations include each of the following, EXCEPT

   A. elevating the public's regard for foster care
   B. the facilitation of adoption by foster parents
   C. influencing legislation that concerns children and natural parents
   D. disseminating information among foster parents

8. "Homeostasis" is a concept that has been traditionally used to describe how

   A. organisms maintain a constant external environment,
   B. organisms keep themselves stable through self-regulating mechanisms
   C. humans tend to form groups or tribes around food supplies
   D. humans display a broad but fixed range of behaviors

9. A practitioner welcomes a client at the door of his office by saying, "Come in and sit down." He gestures to the room and the chair inside. This gesture is a _____ of the practitioner's verbal message

   A. complementation
   B. repetition
   C. regulation
   D. contradiction

10. In interviewing clients, practitioners should be careful to avoid nonverbal behaviors that are generally considered to be negative. These gestures include each of the following, EXCEPT

    A. body rotated slightly away from the client
    B. crossing and recrossing legs
    C. slightly backward body lean
    D. frequent eye contact

11. A practitioner asks himself: "Is our agency's program doing what it had hoped to do?" He is asking himself a _____ question.

    A. client outcome assessment
    B. intervention effectiveness
    C. process evaluation
    D. program evaluation

12. Of the following, which provides the BEST definition of the process of social work?

A. A distinct set of skills that allow the worker to tap into a variety of skills to improve conditions surrounding the client system
B. A helping activity undertaken to improve social functioning through direct involvement with the client or the systems that impact him
C. A series of programmed interventions designed to shape the client and his environment
D. A professional service to people in need who are unwilling or unable to act in their own best interests

13. Which of the following is NOT a basic component of social work "competence," as defined by the NASW?

    A. Accepting responsibility or employment only on the basis of existing competence or the intention to acquire the necessary competence.
    B. Not allowing their personal problems, psychosocial distress, legal problems, substance abuse, or mental health difficulties to interfere with professional judgment and performance.
    C. Basing practice on recognized knowledge, including empirically based knowledge, relevant to social work and social work ethics.
    D. Striving to become and remain proficient in professional practice and the performance of professional functions.

14. For practitioners who hope to draw upon Piaget's theory of cognitive development in their work with clients, probably the biggest shortcoming of his theory is that it

    A. does not examine any cognitive development beyond adolescence
    B. pigeonholes clients into distinct categories
    C. excludes questions of morality
    D. does not examine behavioral components of cognitions

15. Which of the following is true of institutional discrimination?

    A. It is often concealed through legal maneuverings.
    B. It is limited to large, formal organizations.
    C. It is woven into the fabric of society.
    D. It is a construction of the elite.

16. In the solution-focused model of intervention, the best way to solve problems is to

    A. discover when the client is not having a problem, and then build on that
    B. understand the goals and ambitions of the client
    C. determine the function that the problematic behavior serves for the client
    D. define the problem in terms of the client's external environment

17. A child in Piaget's preoperational stage
    I. is capable of altruism
    II. uses transductive reasoning
    III. is egocentric.
    IV. derives thought from sensation and movement

    A. I and II
    B. I, III and IV

C. II and III
D. I, II, III and IV

18. Which of the following is NOT a primary human motive? 18.____

    A. Desire for competence
    B. Avoidance of pain
    C. Thirst
    D. Hunger

19. Summarizing clients' statements is an active listening strategy that is often useful for distilling statements into their important elements. The FIRST step in developing a good summarization of client statements during an interview is to 19.____

    A. covertly restating the message or series of messages to yourself
    B. listening for the presence of "feeling" words
    C. ask the client to summarize for herself
    D. identify any relevant patterns themes, or multiple elements

20. Each of the following is considered to be a desirable outcome of an initial interview with an applicant for social services, EXCEPT that the applicant 20.____

    A. leaves confident of working with the practitioner or case manager toward a satisfactory solution
    B. understands his/her responsibilities in the treatment or intervention
    C. feels free to express him/herself
    D. feeling some rapport with the practitioner or case manager

21. When counseling clients, social work practitioners will generally be effective if they 21.____
    I. are able to recognize and accept their own power
    II. can focus on the present moment
    III. remain in the active process of developing their own counseling style
    IV. are not afraid to offer advice

    A. I and III
    B. I, II and III
    C. II, III and IV
    D. I, II, III and IV

22. According to the NASW's code of ethics, social workers who have direct knowledge of a social work colleague's incompetence should FIRST 22.____

    A. consult with that colleague when feasible and assist the colleague in taking remedial action
    B. take action through the appropriate channels established by the employers or agency
    C. notify the NASW and any appropriate licensing and regulating bodies
    D. solicit the opinion of at least one other social worker with approximately equal qualifications and responsibilities to determine a course of action

23. Countertransference, if recognized by the practitioner, can be a useful element in a client relationship. Often, however, it is not helpful or even hurtful. Hurtful forms typically involve each of the following, EXCEPT countertransference that 23.____

A. causes a practitioner to emit subtle clues that "lead" the client
B. causes a practitioner to adopt the role the client wants us to play in his or her traditional "script"
C. is used at a distance to generate empathy for the client
D. blinds a practitioner from an important area of exploration

24. During any intervention, a social worker's final activities are aimed at _____ in the client's everyday functioning.
    I. stabilizing success
    II. generalizing outcomes
    III. preventing recidivism
    IV. restricting options

    A. I and II
    B. I and III
    C. II, III and IV
    D. I, II, III and IV

25. In the documentation and report writing phase of assessment, a service coordinator's documentation responsibilities usually consist of

    A. social histories and intake summaries
    B. medical and social histories
    C. staff notes and mental status examinations
    D. intake summaries and staff notes

26. A social work practitioner is MOST likely to increase the chances of his clients' connecting with the appropriate services when he

    A. refers clients to other more skilled professionals in the hope that these professionals will be able to determine how best to meet the clients' needs
    B. promotes self determination by providing a list of agencies in the area and allowing the clients to decide who can best meet their needs
    C. acquire expertise in as many areas of social work practice as possible, in order to directly provide needed services
    D. becomes knowledgeable about programs and providers available, and actively brokers needed services

27. One explanation for the steady increase in the divorce rate in the United States is that industrialization and urbanization led to a change in the roles played by family members. This explanation is consistent with the _____ perspective.

    A. symbolic interaction
    B. structural functionalist
    C. subcultural
    D. social conflict

28. One of the most significant criticisms about the use of strategic planning in human services organizations is that it

    A. leaves many stakeholders in the dark about the organization's objectives
    B. limits responsiveness to changing community needs

C. erodes employee morale and commitment to the organizational mission
D. is often too abstract to be useful in day-to-day management

29. The way in which a practitioner conceptualizes a client's problem configuration is known as

   A. conceptualization
   B. the internal working model
   C. mental set
   D. framing

30. Significant factors that have contributed to the changing nature of American families since the 1970s include
   I. an increase in births outside marriage
   II. a greater number of remarriages in which partners bring children from previous relationships
   III. altered gender role expectations
   IV. an increase in the number of partners who divorce or separate

   A. I, II and IV
   B. I and III
   C. III only
   D. I, II, III and IV

31. Culture maintains boundaries in each of the following ways, EXCEPT by

   A. instilling a sense of genuineness about the alternatives peculiar to a society
   B. constructing symbols and meanings
   C. limiting the ranges of acceptable behavior and attitudes
   D. establishing the tendency for people to think of other societies as inferior

32. The solution-focused perspective defines a client who describes a problem but isn't willing to work on solving it as a

   A. resistor
   B. complainant
   C. dam-builder
   D. procrastinator

33. During an assessment interview, a practitioner is trying to identify the range of problems that a client is experiencing. Which of the following communication skills is most appropriately used for this purpose?

   A. Open-ended questions
   B. Closed-ended questions
   C. Confrontation
   D. Interpretation

34. Social workers who have unresolved personal conflicts should

   A. recognize that their problems may interfere with the effectiveness and avoid activities or responses that could harm a client
   B. repress any anxiety-provoking issues in their own lives before attempting to work with others

C. use their experience to lead clients in a mutual resolution of these problems
D. resolve these conflicts before planning a client interventionand ideally, before meeting the client at all.

35. Based largely on the understanding that all people break rules at one time or another, _____ theorists make the assumption that what we call "deviant" is actually part of an overall pattern of normality.   35.____

   A. labeling
   B. social Darwinism
   C. conflict
   D. order

36. Rural clients tend to evaluate social workers on the basis of   36.____

   A. the level of education the worker has achieved
   B. help delivered or problems solved
   C. the type of intervention used
   D. areas of specialization

37. A client is having trouble at work. He tells the practitioner "I have a hard time relating to authority figures." He is describing his problem behavior   37.____

   A. in a way that places responsibility squarely on himself
   B. covertly
   C. in nonbehavioral terms
   D. without any affective cues

38. The practice of limiting a client's right to self-determination in order to protect him or her from self-harm is known in social work as   38.____

   A. gatekeeping
   B. paternalism
   C. delimiting behavior
   D. proxy

39. Which of the following is LEAST likely to be a symptom of stress?   39.____

   A. Emotional instability
   B. Lethargy
   C. Sleep problems
   D. Digestive problems

40. In the traditional clinical model of school social work, a practitioner was probably LEAST likely to execute the role of   40.____

   A. enabler
   B. consultant
   C. supporter
   D. advocate

41. When advocating for a client, the first attempt at advocacy should always be

    A. a legal challenge
    B. a formal appeal
    C. temperate persuasion
    D. widely spread publicity about the client's case

42. During regular meetings with his practitioner, a client has the tendency to ascribe the achievements of others to good luck or easy tasks, while assuming his failures to be due to a lack of ability or experience. The client's thinking is a phenomenon known as

    A. fundamental attribution bias
    B. the Hawthorne effect
    C. self-serving bias
    D. the halo effect

43. The responsibilities of social work intern instructors typically include each of the following, EXCEPT

    A. clearly stating roles and responsibilities of interns in the field
    B. clearly stating the roles and responsibilities of site supervisors
    C. acting on site supervisors' recommendations following a negative intern evaluation
    D. developing clear field placement policies

44. A teenage client has been having problems in school he is constantly being disciplined for being disruptive. Discussions with the client reveal that even though he has lost several privileges at school, he is reluctant to give up his disruptive behavior because of the attention it brings in from his peers. The attention of the client's peers is an example of a(n)

    A. secondary gain
    B. behavioral consequence
    C. negative reinforcement
    D. cognitive dissonance

45. Which of the following is NOT a typical purpose of client self-monitoring?

    A. To shift the burden of decision-making onto the client
    B. To validate the accuracy of the client's reports during interviews
    C. To test out hunches about the problem.
    D. To help practitioner and client gain information about what actually occurs with respect to the problem in real-life situations

46. Which of the following is a "lower-order" human need, as identified in Maslow's hierarchy?

    A. Belonging
    B. Status
    C. Fulfillment
    D. Security

47. Gene, a social worker, finds himself wanting to solve his client's problems with alcohol dependency, which are similar to problems Gene's own son went through several years ago. Gene gives advice and is frustrated when the client doesn't follow through on his suggestions. Gene's emotional reactions to his client are based on

    A. countertransference
    B. nurturing
    C. transference
    D. empathy

48. In the termination phase of treatment, strategies for maintaining client gains may include each of the following, EXCEPT

    A. increasing the client's sense of mastery through realistic praise
    B. anticipating and planning for possible future difficulties
    C. highlighting and specifying the client's role in maintaining change
    D. teaching the client to deal with problems that underlie a coping pattern

49. After receiving a notification about a 10-year-old boy's underperfor-mance at school, a social worker has tried twice to arrange a meeting with the boy's 28-year-old mother, who works long hours as a waitress and has sole responsibility for his care. Both times, the mother has cancelled the meeting at the last minute, citing sudden work conflicts. The social worker schedules an in-home visit to the boy's family but when he arrives, he is told by the boy that the mother is at work. The child's grandmother also lives in the home, but is bedridden, and the boy and his sister help care for her. The family's apartment is in disarray, with dirty dishes stacked in the sink and on the stovetop. Laundry is strewn about in wrinkled piles. The social worker observes no alcohol in the house, and the grandmother, who is cooperative, says that her daughter doesn't drink, and never has.
    As the social worker continues to monitor this family, he should be especially alert for signs of

    A. a personality disorder on the part of the mother
    B. child abuse
    C. substance abuse
    D. child neglect

50. Within practice settings that call upon the practitioner's knowledge and skill at all levels of the organization, the social work profession is considered to be a(n) _____ discipline.

    A. primary
    B. secondary
    C. collegial
    D. ancillary

51. Among gays and lesbians, stress and a lack of emotional support have been shown to contribute to

    A. high rates of alcoholism
    B. promiscuity
    C. identity fragmentation
    D. erratic employment patterns

52. An elderly client is particularly concerned about being "bothered" all the time by a social work practitioner who frequently visits her home. To avoid too much discomfort on the part of the client, the practitioner has the client sign several blank consent forms so that her medical history can be sent to several agencies that might offer supportive services. In this case, the worker has

    A. violated the principle of informed consent
    B. hit upon a key strategy for avoiding burnout
    C. demonstrated ignorance of the eligibility rules for most service agencies
    D. found an ethical strategy for streamlining an often frustrating bureaucracy

53. The most common diagnoses for people who complete suicide are

    A. schizophrenia and substance abuse
    B. depressive illness and borderline personality disorder
    C. depressive illness and alcoholism
    D. schizophrenia and chronic metabolic disease

54. The mother of a 14-year-old girl telephoned crisis services, telling the worker that her son had just locked and barricaded himself in his room. Earlier, she had overheard a conversation between the boy and his girlfriend that was clearly a fight. She is concerned because the boy had tried to overdose after the end of an earlier relationship.
    A worker was immediately dispatched to the residence. After a lengthy conversation in which the worker successfully established rapport with the boy, the boy agreed to let the worker in.
    Thus far, crisis services and the worker have followed the formula of Roberts' Seven-Stage Crisis Intervention Model. As a next step, the worker will attempt to

    A. explore alternatives to suicide, such as inpatient or outpatient services
    B. identify and validate the boy's emotions
    C. develop an action plan with the boy
    D. have the boy identify what he views as the major problem or problems

55. The primary goal of crisis intervention can best be described as

    A. protecting the client from a situation in which he or she has become more likely to experience a traumatic event than other people
    B. helping the client to identify and endure the long-term consequences of a traumatic event
    C. protecting a client from self-harm following a traumatic event
    D. helping the client to identify and cope with the sense of "disequilibrium" in the aftermath of a trauma

56. A practitioner discovers that a client is behaving in a way that is seriously damaging both to himself and a close relative. While respecting the concept of self-determination and confidentiality, the practitioner should

    A. warn the client that he (the practitioner) has an obligation to divulge the client's behavior to the appropriate agency or authority, and then do so
    B. attempt to dissuade the client from further engaging in behavior that is harmful
    C. immediately alert the authorities
    D. refer the client to a social services worker who has more experience in this specific type of behavior

57. In order to serve effectively in rural communities, social work practitioners would most likely need to incorporate the concepts of _____ into their practice.

    A. nature and seasonal fluctuation
    B. self-reliance and mutual aid
    C. land and ownership
    D. religion and spirituality

58. Which of the following is NOT typically included in a service agreement between a practitioner and a client?

    A. Description of the agency's programs and services
    B. Fees for service or arrangements for reimbursement
    C. Theoretical framework for the relationship
    D. Time frames for the provision of services

59. From a legal perspective, case records

    A. belong to the practitioner who created them
    B. belong to the client
    C. belong to the agency at which they are physically held
    D. are for the benefit of the client

60. A practitioner is speaking to a client via cellular phone. The practitioner should be aware that

    I. there is a chance that the call could be intercepted by an unauthorized party
    II. the client may not be in a private place
    III. telephone conversations are not considered to be a public ser vice
    IV. complete privacy cannot be assured

    A. I and II
    B. I, II, and IV
    C. III only
    D. I, II, III and IV

61. The basic assumptions underlying social work administration do NOT include the statement that

    A. each person who works within the agency should be considered a stakeholder in agency outcomes
    B. administration is largely the process of securing and transforming community resources
    C. the major contributions toward the improvement of administration come from management itself
    D. the agency has the primary responsibility for the creation and control of its own destiny

62. Most Asian Americans who are seeking from a social work practitioner are looking for a professional who is

    A. nondirective
    B. problem-focused
    C. goal-oriented
    D. experiential in focus

63. Privileged communication is NOT

    A. widely varying in state-to-state legal definitions
    B. usually waived if a third party is present
    C. particularly difficult to protect when working with married couples
    D. protected no matter what the risks involved

64. In devising a treatment plan, a practitioner begins with client tasks that can be managed fairly easily and with some success, before moving on to the larger issues that are causing problems. In doing so, the practitioner is adhering to the rule of

    A. successive approximations
    B. object orientation
    C. positive reinforcement
    D. mental set

65. "Preparatory empathy" is a process that is used by a practitioner in order to

    A. insure against client deception
    B. streamline an intervention by figuring some things out in advance
    C. choose necessary resources or services
    D. make him more aware of issues or barriers that might be encountered

66. The federal WIC program specifically targets the health and welfare of

    A. abused children
    B. adoptive families
    C. pregnant women and newborn children
    D. unskilled laborers who have been injured on the job

67. Of all Hispanics living the United States, those of Mexican descent account for about _____ percent of the total.

    A. 20
    B. 40
    C. 60
    D. 80

68. From her first few meetings with a client, a social work practitioner has begun to form an impression. If the practitioner seeks out additional information that will help to confirm or deny her existing impressions, she will be engaging in

    A. cognitive integration
    B. active perception
    C. offensive perception
    D. thematic apperception

69. A social worker is using the person-in-environment (PIE) system of client assessment. In describing the environmental problems that affect a client's social functioning, the social worker will rely on six groupings of social system problems. Which of the following is NOT one of the groupings used in the PIE system?

    A. Economic/basic need
    B. Judicial/legal system

C. Physical health
D. Education and training

70. Basic social work values that influence professional practice include each of the following, EXCEPT

   A. self-determination
   B. the inherent uniqueness of a person
   C. individualism
   D. the inherent worth and dignity of a person

70.____

71. Which step in the listening process involves the assignment of meaning to a message?

   A. Encoding
   B. Attending
   C. Understanding
   D. Selecting

71.____

72. Qualitative social work research

   A. observes people in natural settings and focuses on the meaning they assign to experiences.
   B. is analyzed through the use of bivariate methods
   C. details the past in order to understand present conditions
   D. compares statistics from number of cases

72.____

73. When a worker attempts to "cement" a referral, she is attempting to

   A. make sure the client is connected to the suggested resource
   B. make the working relationship into a strong enough bond that the client will be sure to follow through
   C. use software or another evaluative tool that confirms the appropriateness of the client to the proposed resource
   D. suggest to the client in advance that the referral will result in success

73.____

74. In working with a client, a practitioner is careful to avoid singling out one or two obvious client characteristics as the reason for everything the person does. The tendency to do this is known as

   A. stereotyping
   B. scripting
   C. over-attribution
   D. highballing

74.____

75. A group's sense of ethnic identity is affected by the
    I. degree to which the members' physical appearances differ from those in mainstream society
    II. size of the group
    III. amount of power the group has
    IV. extent of assimilation

    A. I only
    B. I and III
    C. II and IV
    D. I, II, III and IV

75.____

KEY (CORRECT ANSWERS)

1. D	16. A	31. A	46. D	61. C
2. D	17. C	32. B	47. A	62. A
3. C	18. A	33. A	48. D	63. D
4. A	19. A	34. A	49. D	64. A
5. D	20. B	35. A	50. A	65. D
6. A	21. B	36. B	51. A	66. C
7. B	22. A	37. C	52. A	67. C
8. B	23. C	38. B	53. C	68. B
9. B	24. A	39. B	54. D	69. C
10. D	25. D	40. D	55. D	70. C
11. D	26. D	41. C	56. A	71. C
12. B	27. B	42. A	57. B	72. A
13. A	28. D	43. C	58. C	73. A
14. A	29. A	44. A	59. B	74. C
15. C	30. D	45. A	60. B	75. D

TEST 2

DIRECTIONS: Each question or incomplete statement is followed by several suggested answers or completions. Select the one that BEST answers the question or completes the statement. *PRINT THE LETTER OF THE CORRECT ANSWER IN THE SPACE AT THE RIGHT.*

1. In the _____ style of conflict management, the parties attempt to separate themselves from the problem.

   A. cooperative
   B. nonconfrontational
   C. mediative
   D. settlement

   1.____

2. The purposes of staff notes, or progress notes, include

   I. recording client's responses to services
   II. connecting a service to a key issue
   III. describing client status
   IV. providing direction for ongoing treatment

   A. I only
   B. I, II and III
   C. III and IV
   D. I, II, III and IV

   2.____

3. A genogram is an assessment tool that

   A. involves DNA sampling
   B. defers consideration of current family relationships
   C. gives a picture of family relationships over at least three generations
   D. uses statistical measures to calculate the probability of an intervention's success

   3.____

4. Which of the following is NOT a belief of stage theorists?

   A. The progression of stages is biologically programmed.
   B. Children pass through the same stages in the same sequence.
   C. Stages are usually marked by age ranges.
   D. As children progress through the stages, the differences between them are quantitative.

   4.____

5. During the opening phase of a client interview, the practitioner should probably spend most of his time and thoughts on

   A. self-disclosure
   B. negotiating a working contract
   C. interpreting behaviors
   D. explaining agency rules and protocols

   5.____

6. Behaviors commonly associated with substance abuse include

   I. a withdrawal from responsibility
   II. unusual outbreaks of temper
   III. abrupt changes in quality or output of work
   IV. wearing sunglasses at inappropriate times

   6.____

A. I and II
B. I, II and III
C. II and IV
D. I, II, III and IV

7. Which of the following would a practitioner typically do FIRST in a problem assessment interview?

    A. Identify client coping skills
    B. Identify the range of client problems
    C. Prioritize and select issues and problems for discussion
    D. Identify consequences of problem behaviors

8. A social worker's primary ethical duty is to

    A. effect social justice
    B. promote the welfare of the client
    C. respect diversity
    D. avoid dependent relationships

9. The person-centered model of human behavior views the major reason for maladjustment as a(n)

    A. failure to set a self-actualizing tendency in motion
    B. inability to establish unconditional positive regard
    C. incongruence between self-concept and experience
    D. unresolved childhood frustrations

10. The person-in-environment (PIE) system of client assessment is a four-factor system. Factor _____ provides a statement of the client's physical health problems.

    A. I
    B. II
    C. III
    D. IV

11. An adolescent client tells her social worker that she feels she is the only person in the world who has ever had such strong unrequited love for another person—the boy who sits next to her in geometry class. The component of adolescent egocentrism being enacted by the girl is the

    A. all-or-none fallacy
    B. imaginary audience
    C. questionable cause
    D. personal fable

12. Research into interpersonal relationships suggests that women often build relationships through shared positive feelings, while men often build relationships through

    A. shared activities
    B. shared opinions
    C. metacommunication
    D. impression management

13. Which of the following is NOT typically a purpose of assessment?

    A. To identify the controlling or contributing variables associated with a client's problem
    B. To launch the first phase of treatment
    C. To educate and motivate the client by sharing views about the problem
    D. To plan effective interventions and strategies

14. Persuading clients to abandon mistaken ways of thinking is a goal of

    A. client-centered therapy
    B. operant conditioning
    C. cognitive therapy
    D. systematic desensitization

15. A practitioner is creating an action plan with an adult client who has decided to leave his current job. Typically, planning such a move requires practitioner and client to move on to

    A. ensure that the work to be done fits an accepted model of treatment
    B. breaking large goals into component parts
    C. making the client aware of the full range of consequences
    D. ensure that this decision meets with the approval of the people who will be affected by it

16. Some of the information in an applicant's file comes from secondary sources. Which of the following is NOT considered a secondary source?

    A. Applicant's family
    B. Referring agency
    C. School
    D. Current staff notes

17. Self-disclosure is considered a "discretionary" response in discussions with clients, because it

    A. is not considered to be therapeutic
    B. is only used if the client requests it
    C. should be used carefully to avoid taking the focus off the client
    D. requires a familiarity with the client's worldview before it is used

18. For a practitioner working from the family systems theory, symptoms of maladjustment in families are usually masked by

    A. the involvement and recommendations of professionals who were previously involved
    B. the presenting crisis or problem that initially brought the family into contact with the agency
    C. abusive relationships
    D. environmental components in the family's community

19. A school social worker is told that one of the kindergartners is running around, out of control, and disrupting the others at naptime. As she attempts to understand the problem, her FIRST step should be to

A. arrange an interview with the school psychologist
B. look into finding an alternative school placement
C. systematically observe the child in the classroom to see how it is managed
D. contact the parents to inform them of the child's behavior problems

20. What is the collective term applied to communication variables such as voice level, pitch, rate, and fluency of speech? 20.____

    A. Kinesics
    B. Paralinguistics
    C. Nonverbal messages
    D. Proxemics

21. Although the terms *counseling* and *interviewing* are sometimes used interchangeably in social work, there are differences that should be noted. Which of the following is NOT one of these differences. 21.____

    A. Interviewing is a responsibility that can be assumed by most practitioners or case managers.
    B. Interviewing is a more basic process for information gathering and problem solving.
    C. Counseling is a more intensive and personal process.
    D. Counseling is often associated with nonprofessional workers, whereas therapy used to indicate professional interventions.

22. A social worker in the _____ role is conducting "macro" practice. 22.____
    I. manager
    II. planner
    III. case manager
    IV. mediator

    A. I and II
    B. I, II and IV
    C. III only
    D. I, II, III and IV

23. The final stage of Elisabeth Kubler-Ross's theory of how people handle the knowledge of their impending death is known as 23.____

    A. denial
    B. bargaining
    C. anger
    D. acceptance

24. Probably the most important factor in establishing a working alliance with a client is the 24.____

    A. client's belief about whether the practitioner attends and understands
    B. accuracy of the practitioner's assessment of the presenting problem(s)
    C. practitioner's effort to be empathetic
    D. client's initial willingness to change

25. During the assessment phase, the practice of _____ means that the practitioner and client are setting specific objectives.

    A. activating resources
    B. framing solutions
    C. defining the problem
    D. weighing alternatives

26. Reflecting and paraphrasing are two active listening strategies often used by practitioners to help clients become more aware of the implications of their own statements. Basically the difference between reflecting and paraphrasing involves the difference between the

    A. client's words and the client's actions
    B. the emotional (affective) and factual (cognitive) content of messages
    C. way the client perceives the world and the way the world actually is
    D. way the client is expressing a message and the way it is being received by the practitioner

27. The process by which people shape social life by adapting to, negotiating with, and changing social structures is known as

    A. determinism
    B. positivism
    C. human agency
    D. ideology

28. Child welfare is a social work practice area that

    A. focuses on issues, problems, and policies related to the well-being of children
    B. administers school lunches and other benefit programs for low-income children
    C. focuses on increasing the educational potential of children
    D. mainly works to broker adoptions

29. The relationship between social work supervisors and supervisees, which parallels the relationship between social worker and client, has been described in terms of basic relational elements. Which of the following is NOT one of these?

    A. Caring
    B. Rapport
    C. Authority
    D. Trust

30. The _____ model attributes the essential characteristics of consensus, cohesion, stability, reciprocity, and cooperation to society.

    A. evolutionary
    B. conflict
    C. order
    D. symbolic interaction

31. Upholding rules, regulations and restrictions of a social services agency which are not always best for the client is a function of the social worker's role known as

    A. gatekeeping
    B. spoilage
    C. advocacy
    D. bureaucratic blindness

32. A social worker and her client have developed a long-range goal. Now they are determining individual steps that will lead to the achievement of that goal. This is a process known as

    A. chunking
    B. prioritizing
    C. partializing
    D. contracting

33. Community surveys, policy analyses, and case histories are examples of

    A. social studies
    B. ecomaps
    C. needs assessments
    D. genograms

34. In a social services agency that serves teenage runaways, an example of a direct service strategy would be

    A. organizing
    B. counseling
    C. gathering information
    D. planning

35. Compared to others in society, those with superior _____ are more likely to support the status quo.

    A. educational achievement
    B. social locations
    C. value systems
    D. incomes

36. "Primary prevention" means

    A. the severity and duration of a disease or disorder have been reduced
    B. clinical means have been used to provide treatment, such as crisis intervention
    C. a disease or disorder is stopped at its source, and the cause is eliminated
    D. the spread of a disease or disorder among people has been limited

37. Under normal circumstances it is considered acceptable practice for a social worker to disclose a client's confidential information to

    I. the practitioner's supervisor as it relates to the supervisory relationship
    II. professionals who are consulted about assessments or interventions
    III. third-party payers for the purpose of justifying treatment decisions
    IV. close family members for the purpose of developing understanding of the client's particular difficulties

A. I only
B. I and II
C. I, II and III
D. I, II, III and IV

38. A client's feelings of powerlessness can be reduced when a social worker adopts each of the following roles, EXCEPT the role of

    A. resource consultant, who connects the client to goods and services
    B. advocate, who acts as the client's protector in social living matters
    C. sensitizer, who helps the client gain knowledge needed to solve problems
    D. educator, who facilitates the learning and skill development needed for goal setting and task completion

39. The _____ model of human services organization management places the greatest value on maximizing the productivity of the organization.

    A. internal process
    B. open-system
    C. rational goal
    D. human relations

40. During an interview, practitioner and client establish a goal for the client to use her time more efficiently at work and at home. This is an example of a _____ goal.

    A. process
    B. survival
    C. treatment
    D. service

41. One reason people often confuse race and ethnicity is because they

    A. are suspicious of people who are different from themselves
    B. are unaware that race is cultural and ethnicity is biological
    C. see cultural differences and define race in specific, often inaccurate ways
    D. have met few people outside their own race

42. Dual relationships between a practitioner and a client, according to the NASW:

    A. should not be formed if there is any possibility for exploitation or potential harm to the client
    B. are usually an unavoidable part of professional practice
    C. are generally acceptable if social workers take steps to protect clients
    D. are generally acceptable if social workers are careful to avoid legal problems that could damage the status of the social work profession

43. In a family intervention that implements the structural model, the family will be expected to

    A. submit to the direction of the practitioner
    B. solve their own problems
    C. shift their internal alliances
    D. shift blame to the external environment

44. In diversion programs, social workers typically provide

   A. case management services with probation officers in an attempt to prevent recidivism
   B. consultation services about early-release programs for juvenile offenders
   C. counseling services through a network of lay professionals
   D. crisis intervention or referral services aimed at avoiding imprisonment

45. In hospital social work, an example of macropractice would be

   A. connecting with community providers to maintain understanding of community needs
   B. increasing health provider awareness of clients' home environment
   C. engaging clients in planning for their immediate future after discharge
   D. educating clients and families about the implications of a particular illness or disorder

46. A client tells a practitioner that he is distraught over the end of his marriage and wishes he could "just go to sleep forever, be at peace, and not have to feel this pain any more." The practitioner should

   A. assess whether the client is suicidal and intervene if necessary
   B. recognize that such statements are often merely a "cry for help" and urge the client to focus on more practical issues
   C. contact the client's wife and determine whether there is a chance to reconcile
   D. immediately commit the client to a psychiatric facility

47. The presenting problems of most African American clients are rooted in

   A. genetics
   B. personality deficits
   C. stress from external systems
   D. unresolved family conflicts

48. A solution-focused intervention would most likely involve the goal of

   A. a first-order change in the client system
   B. behavioral continuity
   C. a perceptual shift from talking about problems to talking about how to solve them
   D. determining exactly how a problem came into being

49. During an interview in which a client is being evaluated, the client should understand that the

   A. information gained during the interview may be the basis of a report on the client
   B. questions will not be upsetting to him/her
   C. interview will focus on the client's well-being
   D. he or she has implicitly entered into a service contract

50. The _____ theory of rural social work asserts that there are distinct differences between rural and urban areas, and that the urban end of the continuum is associated with social pathology.

A. classical
B. subcultural
C. compositional
D. determinist

51. During the supervisory discussion of a client case, the FIRST topic of discussion should typically be

    A. client dynamics and problems
    B. alternative intervention strategies
    C. a tentative assessment or diagnosis
    D. selection of a general treatment approach

52. The millions of Asian Americans living in the United States today represent a generally _____ population.

    A. prosperous
    B. culturally homogeneous
    C. mainstreamed
    D. heterogeneous

53. Most legal issues encountered by social work practitioners involve

    A. complaints of improper conduct
    B. being sued for negligence or malpractice
    C. being prosecuted for crimes
    D. acting as witnesses in litigation

54. The initial recommended response to a client who is suicidal is

    A. hospitalization and observation
    B. identifying the client's level of seriousness
    C. problem-solving training
    D. crisis intervention and a functional assessment of the suicidal behavior

55. The most common client reactions to the termination of direct social service include each of the following, EXCEPT

    A. pride
    B. ambivalence
    C. satisfaction
    D. denial

56. Most referrals to human service professionals are made by

    A. school systems
    B. health care workers
    C. the courts
    D. word of mouth from friends or family members

57. The term "handicap" refers to a(n)

    A. obstruction that prevents an interface between a disability and the environment
    B. an impairment that limits one's daily activities

C. inability to perform tasks at a level that is generally considered to be socially acceptable
D. loss of use or function of an organ or bodily system

58. When writing case notes, practitioners should always
    I. keep in mind that others may read the notes
    II. compose them immediately after a client meeting
    III. provide as much detail as possible
    IV. use shorthand

    A. I and II
    B. II only
    C. I, II and III
    D. I, II, III and

59. The most frequent cause of child death is

    A. physical abuse
    B. suicide
    C. being left unsupervised or alone for long periods of time
    D. automobile accidents

60. Clients of social service agencies often disagree with either agency policies or a practitioner's actions, or both. If a client demands to know why a particular action was taken and perhaps reverse it, he or she is exercising a right to

    A. confidentiality
    B. due process
    C. privileged information
    D. informed consent

61. Content theories of human motivation argue that

    A. most people dislike change
    B. external consequences determine behavior
    C. most people are affiliation-oriented
    D. internal needs lead to behavior

62. Once a client's service needs are clear, a social worker often helps the client choose the most appropriate service and negotiates the terms of service delivery. Here, the social worker is acting in the role of

    A. broker
    B. consultant
    C. advocate
    D. coordinator

63. When social work practitioners commit errors in working with gay, lesbian, and bisexual clients, these errors most often stem from the

    A. workers' own unconscious prejudices
    B. failure to recognize clients as homosexual, due to a lack of identifying characteristics
    C. identification of client problems as being caused by their sexuality

D. assumption that client problems are unrelated to social oppression or stigma

64. If included statistically as a form of elder abuse, self-neglect would represent about _____ percent of cases reported to state adult protective services agencies.

    A. 5-10
    B. 20-35
    C. 40-50
    D. 60-75

65. Many social workers, especially those who work in institutional settings, use the brief treatment model in their interventions. Which of the following is NOT one of the core assumptions of this model?

    A. Problems are a normal part of life and not a sign of pathology.
    B. Practitioners believe people can change, and communicate this to their clients.
    C. The purpose of treatment is to develop insight into the underlying causes of problems.
    D. Treatment makes use of what the client brings to it

66. Stan, a Native American college student, is seeking information about work programs in the urban community where he lives. When Stan asks a female practitioner at the local agency about it, the practitioner notices that he makes very little eye contact. The practitioner should recognize that Stan

    A. would be more likely to look into her eyes if she were a male
    B. is not likely to follow through with the practitioner's recommendations or referrals
    C. is likely to view direct eye contact as a lack of respect
    D. does not express much faith in the practitioner's abilities

67. The tendency of people to perceive what they expect to perceive is a phenomenon known as

    A. self-serving bias
    B. perceptual set
    C. filtration
    D. fundamental attribution bias

68. A person's satisfaction with communication is based upon a theoretical "sum total" of the positive and negative elements in a message. This sum is a phenomenon known as message

    A. validity
    B. salience
    C. solidity
    D. valence

69. Data about how long or how often a problem occurs before an intervention are known as _____ data.

    A. raw
    B. norming
    C. baseline
    D. skewed

70. In _____ social work, assessment is also known as functional analysis.

    A. narrative
    B. behavioral
    C. feminist
    D. cognitive

71. During an assessment interview, a practitioner asks a client: "How do you feel about the fact that your drinking has harmed your relationship with your daughter?" The practitioner is trying to identify _____ consequences of the client's problem.

    A. contextual
    B. affective
    C. behavioral
    D. somatic

72. For social work research to have a meaningful function, it must be applied by practitioners. One of the major reasons practitioners fail to apply the results of research is that

    A. there is no standard methodology that would make results universally applicable
    B. many studies lack relevance to day-to-day practice decisions
    C. there is still widespread theoretical bias in the design of many studies
    D. most practitioners don't conduct research themselves

73. Of the following social sciences, social work draws most of its professional expertise from

    A. psychology
    B. economics
    C. sociology
    D. anthropology

74. In her meetings with a client, a practitioner has begun to form the perception that he may be using a combination of alcohol and illegal drugs. She decides, during subsequent meetings, to engage in "direct perception checking" in order to confirm or deny this perception. This will involve

    A. paying careful attention to the client's tone of voice
    B. observing the client's behaviors to discover cues that will either confirm or deny her impressions
    C. asking the client if he has a drug or drinking problem
    D. listening more intently to the client's words and language

75. Though practitioner self-disclosure can be a useful tool for helping clients, it is most helpful when its use is carefully assessed beforehand. Generally, practitioners should AVOID making self-disclosure statements

    A. as concise as possible
    B. as a way of introducing oneself to the client
    C. in a way that will regulate the role distance between practitioner and client
    D. similar in content and mood to the client's messages

KEY (CORRECT ANSWERS)

1.	A	16.	D	31.	A	46.	A	61.	D
2.	D	17.	C	32.	C	47.	C	62.	A
3.	C	18.	B	33.	A	48.	C	63.	B
4.	D	19.	C	34.	B	49.	A	64.	C
5.	B	20.	B	35.	B	50.	A	65.	C
6.	D	21.	D	36.	C	51.	A	66.	C
7.	C	22.	A	37.	B	52.	D	67.	B
8.	B	23.	D	38.	B	53.	D	68.	D
9.	C	24.	A	39.	C	54.	D	69.	C
10.	D	25.	B	40.	C	55.	D	70.	B
11.	D	26.	B	41.	C	56.	D	71.	B
12.	A	27.	C	42.	A	57.	A	72.	B
13.	B	28.	A	43.	B	58.	C	73.	A
14.	C	29.	C	44.	D	59.	C	74.	B
15.	B	30.	C	45.	A	60.	B	75.	B

EXAMINATION SECTION
TEST 1

DIRECTIONS: Each question or incomplete statement is followed by several suggested answers or completions. Select the one the BEST answers the question or completes the statement. *PRINT THE LETTER OF THE CORRECT ANSWER IN THE SPACE AT THE RIGHT.*

1. Which of the following statements about working with elderly clients in therapy is TRUE? 1.____

    A. Cognitive approaches are usually contraindicated because of the cognitive demands placed on the client.
    B. Elderly clients often become over-dependent on the therapist due to their relative isolation and loneliness.
    C. The therapeutic relationship may be more difficult to form than it would with younger clients
    D. Insight-oriented therapies are usually contraindicated because of the cognitive impairments that typically accompany aging.

2. A 45-year-old client reports to a clinician for an initial consultation upon the advice of her physician. The client complains of headaches, neck pain, stomach and lower back pain, and dizziness. After an initial examination, the client's physician has failed to find any physiological cause for his problems. Which of the following conditions would justify a diagnosis of malingering by the clinician? 2.____

    A. The client demonstrates a psychological need to maintain the "sick role"
    B. Further medical examination confirms the impression that the client's symptoms have no physiological basis
    C. The client feigns symptoms in order to gain an external reward
    D. A clinical presentation characterized by laziness and an "inadequate personality"

3. According to Paul Baltes, individual development across the life span can be described in each of the following ways, EXCEPT 3.____

    A. multidirectional
    B. reversible
    C. nonsequential
    D. intermittent

4. A social worker has been seeing a mother and daughter for several sessions because of the daughter's repeated defiance of the mother. The mother's responses during most of the sessions have been very child-like. If the social worker were to use transactional analysis with this mother and daughter, he might 4.____

    A. confront the child's fearful behaviors
    B. explore mother's feelings toward the child
    C. ask the mother and daughter to perform a role reversal
    D. encourage the mother to talk to the child as "parent to child"

5. A clinician decides to use rational-emotive therapy to help a child who is depressed. The FIRST thing the clinician should do to begin the process is 5.____

A. administer the Reynolds Child Depression Scale
B. interview the child
C. assess the parents and the child for secondary disturbance
D. interview the child's parents and teachers

6. According to the ecological theory of human development and behavior, a "macrosystem" consists of

    A. relations between microsystems or connections between contexts
    B. the patterning of environmental events and transitions over the life course
    C. the attitudes and ideologies of the culture
    D. family, school, peers, and church groups

7. During a client interview, the social worker tends to phrase his questions so that the client gives "yes" or "no" answers. The overall effect on the communication process will be that

    A. the social worker will be able to develop a clear chronological picture of the presenting problem
    B. the client's attitudes and beliefs will eventually be revealed
    C. very little useful information will be elicited
    D. the client will likely become wary and defensive

8. A client has been forced by the court to attend therapy with a social worker. From a clinical standpoint, it will be MOST important for the social worker to address

    A. the client's ability to form a relationship with the social worker
    B. the client's ambivalence about treatment
    C. the nature of the client's offense
    D. the latent factors in the client's legal problems

9. Which of the following does NOT typically characterize a therapy group in its early stages?

    A. Relatively stereotyped and restricted content and communication style
    B. A concern for closeness and intimacy
    C. Giving and seeking advice
    D. Hesitancy and dependence

10. A 42-year-old client has complained of intermittent abdominal pains, periodic nausea and vomiting, irregular menstrual periods, and periodic weakness in her limbs. Physical examinations have been normal for the last 3 years. What diagnosis should the woman receive?

    A. Somatization disorder
    B. Undifferentiated somatoform disorder
    C. Hypochondriasis
    D. Pain disorder associated with psychological factors

11. If the head of a counseling agency hires a consultant to help counselors deal with some particularly difficult cases at the agency, the agency is practicing _____ consultation.

A. consultee-centered case
B. consultee-centered administrative
C. program-centered administrative
D. client-centered case

12. In conducting case presentations, it is usually recommended that

    A. discussion be limited to the case at hand rather than additional problems
    B. the practitioner present several cases in one session
    C. practitioner dynamics be discussed before case dynamics
    D. the practitioner present a specific problem rather than the entire case in context

13. Interventions with Native American clients should generally be focused on

    A. building on client strengths to solve a particular problem
    B. removing environmental obstacles to client success
    C. teaching concrete skills to help clients become self-sufficient
    D. restoring a balance between physical well-being and spiritual harmony

14. Service eligibility requirements for social service clients are typically _____ in nature.
    I. Personal
    II. Demographic
    III. Social
    IV. Financial

    A. I and IV
    B. I, III and IV
    C. III and IV
    D. I, II, III and IV

15. Client-centered therapy asserts that each of the following therapist attitudes is necessary to effect positive changes in clients, EXCEPT

    A. genuineness
    B. positive regard
    C. empathy
    D. insightfulness

16. When communicating with the hearing-impaired, a social worker should try to do each of the following, EXCEPT

    A. speak slowly and clearly
    B. reduce background noise
    C. face the patient
    D. gradually increase the volume of his/her voice

17. Which of the following should generally be done the LATEST in a crisis intervention with a client who is a battered woman?

    A. Asking the client to describe briefly what has just happened
    B. Identifying the client's feelings as asking for a perception check
    C. Making sure the client is now safe and protected
    D. Asking the client if she is taking any medication

18. The area of difference between therapist and client that is likely to be MOST influential in a therapeutic relationship is

    A. gender
    B. socioeconomic status
    C. philosophical orientation
    D. culture

19. After a series of traumatic events at a hospital involving a mother and her young daughter, who has been experiencing hypoglycemic seizures throughout the night, the mother, who has been fiercely devoted to her daughter and has remained at her bedside for more than 24 hours, is inadvertently caught by a nurse in the act of preparing an insulin injection for the girl. The mother later admitted to giving the insulin to her daughter. The mother could be said to be suffering from

    A. factitious disorder
    B. dissociative disorder
    C. conversion disorder
    D. somatoform disorder

20. Which of the following, if used during the first 3 months of pregnancy, may cause a cleft palate or other congenital malformation?

    A. Alcohol
    B. Tranquilizers
    C. Cocaine
    D. Nicotine

21. Purposes of the Adult Abuse Protocol, an assessment and intervention guide for the abused adult, include
    I. documenting the violent incident for legal purposes
    II. alerting the involved hospital staff to provide appropriate clinical care
    III. provide a formal support network for the client in recovery

    A. I only
    B. I and II
    C. II and III
    D. I, II, and III

22. Which of the following listening skills is LEAST likely to be used in a client interview that conforms to the behavioral approach?

    A. Open questions
    B. Closed questions
    C. Feedback
    D. Reflection of meaning

23. The most dangerous side effect associated with phenothiazines is

    A. Parkinson-like symptoms
    B. nausea
    C. epileptic seizures
    D. delusional behavior

24. People who are experiencing anomie are said to adapt in one of five ways. Which of the following is NOT one of these?

   A. Martyrdom
   B. Innovation
   C. Rebellion
   D. Ritualism

25. Erikson's second stage of psychosocial development, which occurs in late infancy and toddlerhood (1-3 years), is

   A. initiative vs. guilt
   B. trust vs. mistrust
   C. identity vs. identity confusion
   D. autonomy vs. shame and doubt

26. Questionnaires can be used in preference over other data collection techniques when
   I. anonymity is important
   II. budgets are limited
   III. respondents are literate
   IV. a high response rate is important

   A. I only
   B. I and II
   C. I, II and III
   D. I, II, III and IV

27. Unlike traditional approaches to psychotherapy, cultural approaches try to understand mental illness from the inside—they attempt to clarify the individual or group's experience of the illness within the cultural context. In this way, cultural approaches adopt an _____ perspective.

   A. etiological
   B. endogenous
   C. emic
   D. etic

28. When a person's moral reasoning is controlled by external rewards and punishment, it is said to be

   A. role-focused
   B. preconventional
   C. circular
   D. preoperational

29. Which of the following individuals if probably the most inappropriate candidate for a long-term interactional therapy group?

   A. A secretive anorexic-bulimic client
   B. A man with a history of sexual promiscuity
   C. A client with inadequate ego strength
   D. A person who has been convicted of child molestation

30. It is probably most appropriate for a clinician to view professional and formal assessment instruments, such as the Stanford-Binet, Wecshler, and Q-sort as

    A. providing a full picture of client functions
    B. getting in the way of establishing a healthy client/worker relationship
    C. ways of confirming impressions
    D. uninstrusive means of identifying specific deficits

31. Private-practice clinicians who work full-time calculate that about _____ percent of their gross income goes for operating and overhead expenses if they maintain a full caseload.

    A. 5-15
    B. 20-30
    C. 35-45
    D. 50-70

32. Which of the following is the BEST example of a secondary prevention program?

    A. a community education program
    B. Head Start
    C. Crisis intervention
    D. a rehabilitation program

33. Most definitions of "family" tend to focus on the two most significant manifest functions of the family, which are

    A. production and consumption
    B. procreation and the socialization of children
    C. production and provision of emotional support
    D. procreation and provision of emotional support

34. Within a social services organization, the type of plan that is probably most frequently misunderstood is a(n)

    A. mission
    B. policy
    C. rule
    D. budget

35. In the psychodynamic perspective, a "love" that is based on self-doubt will play itself out as _____ love.

    A. revengeful
    B. sadistic
    C. compulsive
    D. critical

36. In order to help clients generate additional information about their situations, each of the following is an important skill in interviewing, EXCEPT

    A. influencing skills
    B. confrontation
    C. reflection
    D. focusing

37. Which of the following questions is MOST "open" in nature?

    A. What important things have happened during the week?
    B. Where does your daughter live?
    C. Could you tell me a little about your family?
    D. Do you get along with your mother?

38. Generally, the most strongest predictor of social service utilization by Asian American clients is

    A. degree of isolation
    B. severity of condition
    C. acculturation
    D. financial focus of service need

39. The impact of a therapeutic relationship depends on how well a practitioner uses herself or her sensitivity to guide clients in understanding themselves. Which of the following is NOT an important means of doing this?

    A. Exploring thoughts and feelings
    B. Listing alternatives
    C. Reflecting attitude
    D. Modeling behavior

40. For what reason is it sometimes difficult for clinicians to identify depression in young children?

    A. Depression is often manifested in a variety of symptoms which do not appear to be typical of depression
    B. Depression does not exist as a clinical syndrome at that early age
    C. Young children do not have sufficient language to describe how they feel
    D. Young children do not have the capacity for self-observation

41. Which of the following tasks of remarriage is typically performed FIRST?

    A. Community remarriage: establishing relationships outside the marriage
    B. Parental remarriage: establishing bonds with the children of a partner
    C. Legal remarriage: settling financial and other responsibilities toward children and former partners
    D. Economic remarriage: becoming interdependent in terms of financial needs and responsibilities

42. Which of the following approaches to social services policymaking tends to recommend a policy based on previous information about the impact of a policy of existing policies, with a projection of continuing future effectiveness?

    A. Secondary
    B. Rational
    C. Prescriptive
    D. Vertical

43. Most practitioners view _____ as the most important element in bringing about change in clients' lives.

A. effective service linkage
B. a strong support network
C. client skill development
D. the therapeutic relationship

44. Individuals with a diagnosis of _____ have a 6-month history of recurrent, intense, sexually arousing fantasies, urges, or behaviors involving touching and rubbing against a nonconsenting person.

    A. voyeurism
    B. exhibitionism
    C. frotteurism
    D. fetishism

45. A pregnant 14-year-old reports to a social worker complaining about her boyfriend, whom she fights with often because he won't look for work to support her and her child. The girls says she uses cocaine once a week. The social worker should:

    A. maintain confidentiality and continue therapy
    B. consult child protective services, because the girl is a minor and needs protection
    C. consult child protective services, because the girl is abusing the fetus
    D. call the girl's parents for permission to treat her

46. Of those who participate in AA, those most likely to benefit are generally

    A. members of a lower socioeconomic group
    B. women
    C. older drinkers
    D. heavy drinkers

47. Which of the following forms of elder maltreatment is LEAST commonly reported?

    A. Physical abuse
    B. Psychological abuse
    C. Financial abuse
    D. Physical neglect

48. Which of the following is a secondary social work setting?

    A. Child welfare agency
    B. Homeless shelter
    C. Alcohol and drug treatment center
    D. Family service agency

49. In a client interview, a worker may sometimes reflect the client's feelings in a way that is helpful. Which of the following statements about this technique is FALSE?

    A. Reflections in the past tense tend to be more useful than those in the present.
    B. The emotion being reflected should be clearly labeled with a word.
    C. It is often useful to add a contextual word (because, when) to broaden the reflection.
    D. It's important to refer directly to the client in the reflection.

50. The ideal of human development envisioned by ego psychology is

A. consensus and shared values
B. individual development across the life course
C. equality and the absence of alienation and exploitation
D. mutual self-respect and the absence of labeling

51. Probably the most frustrating problem encountered by clients in need of services who apply to a public social services agency is the

    A. stigma attached to those who seek services
    B. means-testing process
    C. inability to consider cases individually
    D. size and complexity of the agency's bureaucratic structure

52. Sample size is social work research has its most direct affect on

    A. internal validity
    B. the ability to infer a causal relationship between variables.
    C. experimental control
    D. generalizability

53. According to Piaget, assimilation occurs when individuals

    A. incorporate new information into their existing knowledge
    B. coordinate sensory experiences with physical actions
    C. adjust to new information
    D. represent the world in words, images and drawings

54. Typically, the relationship between a social worker and a small group differs from that of a social worker and an individual. Which of the following statements is FALSE regarding the relationship between a worker and a small group?

    A. There is greater formality than in a worker/individual relationship.
    B. There is an inherent lack of confidentiality.
    C. A greater feeling of identification usually exists among clients than in a worker/individual relationship.
    D. Acceptance of others is not mandated to other group members.

55. After the review of a case, an HMO decides to deny further payment for sessions for a social worker's client. The worker believes the client would benefit from additional therapy. The BEST approach by the worker would be to

    A. file a complaint against the HMO
    B. consult with the client about his options in this situation
    C. comply with the HMO's request, but only if the limits of treatment were discussed with the client at the beginning of therapy
    D. continue to provide therapy to the client without compensation if necessary until other arrangements can be made

56. The key personality trait in clients who suffer from avoidant personality disorder is

    A. an indifference to human contact
    B. a distaste for other people
    C. a sense of entitlement and lack of empathy
    D. a fear of rejection

57. A clinical supervisor who maintains an "open-door" policy with supervisees is MOST likely to encourage the development of

   A. unstructured supervision that operates on a crisis basis
   B. solution-focused supervision that is focused on client dynamics
   C. a proactive style of interaction that locates and attempts to solve problems early
   D. a warm peer relationship with practitioners who view the supervisor as an equal

58. In a troubled family it sometimes happens that members project their internal conflicts onto others outside them. These projections are known as

   A. triangulations
   B. stable coalitions
   C. detouring coalitions
   D. disengagements

59. The driving force behind a social service agency's resource allocation decisions should be

   A. the distribution between current vs. long-term debt
   B. the available liquid cash resources to cover current debt
   C. assets available for collateral for additional debt
   D. the mission of the organization

60. The easiest measure of data variability to calculate and understand is

   A. mean
   B. standard deviation
   C. range
   D. slope

61. The use of "systems" thinking in social work generally involves each of the following advantages, EXCEPT

   A. it can easily be adapted for the implementation of partial solutions
   B. it ensures that a worker will search for more than one way to look at a situation
   C. it helps the worker to see the world through the eyes of another
   D. it shows that behavior must be understood in the context of a number of factors

62. Sometimes, experiences in another social setting-in which the individual does not have an active role-influence what the individual experiences in an immediate context. This other social setting is described as a(n)

   A. mesosystem
   B. exosystem
   C. milieu
   D. macrosystem

63. A 30-year old man visits a hospital emergency room complaining of extreme nervousness. When told that he'll have to wait for physician, he becomes irritated and argues with the receptionist, and then paces around the waiting room. An initial physical examination reveals a heart rate of 111 and a blood pressure of 170/110. The man says he's felt extremely nervous, off and on, for several days now. Based on this information only, a practitioner should FIRST investigate the possibility that the man

A. is intoxicated with a substance
B. suffers from posttraumatic stress disorder
C. suffers from acute stress disorder
D. has developed generalized anxiety disorder

64. In the stage of a client interview during which the worker and client explore alternatives and confront client incongruities, an important goal is to

    A. work toward resolution of the client's problem
    B. facilitate changes in thoughts, feelings and behaviors in daily life
    C. build a working alliance with the client
    D. discover the client's ideal world

64.____

65. A clinician decides to use Beck's cognitive approach to treat a client with panic disorder. The FIRST goal of intervention would be to for the client to

    A. see how he misinterprets the meaning of his symptoms
    B. identify the antecedents and consequences that are controlling his symptoms
    C. understand how the symptoms are controlling different aspects of his life
    D. identify the underlying causes of his symptoms

65.____

66. Problems associated with labeling in client assessment include
    I. masking clients' subjective experience and coping mechanisms
    II. a perceived loss of control by the practitioner
    III. the constraint and trivialization of clients
    IV. an emphasis on what is wrong, rather than what is right

    A. I and III
    B. I, III and IV
    C. II and IV
    D. I, II, III and IV

66.____

67. The efficiency and effectiveness factors relating to the delivery of social services are evaluated broadly in terms of

    A. influence
    B. summation
    C. accountability
    D. transactional analysis

67.____

68. The functions of an organizational advisory board typically do NOT include

    A. publicizing agency activities
    B. procuring the funds needed to operate the organization
    C. evaluating agency services and recommending improvements
    D. assisting in determining consumer needs

68.____

69. Culturally, the most significantly observed life-cycle transition among African American families is

    A. birth
    B. passing into adulthood
    C. marriage
    D. death

69.____

70. Which of the following is NOT an example of an output goal?

    A. Reduce the number of alcohol-related incidents of domestic violence by one-third (by 250 incidents)
    B. Increase the number of Alcoholics Anonymous and Al-Anon groups in the county by 40% (from 10 to 14) during the coming year.
    C. Provide inpatient treatment services to 235 persons with alcohol dependency problems, supplemented with services to their families.
    D. Develop a special unit for female alcoholics, increasing service from 40 clients a year to 80 a year.

71. Which of the following interviewing skills generally exerts the greatest amount of influence over client talk?

    A. Interpretation
    B. Open questions
    C. Focusing
    D. Paraphrasing

72. A family reports to a private practitioner out of concern for their young son, who repeatedly urinates in his bed at night and in his clothes during the day. The parents' attempts to shape the boy's behavior have failed. In order to assign the boy a diagnosis of enuresis consistent with DSM-IV standards, the practitioner must establish that

    A. the boy is at least 5 years old
    B. the problem occurs at least once a week
    C. the problem has persisted for at least 6 months
    D. the problem is not related to some external stressor

73. Which of the following processes typically occurs EARLIEST in the therapeutic relationship?

    A. Idealization
    B. Individualization
    C. Identification
    D. Individuation

74. Most developmental psychologists prefer longitudinal research designs to cross-sectional research designs, primarily for the reason that longitudinal designs

    A. use the subjects as their own experimental controls
    B. are much less likely to be influenced by cultural changes that occur over time
    C. offer the advantage of between-subjects comparisons
    D. usually yield results more quickly

75. Most social work professionals agree that paternalism may be justifiable if clients 75.____
    I. are not mentally competent
    II. might harm themselves seriously
    III. have repeatedly proven incapable of caring for themselves
    IV. do not voluntarily consent to a social worker's intervention plan

    A. I and II
    B. III only
    C. I, II, III and IV
    D. None of the above

KEY (CORRECT ANSWERS)

1. C	16. D	31. B	46. C	61. A
2. C	17. A	32. C	47. A	62. B
3. D	18. D	33. B	48. C	63. A
4. D	19. A	34. B	49. A	64. A
5. D	20. B	35. C	50. B	65. A
6. C	21. B	36. C	51. D	66. B
7. C	22. D	37. C	52. D	67. C
8. B	23. A	38. C	53. C	68. B
9. B	24. A	39. B	54. A	69. D
10. B	25. D	40. A	55. B	70. A
11. D	26. C	41. A	56. D	71. A
12. A	27. C	42. C	57. A	72. A
13. D	28. B	43. D	58. C	73. B
14. B	29. A	44. C	59. D	74. A
15. D	30. C	45. A	60. C	75. A

TEST 2

DIRECTIONS: Each question or incomplete statement is followed by several suggested answers or completions. Select the one the BEST answers the question or completes the statement PRINT THE LETTER OF THE CORRECT ANSWER IN THE SPACE AT THE RIGHT.

1. The primary purpose of assessment in clinical social work is to

   A. help set appropriate goals and objectives for treatment
   B. provide a means of measuring treatment progress and outcome
   C. identify an appropriate DSM-IV diagnosis
   D. help establish meaningful communication with other providers and insurers

2. An adolescent client, while discussing the murder of her mother by her father, relates the events in a detached, matter-of-fact manner. When emotional blunting of this type occurs in conjunction with _____ , a strong likelihood exists that the client is psychotic and in need of psychiatric evaluation.

   A. alcohol and/or drug abuse
   B. thought disorder
   C. unipolar disorder
   D. poor self-concept

3. A social worker in private practice receives a phone call from a prospective client who says that she wants to get to know the worker, free of charge, before beginning treatment. The worker should:

   A. outline his fee policy for the client
   B. see the client
   C. tell the client there will be no charge for the session if the worker decides he cannot work with her
   D. inform the client that this isn't possible

4. A clinician in family treatment is dealing with an "undifferentiated ego mass." Which of the following would be an element of the intervention?

   A. Forming and join an "emotionally triangle" in the family system in order to reduce anxiety from within
   B. Working individually with the most differentiated family member, because he/she is most capable of breaking habitual pathological patterns
   C. Unbalancing the family's homeostasis by promoting confrontations among family members
   D. Working individually with the least differentiated family member in order to bring him/her up to the level of the more differentiated family members

5. A client with a long history of depression visits a clinician for the first time. While the client is hopeful that the clinician can help with his problem, he says he cannot sign a "non-suicide" contract, and he insists on the additional condition that the clinician not involuntarily hospitalize him for extreme suicidal thoughts. The clinician should

A. inform the client that she cannot make this promise under any circumstances
B. take a medical and social history before deciding to treat this client
C. try to persuade the client to seek hospitalization for treatment
D. start a course of antidepressants and check with the client in a few weeks to see if he's changed his mind

6. Generally, the thinking today regarding phenotype and genotype is that

   A. phenotype reveals certain aspects of genotype
   B. phenotype and genotype have a bidirectional influence on each other
   C. phenotype and genotype have no relation to each other
   D. phenotype does not indicate anything about genotype

7. Within the context of employee evaluation at a social services agency, the practice of "banding"

   A. is not considered useful because it increases the likelihood that a selection technique will have an adverse impact
   B. may not reduce adverse impact unless it is combined with a minority preference component
   C. is considered useful for tracking the success rates of employees who have been hired using a particular selection technique
   D. is preferable to other techniques because it is more likely to eliminate problems related to adverse impact

8. To make acceptance clear to the client in the early stages of building the therapeutic relationship, it's important for the practitioner to
   I. maintain eye contact with the client
   II. maintain facial expressions that are consistent with the client's emotions
   III. keep an appropriate distance away from the client—more than arm's length
   IV. avoid crossing his/her arms while listening

   A. I only
   B. I and II
   C. I, II and IV
   D. I, II, III and IV

9. Which of the following clinician roles will generally be LEAST important for a social worker's crisis intervention practice in an emergency room setting?

   A. Educator
   B. Activist
   C. Coordinator
   D. Broker

10. According to Dane and Simon, one of the predictable problems faced by social workers in secondary practices settings is the "marginality of token status." This means that

    A. in a given secondary setting, social workers are few and their visibility is high
    B. social work is devalued as "women's work" in settings that are predominantly male in composition
    C. there is a discrepancy between the values of the social work profession and the dominant profession of the organization

D. a worker who is responsible for developing a helping relationship with the client in an effort to solve problems must also perform in a role that reinforces the norms of the organizational setting

11. Which of the following listening skills is MOST likely to be used in a client interview that conforms to the client-centered approach?

    A. Open questions
    B. Paraphrasing
    C. Closed questions
    D. Interpretation/refraining

12. Most practitioners, when they begin their careers and begin a relationship with their supervisors, desire help in each of the following areas, EXCEPT

    A. developing skills
    B. finding a specialized niche
    C. fostering self-awareness
    D. applying theory

13. According to Lewis, the primary difference between a "healthy" and a "faltering" family appears to be in the relationship between

    A. the children
    B. the married couple
    C. the mother and the child/children
    D. the father and the child/children

14. Which of the following tasks is NOT generally appropriate for paraprofessionals in a social service agency?

    A. Arranging client transportation
    B. Referring clients to appropriate helping professionals
    C. Completing forms requesting services from other agencies
    D. Conducting intake histories

15. Which of the following term denotes the "pitch" of the voice?

    A. Tone
    B. Resonance
    C. Inflection
    D. Volume

16. The "constructivist" model of social work holds that clients' conceptions of reality are a product of

    A. experience
    B. deeds
    C. ideals
    D. language

17. Which of the following is an argument commonly given by social work practitioners AGAINST the use of worker-client contracting in the therapeutic relationship?

A. Expanded malpractice risks
B. Greater likelihood of misunderstandings about expectations
C. Increased likelihood of premature termination
D. Forces a legal requirement onto the client that damages the status of the "helping" relationship

18. The symptoms of people with somatization disorder must include the following:
    I. Four pain symptoms in different sites
    II. Two gastrointestinal symptoms without pain
    III. One sexual symptom without pain
    IV. One pseudoneurological symptom without pain

    A. I only
    B. I or II
    C. II, III and IV
    D. I, II, III and IV

19. During a family intervention session, the teen-age daughter is sitting silently in a corner of the room with her arms folded across her chest. To engage the daughter in the process, clinician using the structural model would

    A. sit next to her and tell her what she's doing is okay and makes perfect sense
    B. direct her to be participate in the agreed-upon intervention
    C. reward and praise her when and if she does speak
    D. ignore her and wait for her to speak when she's ready

20. It is common for Native American or Latino families to ascribe family status to close friends. These friends are said to take on the status of

    A. modified extended members
    B. referents
    C. fictive relatives
    D. de facto kin

21. Advantages to a shared partnership in private social work practice include
    I. Cost savings in office space
    II. Minimal problems in coverage and consultation
    III. Increased income- and client-building opportunities
    IV. Enhanced credibility with other professional groups

    A. I only
    B. I and II
    C. I, III and IV
    D. I, II, III and IV

22. A social worker is interviewing a client who is a recent immigrant from China. In general, the social worker should avoid

    A. attentive body language
    B. sustained eye contact
    C. open-ended questions
    D. verbal tracking

23. Which of the following is NOT a theory of psychoanalysis? 23.____

    A. The therapist should relate as a real, genuine person.
    B. Mental illness is not an accepted concept.
    C. Insight into problems is insufficient for producing change.
    D. Clients are not responsible for their deviant behaviors.

24. The NASW code states explicitly that a social worker has an ethical duty to provide voluntary public service that benefits society as a whole. Probably the most appropriate way to do this is to 24.____

    A. join and participate in professional organizations or associations
    B. engage in individual advocacy
    C. engage in class advocacy
    D. run for public office

25. Sherman and Wenocur propose six ways for social services workers to resolve their feelings of alienation from the agency. Of these, the most productive is 25.____

    A. withdrawal
    B. functional non-capitulation
    C. niche-finding
    D. capitulation

26. In the psychodynamic perspective, "falling in love" is best described as 26.____

    A. the unrealistic search for the perfect partner
    B. a sign that inner needs are finally being met
    C. an idealization of the sexual drive
    D. an irrational process

27. Which of the following relationships is an example of a purchase of service agreement? 27.____

    A. A child protective services agency contracts with a family services agency to provide counseling to children who have suffered abuse or neglect.
    B. A psychotherapist refers a client to a general assistance agency for help with financial management.
    C. A family services agency hires the legal advisors of the local hospital to help with a malpractice suit.
    D. A general assistance client applies for and is given food stamps to supplement his income

28. According to Freud, which of the following defense mechanisms is ALWAYS involved in neurotic behavior? 28.____

    A. sublimation
    B. regression
    C. anger
    D. repression

29. In the transactional view of human behavior, 29.____

    A. it is believed that human potential is limitless
    B. people are motivated primarily by the potential for profit

C. the primary issue is the tension between individual and collective well-being
D. people are seen as individual systems, separate from their social context

30. The client of a private practitioner complains of frequent periods of dizziness during which he experiences several unsettling feelings: he feels completely separate from his mind and body, as if he's floating and watching himself from above. The client says that during these episodes he sometimes wonders whether he's a real person or some machine that's programmed by someone else. The client is aware that the feelings are a product of his mind, but he can't control them, though he has been keeping them to himself and not telling family or friends about them. The most appropriate diagnosis for this client is

30.____

A. dementia, not otherwise specified
B. depersonalization disorder
C. delusional disorder
D. schizophreniform disorder

31. During an initial interview, a client tells the social worker that he is gay and has AIDS. For the worker and this client to have an effective long-term therapeutic relationship, it is most important for the worker to be:

31.____

A. gay
B. non-homophobic
C. ready to refer the client out
D. comfortable dealing with issues of sexuality and safe sex

32. Which of the following statements is TRUE?

32.____

A. There is no consistent correlation between ethnic, racial, or socioeconomic status and the likelihood of child abuse or neglect.
B. Mothers are more likely to be implicated in cases of abuse and neglect than fathers.
C. In general, the likelihood that a child will experience neglect decreases with age.
D. Boys are twice as likely as girls to experience abuse or neglect.

33. As a social worker leads a therapy group, a client offers constructive feedback to another client in the group, but the feedback is offered in clear irritation and agitation. The rest of the group becomes angry at the first client. The social worker should:

33.____

A. point out what the first client did well, and then offer constructive criticism
B. see the first client in an individual session to give him feedback on his performance
C. ask the group to point out what the first client has done wrong
D. focus on the needs of the client who has just received negative feedback

34. A practitioner in private practice is visited by a mother and her, an exceptionally bright 11-year-old who is not at all liked by his peers. Their dislike has become so strong that they continually tease and taunt the boy, and he has complained bitterly to his mother. Probably the most useful means of assessment in this situation would be for the practitioner to

34.____

A. arrange situations in which the boy's behavior around other children can be observed
B. begin a course of insight-oriented treatment

C. gently question the boy about what he believes might be causing the problem
D. set up a role-playing exercise in which the boy assumes the role of one of his classmates

35. In removing personal barriers to achievement for clients of color, interventions should be aimed at

    A. distributing resources through information/education
    B. actively encouraging family involvement
    C. recognizing and affirming client system strengths
    D. improving educational/vocational opportunities through greater teacher/employer awareness of diversity, history and customs

36. Which of the following is NOT a type of behavioral intervention?

    A. Systematic desensitization
    B. Assertiveness training
    C. Script analysis
    D. Contingency contracting

37. In couples therapy, it is most important for the social worker to

    A. establish rapport with each partner
    B. maintain confidentiality
    C. cut through the denial
    D. teach communication skills

38. A clinician collects different kinds of data—for example, interviews and observations—which may include both qualitative and quantitative data, for the purpose of studying the same research question. This is an example of

    A. triangulation
    B. cross-classification
    C. rival hypotheses
    D. validation

39. Ivan Nye and his associates, applying the social exchange theory to family life, concluded that behavioral choices made by family members follow a specific, rank-order pattern, beginning with choices from alternatives

    A. from which they anticipate the fewest costs
    B. that provide better immediate outcomes
    C. from which they expect the most profit
    D. that promise better long-term outcomes

40. Of the types of adolescents listed below, psychodynamic interventions will probably be MOST useful for those

    A. who are addicted and in denial
    B. with oppositional/conduct disorder
    C. who are clinically depressed
    D. with ADHD

41. A family has been seeing a social worker for almost one year, after receiving a court referral—their 15-year-old son was found guilty of sexually molesting their 7-year-old daughter. The son has been in foster care for the last year and has been receiving individual and group therapy. In one month, he is due to begin visitations at home. The social worker should

    A. reiterate to the family what they've learned about the "cycle of incest"
    B. include the son in a family therapy session during his first visitation
    C. contact the son's individual and group therapists for copies of their opinions as to his readiness for family therapy, and coordinate treatment with them
    D. review the family's plans for what will take place in terms of the son's interactions with his sister during initial visitations

42. Which of the following question stems is particularly useful to social workers in client interviews, because it is simultaneously open and closed?

    A. What
    B. Could
    C. Is
    D. How

43. Which of the following statements is NOT characteristic of ego psychology?

    A. The social environment shapes the personality
    B. Problems are almost exclusively the function of deficits in coping capacity
    C. The ego mediates between the individual and the environment
    D. The ego is the part of the personality that allows for successful adaptation to the environment.

44. Questioning is one of the most important means for supervisors to help practitioners reflect on their own work. Which of the following is a guideline to for a supervisor to use in questioning an practitioner?

    A. When the supervisor wonders whether the practitioner has adequate knowledge of the case or diagnosis, to make treatment decision, the supervisor should move from specific to general questions.
    B. Beginning questions should be specific in nature and answered specifically.
    C. When general supervisory questions result in answers that reveal thorough knowledge of the case, the supervisor can move to questions related to treatment and intervention strategies.
    D. Questions related to treatment strategies and techniques should be more specific than questions related to diagnostic understanding.

45. In applying the ethical concept of client self-determination, a social worker upholds:

    A. the importance of helping clients make healthy choices and decisions
    B. the right and need of clients to make their own choices and decisions
    C. the importance of helping clients achieve their fullest potential
    D. the right of clients to seek help in making choices and decisions

46. According to Bowen, families deal with anxiety and tension in one of four ways. Which of the following is NOT one of these?

A. Increased emotional distance between spouses
B. Increased emotional distance between siblings
C. Physical or emotional dysfunction in a spouse
D. Impairment in a child

47. Which of the following offers the BEST example of a double-bind paradox?

    A. A father who masks hostility with a too-loving attitude
    B. An authoritarian mother
    C. A passive mother and a hostile son
    D. An aggressive mother and a timid son

48. Which of the following is a phenotypical definition of gender?

    A. Genital gender
    B. Hormonal gender
    C. Organal gender
    D. Chromosomal gender

49. Which of the following approaches to social services policymaking is designed to meet a long-term need, such as education?

    A. Formative
    B. Residual
    C. External
    D. Investment

50. In the early stages of a therapeutic relationship, the practitioner brings the focus of discussions onto the client herself, and affirming her willingness and ability to bring about necessary change. Probably the next stage for this relationship will be to

    A. connect various elements of current client problems to patterns of their life experience
    B. client internalization of appropriate goals, attitudes and behaviors
    C. creating structures and patterns of learning and awareness
    D. recognizing and admiring client abilities to grow independent and create something valuable

51. Which of the following ethnic groups are generally LEAST likely to the placement of older relations into a nursing home?

    A. Latino
    B. Chinese-American
    C. African-American
    D. Jewish-American

52. The general consensus among clinical social workers and psychologists is that a person in crisis is characterized by each of the following, EXCEPT

    A. appearing unable to modify or lessen the impact of stressful events with traditional coping methods
    B. experiencing a serious loss of function
    C. experiencing increased fear, tension and/or confusion
    D. exhibiting a high level of subjective discomfort

53. Within a social services organization, zero-based budgeting
    I. requires that a program start from scratch
    II. requires that a program justify each dollar requested
    III. is calculated annually
    IV. rolls unused funds into the next program

    A. I only
    B. I and II
    C. I, II and III
    D. I, II, III and IV

54. In the theoretical construct of self psychology, drives are seen as more _____ than in the Freudian approach.

    A. social
    B. libidmal
    C. aggressive
    D. instinctual

55. Among social work clinicians, one of the major problems with the concept of acceptance in a therapeutic relationship is that

    A. clinicians often become overinvolved and make the client's needs into their own
    B. the duration of such relationships usually doesn't allow for acceptance
    C. clinicians often confuse it with liking the person or approving of client behaviors
    D. clients often don't care whether they are accepted or not as long as their problem is solved

56. During the assessment phase of treatment for the family of a child with conduct disorder, the practitioner should focus attention on each of the following, EXCEPT

    A. information about cognitive/emotional reactions to the presenting problem
    B. solutions already attempted by the family
    C. the reasons why people react to the presenting problem in the ways that they do
    D. family myths

57. Which of the following is NOT a recent professional trend that has supported the need for clinical supervision of practitioners?

    A. Changes in professional standards
    B. Resurgence of clinical practice
    C. Complex external controls on practice structure
    D. Decreasing role of social work in mental illness treatment

58. During an initial interview session with a family, the social worker observes that family therapist notices that whenever the mother talks, the father and son contradict what she says and criticize her. The father and son's behavior is best described as:

    A. triangulation
    B. scapegoating
    C. a coalition
    D. positive feedback

59. In making her assessment of the occurrence of depression in a community, a practitioner begins to worry that the problem is not as serious as has been suggested by several recent well-publicized events. The practitioner should

   A. rely on clients' definitions of their individual problems
   B. put her theories and preconceptions on hold until she has gathered more information
   C. engage in self-exploration to heighten sensitivity to misplaced assumptions and expectations
   D. check statistical data and data on non-occurrence

59.____

60. In order to be accurate, a paraphrase of a client's statements must contain certain elements. Which of the following is NOT necessarily one of these?

   A. A succinct summary of what the client said, in the same order it was said
   B. A brief signal at the end of the paraphrase that asks whether it is accurate
   C. A sentence stem using some aspect of the client's mode of receiving information
   D. The key words and constructs used by the client to describe the situation or person.

60.____

61. Which of the following approaches to social services policymaking focuses on a specific need, such as food stamps?

   A. Institutional
   B. Consumption
   C. Coalition
   D. Prescriptive

61.____

62. By far, the most readily available data in assessment are the anecdotal data provided in interviews with the client. This type of information carries the risk of

   A. masking the client's perceptions of his own experience
   B. a focus on client deficits
   C. "pigeon-holing" the client in the worker's eyes into a neat category of presenting problem
   D. worker counter-transference

62.____

63. The Rational Decision-Making Model is used by some social service administrators in program evaluation and design. In the first stage of the model, problem formulation, administrators
   I. identify stakeholders in the evaluation
   II. specify the relationship between the evaluation and the program
   III. specify types of data to be collected
   IV. clarify the objectives of the evaluation

   A. I and II
   B. I and IV
   C. II, III and IV
   D. I, II, III and IV

63.____

64. In the conduct of life span research, effects that are due to a subject's time of birth, but which are unrelated to age, are known as

64.____

A. age-graded influences
B. chronosystems
C. normative life events
D. cohort effects

65. A practitioner incrementally adds specific treatment components to a client's treatment package, in order to monitor their collective impact. This type of intervention is known as a _____ treatment strategy.

    A. dismantling
    B. dichotomous
    C. constructive
    D. parametric

66. One of the clinician's tasks in crisis intervention is to restore a client's cognitive functioning. In developing cognitive mastery, the client must FIRST

    A. restructure, rebuild, and replace irrational beliefs with new, realistic cognitions
    B. obtain a realistic understanding of what happened and what led to the crisis
    C. explore feelings and emotions surrounding the incident
    D. understand the specific meaning the event has for him or her

67. Which of the following is NOT a type of "in-kind" social service program?

    A. Food stamps
    B. Public housing
    C. General assistance
    D. Medical assistance

68. Which of the following statements about child abuse/maltreatment is FALSE?

    A. It occurs in nearly half of all families.
    B. It is usually mild to moderate in severity.
    C. It is a diverse condition.
    D. It is only partially caused by parental personality characteristics.

69. In social work practice, the corrective experience that allows clients to experience themselves differently, and thereafter make changes, begins as a function of

    A. the client's willingness to change
    B. how much the client is able to trust the practitioner to help him make the right decisions about how to change
    C. the degree to which the practitioner can establish an empathic understanding of the client and his situation
    D. the degree to which the practitioner can establish a sense of urgency for change

70. During an initial interview with a divorced 37-year-old man, the client reports that he suspects his ex-wife, who is the custodial parent of their daughter, of abusing her. The MOST appropriate response for the worker would be to

    A. ask the client whether he has reported the abuse
    B. explore the factors that have led the client to believe this
    C. begin therapy cautiously, mindful of the possibility that the client may be using this allegation to obtain custody of his daughter

D. report child abuse in accord with a social worker's legal mandate to make
E. a suspected child abuse report whenever he or she hears about possible child abuse

71. Studies comparing the personalities of lesbian and heterosexual females have found that

    A. lesbian women are less defensive than heterosexual women
    B. lesbian women are higher in neuroticism than heterosexual women
    C. lesbian women and heterosexual women are about equally well-adjusted
    D. lesbian women are less confident than heterosexual women

72. Which of the following is a significant benefit associated with the psychoanalytical model of intervention?

    A. easily operationalized concepts
    B. attention to personality development across the entire human life span
    C. clear recognition of the subconscious in psychological functioning
    D. pan-cultural theoretical base

73. Which of the following investigative strategies is designed to achieve a precise determination of a behavior's causes?

    A. Random assignment
    B. Correlational
    C. Longitudinal
    D. Experimental

74. As part of an evaluation program, a social worker records the number of times a child replies to a specific parental request The observational method used here is

    A. time sampling
    B. recording latency
    C. counting discriminated operants
    D. frequency count

75. Which of the following questions or statements is MOST likely to be used during a client interview by a social worker using the Rogerian model?

    A. On the other hand; you see your ideal self as someone who can excel at managing both a career and a family.
    B. You say you often act awkwardly in social situations, and you'd like to develop some social skills?
    C. I think you've described your short-term and long-term goals pretty clearly.
    D. I'm beginning to see the difference here between your present situation and your desired outcome.

KEY (CORRECT ANSWERS)

1. A	16. D	31. B	46. B	61. B
2. B	17. D	32. B	47. A	62. D
3. A	18. D	33. A	48. A	63. B
4. C	19. A	34. A	49. D	64. D
5. A	20. C	35. C	50. C	65. C
6. D	21. D	36. C	51. B	66. B
7. B	22. B	37. D	52. B	67. C
8. C	23. D	38. A	53. B	68. A
9. B	24. C	39. C	54. A	69. C
10. A	25. B	40. C	55. C	70. B
11. B	26. D	41. C	56. C	71. C
12. B	27. A	42. B	57. D	72. C
13. B	28. D	43. B	58. C	73. D
14. B	29. C	44. C	59. D	74. C
15. C	30. B	45. B	60. A	75. A

EXAMINATION SECTION
TEST 1

DIRECTIONS: Each question or incomplete statement is followed by several suggested answers or completions. Select the one the BEST answers the question or completes the statement. *PRINT THE LETTER OF THE CORRECT ANSWER IN THE SPACE AT THE RIGHT.*

1. At the outset of treatment, a client tells the social worker that she must promise never to involuntarily hospitalize her, no matter how depressed or suicidal she may seem. In formulating a response to this request, the social worker should use the underlying ethical principle of

    A. the need to do whatever is necessary to maintain a therapeutic relationship with a client
    B. never making a promise that is in conflict with legal and ethical requirements
    C. the client"s right to self-determination
    D. the understanding that the client has legitimate, defensible reasons for making this request

2. For a Gestalt therapist, a primary goal of treatment is to help the client

    A. integrate the present with his/her past and future
    B. develop a "success identity"
    C. integrate the functioning of his/her mind and body
    D. incorporate the external into the internal

3. What is the term for a social system that is part of a larger system and made up of several smaller systems?

    A. Focal system
    B. Schema
    C. Holon
    D. Gemeinschaft

4. The most commonly occurring psychological disorders are _____ disorders.

    A. Dissociative
    B. Psychosexual
    C. Mood
    D. Somatoform

5. In the early stages of problem-solving communication training with a family, the practitioner should FIRST assess

    A. family cognitions about communication/arguments
    B. the history of the problem
    C. family assets
    D. specific skill deficits

6. An intern at an agency for the chronically mentally ill meets with a 24-year-old client who has been referred by his family doctor. The primary basis for this referral is the client's isolation from peers and general lack of social skills. In many ways, the client reminds the intern of the quiet, studious friends she made in graduate school, who had very little time to socialize because of studies and part-time jobs. The client tells the intern he doesn't think he belongs in this place, and she silently agrees, though her supervisor and more experienced workers seem to believe that this is the right place for him. In her assessment of this client's situation, the intern has relied on the _____ heuristic.

   A. theoretical
   B. schematic
   C. availability
   D. representativeness

7. Which of the following types of feminism proposes that men and women have different values due to the structure of sex and gender roles in society?

   A. socialist
   B. reactionary
   C. radical
   D. liberal

8. The most significant problem with establishing "comparable worth" at an agency is that

   A. males and females may use different strategies to reach the same decision or solution
   B. the job evaluation techniques themselves may be gender-biased
   C. job evaluation techniques are not as useful for very complex jobs
   D. it is difficult to compare achievement across different domains

9. A social worker decides that solution-focused therapy is the most appropriate approach for a family that has come to see her about financial problems. The social worker's FIRST intervention would be to

   A. discuss time constraints and make sure the family knows the intervention will be brief
   B. get a clear picture of how the system functions
   C. get a history of the origins of the symptoms
   D. discuss how things would be for the family if the problem was already solved

10. Social service agencies, in attempting to make a certain program more efficient and useful, may sometimes get lost in pursuing a prescribed means of service delivery at the expense of accomplishing program goals. This is known as

    A. output loss
    B. goal displacement
    C. bounded rationality
    D. organizational shaping

11. According to Elkind, the most significant descriptor of adolescent thought is

    A. concrete
    B. irrational

C. egocentric
D. moralistic

12. In a program evaluation, which type of data is concerned primarily with whether or not the program goals are being met?

    A. throughput
    B. process
    C. product
    D. input

13. Which of the following problems or disorders is LEAST likely to be changed through psychotherapy?

    A. Anorexia nervosa
    B. Conduct disorder
    C. Antisocial personality disorder
    D. Compulsive behavior

14. The record-keeping requirements at a typical social services agency require the completion of a review treatment plan at an interval no longer than

    A. after every client contact
    B. weekly
    C. every 30 days
    D. every 90 days

15. For social workers, it is usually most appropriate to view a woman's separation from an abusive husband as

    A. a series of losses which initiates a mourning process
    B. a solution that must be accomplished as quickly as possible
    C. a partial process at best if children are involved
    D. the best of all possible solutions to the problem of domestic abuse

16. Formative policy research at social services agencies

    A. is usually conducted in response to legislative mandates
    B. focuses on policy development rather than on its impact on clients and agencies
    C. identifies social policy as the independent variable
    D. is based entirely on output goals

17. Abusive families are most often characterized by

    A. openness and affection
    B. rigid boundaries and clear roles
    C. a strong parental subsystem
    D. denial and enmeshed boundaries

18. The principal assessment tool for clinicians working from the intergenerational perspective on the family is the

    A. life cycle matrix
    B. social history

C. genogram
D. ecomap

19. The "output goals" of a social service program are MOST likely to include

    A. specified ratings of services by clients on a standardized scale
    B. observable effects on a given community or clientele
    C. the number of units of service provided
    D. the number of clients served

20. A 35-year-old client, a high school teacher, reports to a practitioner at an outpatient clinic and reports the following incident: he, a high school teacher, was in the middle of a lesson during a class period that had been particularly difficult for him over the past several months, because the class was large and often noisy. During the middle of today's lesson, the client suddenly began to sweat profusely and his heart started to race. He continued with the lesson but soon felt dizzy and fearful that he was about to die. The feeling was so overwhelming that he had to leave the class unattended and retreat to the teacher's lounge, where he was found sitting alone and trembling. The client's physician has found no evidence of medical problems. The most likely DSM-IV diagnosis for this client would be

    A. panic disorder
    B. posttraumatic stress disorder
    C. dissociative disorder
    D. social phobia

21. Which of the following statements reveals a client with a formal-operational emotional orientation?

    A. I'm so sad right now that my stomach hurts. I haven't eaten all day.
    B. I suppose there are two different ways of looking at this. On one hand, these arguments are really painful, but I know I have to set limits for my son and it's part of my role as a parent. I know he needs to find his own space, but his decisions are sometimes questionable.
    C. I feel great about the new relationship I'm in. I think I've met the perfect man.
    D. As I think about it, I feel bad because it seems as if we've been arguing a lot lately. It's almost a ritual--every time I get ready to leave the house, an argument starts.

22. The purpose of the mental status examination in psychotherapy is

    A. personality testing
    B. to make a diagnosis
    C. reality testing
    D. to determine the severity of psychotic symptoms

23. Which of the following interviewing skills is most useful for discovering the deeply held thoughts and feelings underlying the client's experience?

    A. Confrontation
    B. Open-ended questioning
    C. Focusing
    D. Reflection of meaning

24. A client who has a history of hypomanic and major depressive episodes would have a diagnosis of

    A. Hypomanic disorder
    B. Cyclothymic disorder
    C. Bipolar I disorder
    D. Bipolar II disorder

25. Which of the following theoretical frameworks establishes equity and distributive justice as its ideal ends of development

    A. Behavioral/social exchange
    B. Ego psychology
    C. Symbolic interactionism
    D. Structural functionalism

26. A "Theory X" manager in an organization is likely to

    A. adopt a team approach to problem-solving
    B. use tangible rewards and sanctions to shape employee behavior
    C. work to set up and maintain a work environment that promotes growth and creativity
    D. assume that subordinates want to work toward organization goal attainment

27. Which of the following is generally NOT recommended as part of an intervention with a Native American client who follows older traditions?

    A. Serving food
    B. Emphasizing the past
    C. Giving gifts
    D. Including friends and family

28. The process of transforming a piece of legislation into a specific program or policy, by means of identifying specific guidelines and operating procedures to be used in administering the program, is known as

    A. rationalization
    B. promulgation
    C. consignment
    D. confederation

29. Which of the following is NOT an ego-defense mechanism?

    A. Regression
    B. Reality testing
    C. Displacement
    D. Sublimation

30. Which of the following is probably the MOST appropriate candidate for an intensive, heterogeneous outpatient therapy group?

    A. A paranoid person
    B. A person with bipolar II disorder

C. An alcoholic or drug addict
D. A person with brain damage

31. In removing intracultural barriers to achievement for clients of color, interventions should be aimed at

    A. active encouragement of family involvement
    B. recognition and affirmation of client system strengths
    C. changes in institutional policies, practices, and administration
    D. improved educational/vocational opportunities through greater teacher/employer awareness of diversity, history and customs

32. Which of the following is a means-tested program?

    A. Medicare
    B. Social Security
    C. Public education
    D. Police protection

33. One of the greatest risks associated with too little self-disclosure in the group therapy process is

    A. severely limited reality testing
    B. low group cohesiveness
    C. yielding an inappropriate amount of member control
    D. severe dependence

34. In behavioral therapy, the systematic desensitization process, usually performed by disassociating a neutral stimulus from a situation that has created fear or anxiety, is also known as

    A. extinction
    B. aversion therapy
    C. overcorrection
    D. counterconditioning

35. The primary function of reflecting feelings during a client interview is to

    A. help the client sort out mixed or ambivalent feelings
    B. grounding the worker and client in concrete experience
    C. bring out additional details of the client's emotional world
    D. make implicit, sometimes hidden emotions clear to the client

36. Which of the following is NOT a privileged relationship during the prosecution of child abuse?

    A. Priest-confessor
    B. Lawyer-client
    C. Psychotherapist-patient
    D. Physician-patient

37. According to ego psychology, the ego

A. mediates between erotic energies and superego constraints
B. is a drive for pleasure
C. imposes a set of rules to control unbridled pleasure-seeking
D. offers ideals for the individual to strive for

38. Which of the following statements reveals a discrepancy that is external to the speaker? 38.____

A. I don't mind talking about that at all.
B. I wanted to go to business school, but my grades weren't good enough.
C. My mother is a saint, but she doesn't respect me.
D. This is a nice office. It's too bad it's in this neighborhood.

39. During an intake interview for a woman who has committed a violent crime, the clinician notes that whenever the woman talks of the act she does so without any emotion–anger, shame, guilt, or sadness–whatsoever. From the psychoanalytic perspective, the woman is using the defense mechanism of 39.____

A. isolation
B. fantasy formation
C. repression
D. rationalization

40. A humanist, looking at an individual's misbehavior, would conclude that a person who acts badly is 40.____

A. suffering from a kind of illness
B. experiencing a detachment from her moral compass
C. willfully disregarding the norms which characterize her community
D. reacting to the deprivation of her basic needs

41. Clinicians in private practice are generally paid for 41.____
   I. direct services to clients
   II. number of hours on the job
   III. indirect services

A. I only
B. I and II
C. II only
D. I, II and III

42. A clinician is meeting with a transactional group for the first time and works intensely at studying the members and their transactions. In the early stages of work with this group, the clinician's greatest challenge is likely to be 42.____

A. defusing conflict between members
B. identifying the self-talk or cognitions that lie behind a transaction
C. heading off the tendency toward subgroupings
D. determining which ego state a transaction comes from

43. A social worker has been seeing a client for several months and has developed a good working relationship. The client loses her job and cannot afford to pay for therapy. Under the social worker's professional code and value system, the BEST option in this case would be to 43.____

A. refer the client to low-cost therapy from another provider
B. allow the client to divert payments until she gets another job
C. provide the therapy free of charge until the client can find employment
D. reduce the fee for this client and/or offer her shorter sessions

44. "Acceptance" in the therapeutic relationship mean that the practitioner
    I. separates the client from her behavior
    II. indicates approval of the client's behavior
    III. expresses sympathy for the client
    IV. demonstrates tolerance for client's behavior

    A. I only
    B. I and II
    C. II, III and IV
    D. I, II, III and IV

45. According to Papernow, most people first enter a stepfamily with

    A. a clear awareness of the reality of their situation
    B. a growing sense of realistic intimacy with new family members
    C. the fantasy that they will rescue the new partner and any children from the deficiencies of a previous marriage
    D. a feeling of resentment toward new family members who place new demands on their time, money, and other resources

46. An ideal therapeutic relationship in social work is one that

    A. connects the client with the proper support services
    B. allows and helps the client's capacity to work out his own issues
    C. is an ongoing source of support
    D. the client can rely upon as a problem-solving tool

47. Which of the following is NOT characteristic of a clinician who is conducting reality therapy with a client?

    A. Viewing mental illness labels as destructive
    B. Focusing on behavior rather than feelings
    C. Discouraging value judgements
    D. Not offering sympathy

48. In general, a DSM-IV diagnosis of a specific disorder includes a criterion of

    A. no medical involvement
    B. a clinically significant impairment or distress in a social or occupational area
    C. an identifiable etiology
    D. distress that has exceeded a period of 8 weeks

49. A client interview is interrupted by a long silence that makes the social worker uncomfortable. The FIRST thing the social worker should do is

    A. inform the client that of his/her (the worker's) discomfort and observe the client's reaction
    B. restate the last words spoken by the client

C. say, "I wonder why you're so quiet"
D. study the client to see if he/she appears comfortable with the silence

50. A social worker is seeing a Latino family that immigrated to the United States several years ago. The social worker is not Latino. The family often arrive late for their sessions, causing some scheduling problems—and mild annoyance—for the social worker. The best way for the social worker to handle this would be to

   A. be aware that time may be perceived differently in their culture and invite them to discuss what being late means to them
   B. understand that being late is probably an expression of cultural resistance to disclosing family issues
   C. be aware that time may be perceived differently in their culture, and take a more flexible approach to beginning scheduled sessions
   D. consider referring the family to a Hispanic therapist

51. The foundation of clinical supervisory techniques—and the focus of supervision—is/are typically

   A. case material
   B. educational assessment
   C. long-term practitioner development goals
   D. practitioner attitudes and values

52. A practitioner grew up as the oldest child of alcoholic parents, and was often placed in the role of parent to his three younger siblings. In order to establish solid therapeutic relationships with his clients, the most important challenge this practitioner will probably face is

   A. being able to trust that clients have the capacity to work through their problems
   B. being able to see clearly the problems faced by alcoholic clients
   C. the risk that he will impose an undue level of responsibility on clients early in the intervention process
   D. a lack of faith in his ability to help clients change

53. A married couple and their two teenage sons see a clinician for the first time for help with what they view as an unhealthy spirit of competition between the two boys. The clinician observes the family's interactions and characterizes them as high-functioning and relatively flexible. Which of the following models of intervention is probably MOST appropriate for this family?

   A. Structural-functional
   B. Strategic
   C. Experiential
   D. Solution-focused

54. According to the lifespan perspective of human development and behavior, development is NOT

   A. contextual
   B. historically embedded
   C. unidirectional
   D. lifelong

55. The sole motivation for a client's feigning illness in factitious disorder is to

    A. obtain prescription drugs
    B. draw attention away from his/her psychological problems
    C. assume a sick role.
    D. escape material and everyday responsibilities

56. In school, an 8-year-old boy has considerably impaired social interactions with other children, along with severely impaired language skills. The boy also pulls at his hair constantly, sometimes leaving ragged bald patches, and often bites himself, leaving wounds and scars that his parents have made the primary concern for treatment. Appropriate diagnoses for this boy include
    I. Asperger's disorder
    II. Stereotypic movement disorder
    III. Autism
    IV. Mental retardation

    A. I and II
    B. II and III
    C. III only
    D. IV only

57. In order to ensure a margin of error no greater than 5%, what is the size of the sample required to represent a population of 10,000?

    A. 108
    B. 370
    C. 1235
    D. 9,500

58. Social learning theory recognizes each of the following as a key factor in human development, EXCEPT

    A. cognition
    B. heredity
    C. behavior
    D. environment

59. According to Annon, clients in sex therapy need interventions at very specific levels. The first of these levels is

    A. specific suggestions
    B. intensive therapy
    C. limited information
    D. permission

60. Which of the following is named as the etiological agent for adjustment disorder?

    A. Depressed mood
    B. Stress
    C. Sudden trauma
    D. Organic chemistry imbalance

61. Social workers generally observe several distinct characteristics in the life cycle of poor African-American families. Which of the following is NOT one of these?

    A. Households that are frequently female-headed and isolated from the community
    B. A scarceness of resources that compels a reliance on government institutions
    C. A truncated life cycle with less time to resolve developmental tasks
    D. A life cycle punctuated by numerous unpredictable life events

62. A 50-year-old client has been significantly depressed for more than a year. For the past two months, the client has been convinced that he has developed lung cancer. The most appropriate DSM-IV diagnosis for the client would be

    A. conversion disorder
    B. major depressive episode
    C. somatoform disorder, not otherwise specified
    D. hypochondriasis

63. Persuasive arguments for flexible-rate fee schedules include
    I. Services more accessible to disadvantaged clients
    II. Endorsements of insurers and other third-party organizations
    III. No means testing
    IV. Consistency with consumer protection laws

    A. I only
    B. I and III
    C. I, II and IV
    D. I, II, III and IV

64. The psychoanalytical perspective views _____ as the most powerful and pervasive defense mechanism.

    A. projection
    B. rationalization
    C. repression
    D. denial

65. Which of the following approaches to client interviewing is MOST likely to make use of interpretation or refraining?

    A. Psychodynamic
    B. Solution-focused
    C. Client-centered
    D. Behavioral

66. When a clinician is on a provider panel for a managed health care company, he or she:

    A. is guaranteed a certain number of referrals from this company per year.
    B. has met the qualifications for company, and has no guarantee of referrals.
    C. agree to see any referral within your specialty.
    D. will receive a full fee from the company when he/she sees a client

67. When a therapeutic relationship is functioning on the cognitive level, the therapist will probably engage in each of the following processes, EXCEPT

A. highlighting inconsistencies
B. reassuring
C. refraining
D. asking key questions

68. Several days after losing her job, a woman becomes so depressed that she is unable to get out of bed until well into the afternoon, and rarely leaves her home. By the time she reports to a practitioner for treatment, she has been depressed and had trouble sleeping for about 4 months. The most appropriate DSM-IV diagnosis for this client is

    A. major depressive episode
    B. dysthmic disorder
    C. adjustment disorder with depressed mood
    D. depressive disorder, not otherwise specified

69. The NASW code's prohibition of dual relationships is most likely to be challenged by social workers who

    A. are part of an interdisciplinary team
    B. live and work in rural areas
    C. are involved in direct practice
    D. perform supervisory functions

70. Many practitioners make use of informal assessment instruments such as self-reporting questionnaires, indexes, and profiles. The main risk associated with these instruments as assessment tools is that they

    A. often put the client on the defensive
    B. may place too much emphasis on relatively unimportant details
    C. suggest that the practitioner may be lazy or incompetent
    D. often provoke client dissembling

71. The term "active listening" mostly refers to a person's ability to

    A. indicate with numerous physical cues that he/she is listening
    B. take an active role in determining which information is provided by the client
    C. concentrate on what is being said
    D. both listen to the client and accomplish other meaningful tasks at the same time

72. Which of the following is a latent function of the family unit?

    A. Economic production
    B. Socialization of children
    C. Provision of emotional support to members
    D. Contribution to institutional arrangements

73. Current knowledge of post-traumatic stress disorder (PTSD) indicates that if the initial stage of anxiety and obsession with the trauma persist for longer than _____, the patient then enters stage 2, or acute PTSD.

    A. 5-10 days
    B. 4-6 weeks
    C. 8-12 weeks
    D. 3-6 months

74. After making contact with a person in crisis and establishing a relationship, a clinician faces the task of examining the dimensions of the problem, in order to define it. Which of the following is NOT typically a task of this phase of crisis intervention?

    A. Exploring alternatives
    B. Assessing the dangerousness or lethality of the situation
    C. Identifying the precipitating event that led to the crisis
    D. Detailing a client's previous coping methods

75. In general, administrative evaluation at a social services agency differs from practice evaluation in that administrative evaluation is

    A. external to the supervisory relationship
    B. continuous
    C. basically self-contained
    D. specific

KEY (CORRECT ANSWERS)

1.	B	16.	B	31.	A	46.	B	61.	A
2.	C	17.	D	32.	A	47.	C	62.	B
3.	C	18.	C	33.	A	48.	B	63.	A
4.	C	19.	C	34.	D	49.	D	64.	C
5.	D	20.	A	35.	D	50.	A	65.	A
6.	D	21.	D	36.	D	51.	A	66.	B
7.	A	22.	C	37.	A	52.	A	67.	B
8.	B	23.	D	38.	B	53.	D	68.	C
9.	D	24.	D	39.	A	54.	C	69.	B
10.	B	25.	A	40.	D	55.	C	70.	B
11.	C	26.	B	41.	A	56.	B	71.	C
12.	C	27.	B	42.	D	57.	B	72.	D
13.	C	28.	B	43.	D	58.	B	73.	B
14.	D	29.	B	44.	A	59.	D	74.	A
15.	A	30.	B	45.	C	60.	B	75.	A

TEST 2

DIRECTIONS: Each question or incomplete statement is followed by several suggested answers or completions. Select the one the BEST answers the question or completes the statement. *PRINT THE LETTER OF THE CORRECT ANSWER IN THE SPACE AT THE RIGHT.*

1. An 18-year-old girl is brought into a hospital emergency room by her family, who reported that she experienced sudden blindness. She had been arguing with her mother about why her mother was so much stricter with her than her father, when her mother suddenly blurted out that she and the father were seeking a divorce. The girl continued to argue for several minutes but then suddenly stopped and announced that she couldn't see anything. An examination reveals no neurological deficits. The client should most likely receive a diagnosis of

    A. conversion disorder
    B. somatoform disorder, not otherwise specified
    C. dissociative disorder
    D. hypochondriasis

2. An important difference between brief psychotherapy and crisis intervention is that

    A. brief therapy focuses on pathology
    B. crisis intervention focuses on specific issues
    C. brief therapy focuses on specific issues
    D. crisis intervention focuses on pathology

3. During an evaluation session in which the supervisor and practitioner are discussing the progress of the practitioner's current caseload, the practitioner admits to being unhappy with the overall progress of his clients, but attributes it to problems he has been experiencing because of excessive pressure placed on him by the supervisor. At this point in the evaluation, the supervisor should

    A. reassure the practitioner that whatever pressures have been placed on him have been for the benefit of his professional development
    B. apologize and suggest that the practitioner think of ways in which the supervisory relationship can be made more comfortable
    C. try to steer the focus of the discussion toward client progress
    D. remind the practitioner that he is the one ultimately responsible for handling the pressures that come with social work practice

4. In the time series design of program evaluation, the primary threat to internal validity is

    A. history
    B. selection
    C. testing
    D. regression to the mean

5. A client tells her clinician that members of an international espionage ring are after her to torture her and find out what she knows. She suspects that there are higher forces at work behind her persecution, but she can't tell the clinician what these forces are. Her beliefs have interfered with her work and social life for more than a year. The most appropriate diagnosis for this client is

A. psychotic disorder, not otherwise specified
   B. schizophrenia, paranoid type
   C. delusional disorder
   D. schizoaffective disorder

6. Which of the following factors is NOT typically associated with ethnicity?

   A. Language
   B. Physical type
   C. Economic status
   D. Culture

7. A 19-year-old male client's father calls the social worker and requests information about his son's treatment. In this situation, the social worker should

   A. confirm that the son is in treatment but give no other information
   B. tell the father about his son's progress but not reveal any specifics
   C. set up a conjoint therapy session
   D. refuse to reveal any information

8. In an approach-avoidance conflict, as the person nears the goal,

   A. attraction and aversion both increase
   B. attraction and aversion both decrease
   C. attraction increases and aversion decreases
   D. atraction decreases and aversion increases

9. According the Herzberg's model of employee motivation, which of the following is a "hygiene" factor?

   A. Potential for growth
   B. Interesting, challenging work
   C. Freedom
   D. Salary

10. A disturbance of consciousness accompanied by some changes in cognition is the distinguishing feature of

    A. schizophrenia
    B. dementia
    C. delusion
    D. delirium

11. Public and private social service agencies generally differ in each of the following ways, EXCEPT

    A. practitioner certification requirements
    B. philosophy of service
    C. service eligibility requirements
    D. scope of services

12. Consistently, an employee is observed to be extremely friendly toward his boss, whom he really despises. From a Freudian perspective, the employee is exhibiting

A. reaction formation
B. isolation of affect
C. projection
D. sublimation

13. The purpose of an explanatory design for practice evaluation is to

    A. determine the causes of specific client behaviors
    B. examine and reflect on the intervention being used
    C. examine the impact of the intervention on the target behavior
    D. monitor client progress

14. Which of the following neurotransmitters or neuropeptides is generally deficient in clients with anorexia nervosa?

    A. Serotonin
    B. Cholecystokinin
    C. Dopamine
    D. Neuropeptide Y

15. Services that are provided to clients without a means test are described as

    A. pro-rated
    B. contributory
    C. eclectic
    D. universal

16. In a family intervention formed in the strategic model, a clinician who uses a "restraining strategy" will begin the intervention by

    A. warning the family of the danger of continuing its symptomatic behavior
    B. directing the family to stop its symptomatic behavior
    C. warning the family of the negative consequences of behavioral change
    D. instructing the family to engage in only nonsymptomatic behavior

17. The primary disadvantage associated with purchase-of-service agreements in social services is

    A. higher agency costs
    B. further fragmentation of the social service system
    C. decreased innovation in problem-solving
    D. diminished scope of services

18. Roles in the alcoholic family system have been labeled by Wegscheider and others. Typically, the youngest child in an alcoholic family occupies the role of

    A. mascot
    B. lost child
    C. hero
    D. scapegoat

19. The primary purpose for using confrontation in a client interview is to

A. teach mediation and conflict resolution skills
B. activate the client's potential for change
C. identify mixed messages in behaviors and thoughts or feelings
D. identify the processes the client uses to make changes

20. A clinician at a mental health clinic decides to work from the perspective of Rogers client-centered therapy. If the counselor goes against the policy of the clinic and decides to reject the use of diagnosis, it will be because from the person-centered perspective, 20.____

    A. the validity of diagnostic labels has not been empirically demonstrated
    B. diagnosis forces the therapist, rather than the client, to assume the expert role
    C. labeling results in an incongruence between self and experience
    D. labeling discourages the process of in-depth interpretation of the client's behavior

21. Which of the following interventions is one of the most frequently used therapies in the treatment of phobias? 21.____

    A. Exposure therapy
    B. Object relations
    C. Extinction
    D. Social skills training

22. Which of the following statements about therapeutic group composition is generally FALSE? 22.____

    A. Task groups that are homogeneous are less productive and cohesive than heterogeneous groups.
    B. Homogeneous groups of task-oriented, high-structure, impersonal people function as effective, change-producing human relations groups.
    C. Heterogeneous encounter groups are more effective in producing greater self-actualization of members.
    D. Homogeneous groups of person-oriented, low-structure people do not generally function as effective human relations groups.

23. When behaviors are known and categorized prior to an observation, and the intention is to collect quantitative data, the method of choice is 23.____

    A. structured observation
    B. the Likert scale
    C. participant observation
    D. structured interview

24. A client who was abused as a child, whenever speaking of her parents, tends to cast the father in the most negative light possible, describing his as evil and every encounter with him as a disaster. Of her mother, however, she has only the most glowing praise, often referring to her as a saint. From a psychodynamic perspective, the client is using the defense mechanism known as 24.____

    A. reaction formation
    B. primitive idealization
    C. projection
    D. splitting

25. In the transactional analysis model of social intercourse, the safest type of interaction is   25.____

    A. a game
    B. intimate
    C. ritualistic
    D. a pastime

26. Dissociative amnesia is usually   26.____
    I. related to the inability to recall important personal information
    II. retrograde
    III. selective
    IV. accompanied by apraxia

    A. I and II
    B. II and III
    C. I, II and III
    D. II, III and IV

27. People often have difficulty receiving information because of an impairment or other barrier. Which of these will probably NOT help such a person to better understand a message?   27.____

    A. Repeating the message
    B. Changing the sequence of the message
    C. Changing the form in which the message is transmitted
    D. Using an interpreter

28. A social worker is working with an autistic child who is mute. The major goal of intervention is the development of language. The social worker begins by rewarding the child with food whenever he vocalizes. The social worker then begins to reward the child only when his vocalizations occur within ten seconds of the social worker's vocalization, then only if the child's vocalizations resemble the social worker's, and so on, until the child's vocalizations are identical to those of the social worker. The technique is used until the child is eventually using words and sentences. This technique is known as: 28.____

    A. counterconditioning
    B. chaining
    C. shaping
    D. prompting

29. Potential limitations on confidentiality should be discussed with a client   29.____

    A. when the social worker determines it to be appropriate
    B. at the onset of the professional relationship
    C. at the onset of the professional relationship and thereafter as needed
    D. and documented in writing as soon as possible

30. Other than describing a client's problem in a way that imposes meaning on a large amount of information, the primary cognitive task of assessment is to   30.____

    A. establish client comfort with the therapeutic plan
    B. selectively focus on the information that will be most useful to the treatment planning process

C. infer whether a specific groups of facts or observations belongs to a larger known category of problems
D. identify the client's feelings of concern

31. The status of the practitioner/client therapeutic relationship is seen as an important aspect of therapy in each of the following models, EXCEPT

    A. ecosystems
    B. psychoanalysis
    C. client-centered
    D. behavioral

32. Among the skills important to effective communication with clients, the most sophisticated and complex is/are

    A. encouraging, paraphrasing, and summarization
    B. confrontation
    C. influencing skills
    D. open and closed questions

33. The _____ approach to human behavior attempts to describe behaviors in ways that allow for generalization across cultures.

    A. etic
    B. holistic
    C. emic
    D. pluralist

34. The most widely-used bivariate statistical measure in social work is

    A. regression analysis
    B. cross-tabulation
    C. slope/drift
    D. correlation

35. Which of the following statements is most abstract?

    A. Last night my mother told me I was a disappointment.
    B. I cry all day long. I can't eat.
    C. My daughter just sent me a letter.
    D. My family is very close.

36. Each of the following is viewed by clinicians as an important element of the therapeutic relationship, EXCEPT

    A. confidentiality
    B. dependability
    C. sympathy
    D. confidence

37. The _____ theory of human development holds that human behavior is strongly influenced by biology, is tied to evolution, and is characterized by critical and sensitive periods.

A. Biosocial
B. Ecological
C. Social learning
D. Ethological

38. The residual model of social welfare
   I. is developed piecemeal as a reaction to the development of social problems, rather than in anticipation of them
   II. views government as the last line of defense for people experiencing problems
   III. views family and work as the first line of defense
   IV. expects individuals to have trouble meeting the needs of modem living

   A. I only
   B. I and II
   C. I, II, and III
   D. I, II, III and IV

39. One of the helping models for multiproblem families is the Multiple-Impact Family-Therapy (MIFT) model, which includes each of the following elements, EXCEPT

   A. a long-term, client-centered approach
   B. an extended session format
   C. use of a team of professionals who work directly with the family
   D. immediate response to a request for service

40. Which of the following has NOT been a factor in the recent growth of the for-profit sector of social services in the United States?

   A. The ability of for-profit agencies to offer more stable financial sources of income than other investments
   B. The historical ability of private-sector solutions to solve problems that the government has failed to solve
   C. The growing complexity and number of problems experienced by the disadvantaged
   D. The existence of for-profit opportunities outside of public health insurance benefits

41. Which of the following is NOT typically a factor used by private clinicians to determine fees for clients?

   A. The amount charged by local psychiatrists of equal experience
   B. What the worker thinks will be the most attractive rate to the clientele she hopes to attract
   C. What third-party financing organizations identify as reasonable and customary charges
   D. How much other helping professionals charge for such services

42. Erikson's final stage of psychosocial development, experienced during late adulthood, is

   A. industry vs. inferiority
   B. generativity vs. stagnation
   C. intimacy vs. isolation
   D. integrity vs. despair

43. Which of the following approaches to social services policymaking assess the process of moving from the identification of a social problem to implementing a policy and assessing the impact the policy has on the original problem?

    A. Prescriptive
    B. Investment
    C. Cause and consequences
    D. Formative

44. Research suggests that negative emotional effects from divorce are LEAST likely to impact

    A. women who do not remarry
    B. women who remarry
    C. men who do not remarry
    D. men who remarry

45. Closed questions typically do NOT begin with the word

    A. how
    B. is
    C. do
    D. are

46. In order to receive a diagnosis of acute stress disorder that conforms to DSM-IV standards, a client's symptoms must occur within _____ of a traumatic event.

    A. 5 days
    B. 4 weeks
    C. 3 months
    D. 6 months

47. Which of the following types of programs is typically administered exclusively at the county level?

    A. Food stamps
    B. AFDC
    C. Medical assistance
    D. General assistance

48. In the clinical supervision of a social work practitioner, a good general policy is to

    A. begin with technical skill learning and then move to theoretical and perspective learning
    B. begin with perspective learning and then move to technical skill learning
    C. teach a supervisee technical skills and theory simultaneously
    D. avoid both technical skills and theory and instead focus on smaller, concrete problems faced by the practitioner

49. Approximately what percentage of child maltreatment/abuse cases involve sexual abuse?

    A. 5   B. 10   C. 30   D. 50

50. In the United States, most social policy is formulated

   A. by individual agency boards
   B. in a de facto manner by the direct practice of social workers
   C. through legislation
   D. by state boards

51. Which of the following terms is used to describe memory loss that has a purely psychological cause?

   A. Anterograde
   B. Organic
   C. Retrograde
   D. Inorganic

52. Which of the following statements reveals a client with a sensorimotor emotional orientation?

   A. A lot of us are angry. I know my boss is busy, but his forgetting to sign the payroll is going to cost some of us our weekend plans.
   B. I'm feeling lost I start to tremble when I go out in public.
   C. It seems that every time my wife is late meeting me somewhere, I get really angry with her. My time is valuable.
   D. I feel really angry because my best friend borrowed my car without asking.

53. In order to receive a diagnosis of adjustment disorder that conforms to DSM-IV standards, a client's symptoms must occur within _____ of a traumatic event

   A. 5 days
   B. 4 weeks
   C. 3 months
   D. 6 months

54. In the static-group comparison design of program evaluation, the primary threat to external validity is

   A. maturation-treatment interaction
   B. selection-treatment interaction
   C. reactive effects
   D. history-treatment interaction

55. According to Ainsworth, a "Type B" baby

   A. exhibits insecurity by avoiding the mother
   B. exhibits insecurity by resisting the mother
   C. exhibits insecurity by clinging to the mother
   D. uses the mother as a secure base from which to explore the environment

56. Which of the following is a primary social work setting?

A. Community center
B. Child protective services agency
C. Hospital
D. Nursing home

57. A client is a 40-year-old man who works as a night custodian at a local bank building. He keeps to himself and seems to have no interests outside his job, his stamp collection, and his two cats. He lives alone in a small apartment, has no close friends, and appears to have to interest in making friends. If this client is to receive a DSM-IV diagnosis, what would it be?

   A. Avoidant personality disorder
   B. Schizoid personality disorder
   C. Antisocial personality disorder
   D. No diagnosis—the man's isolation is not a disorder

57._____

58. A social or financial service that requires an applicant to prove financial need in order to receive the service is described as

   A. means-tested
   B. prescriptive
   C. residual
   D. eclectic

58._____

59. The initial aim in treating a client with conversion disorder is

   A. removal of the symptom
   B. determining predisposing factors
   C. forming a description of interpersonal relationships
   D. discovering precipitating stressors

59._____

60. Which of the following is NOT a preexperimental design for program evaluation?

   A. One-group pretest/posttest
   B. Client satisfaction surveys
   C. Static-group comparison
   D. Solomon four-group approach

60._____

61. In their definition of "family," many Asian Americans, especially Chinese Americans, are likely to include
   I. members of the nuclear family
   II. members of the extended family
   III. the informal network of community relations
   IV. all their ancestors and descendants

   A. I and II
   B. I, II and III
   C. I, II and IV
   D. I, II, III and IV

61._____

62. Within the context of the therapeutic relationship, practitioners and clients deal either explicitly or implicitly with

    I. past experiences that have affected abilities to relate to others
    II. the present physical, emotional, and perceptual state of the transaction
    III. each person's expectations of the process

    A. I only
    B. I and II
    C. II and III
    D. I, II and II

63. Assertiveness and social skills training are interventions MOST likely to be useful to clients with

    A. panic disorder with agoraphobia
    B. avoidant personality disorder
    C. narcissistic personality disorder
    D. schizoid personality disorder

64. A client reports to a practitioner at an outpatient care clinic in clear psychological distress, exhibiting paranoia and severe anxiety. The clinician is certain that the client has some form of anxiety disorder. The patient has severe liver disease, but the clinician can't determine whether this is a factor; it's possible that the problem is related to other factors such as the client's persistent substance abuse. The most likely DSM-IV diagnosis would be Anxiety Disorder,

    A. provisional
    B. not otherwise specified
    C. with generalized anxiety
    D. undifferentiated

65. Which of the following is NOT generally a guideline for supervisors to follow regarding case presentation?

    A. The presentation should be organized around questions to be answered.
    B. The supervisor should present a case first.
    C. The presentation should progress from practitioner dynamics to client dynamics.
    D. The presentation should be based on written or audiovisual material.

66. A thirty-five-year-old client was referred by a friend because of her sadness and talk of suicide, which were brought on by the death of her lover several years ago but never fully subsided. A practitioner working from the existential viewpoint would view the goal of assessment with this client as

    A. an in-depth understanding of her subjective experience
    B. identifying the support resources already available to her
    C. the identification of situations and stimuli that reinforce her depressive responses
    D. achieving transference

67. Which of the following processes typically occurs LATEST in the therapeutic relationship?

    A. Individuation
    B. Idealization

C. Individualization
D. Identification

68. A social worker has been seeing a client who whose wife left him and moved out of state with the children. During a session, the client says he wishes he could find out where she lives, so he could make her pay for what she's done. The social worker should

    A. call domestic violence experts and document the statement
    B. call domestic violence experts and get legal advice
    C. call the police
    D. try to find the ex-wife and warn her

69. Some Marxist-oriented behavioral theorists believe that when individuals meet in face-to-face encounters, they make several different adaptations. For example, when individuals of different classes meet, the interaction tends to be very narrow and role-prescribed. This is an example of _____ generalization.

    A. means-end
    B. feelings
    C. control-purposiveness
    D. detachment

70. A practitioner using rational-emotive therapy to help a child who is depressed has gathered information from the child's parents and teachers, and has collected formal assessment instruments that were completed by the parents and the child. The practitioner then meets with the parents and the child together, and asks the parents a series of questions about their child's symptoms and their history of attempts to deal with the problem. The practitioner's NEXT step should be to

    A. question both the parents and the child about treatment goals
    B. assess the parents and the child for secondary disturbance
    C. ask for the child's opinion of her parents' statements
    D. assess the practical and/or emotional problems presented

71. The record-keeping requirements at a typical social services agency require the completion of progress notes at an interval no longer than

    A. after every client contact
    B. weekly
    C. every 30 days
    D. every 90 days

72. NASW policy regarding foster care and transracial adoption states that placement decisions should reflect a child's need for

    A. basic material comforts
    B. continuity
    C. ethnic/racial integrity
    D. a stimulating, challenging environment

73. Which of the following statements about the behavioral approach to treatment is FALSE?

A. Behavioral interventions are intended to modify only certain, limited aspects of human behavior
B. Under certain conditions, behaviorists are concerned with affect and cognitions
C. Behaviorists prefer observation over introspection
D. Behaviorists believe that a client's symptoms are merely observable behaviors that have been labeled as problematic

74. Within the family life-cycle perspective, divorces are sometimes referred to as 74.____

    A. derailments
    B. dislocations
    C. non-normative crises
    D. ruptures

75. Which of the following statements is TRUE regarding summative program evaluations? 75.____

    A. Interpretive approaches using qualitative data are particularly useful.
    B. They make no attempt to determine causality.
    C. Validity is a central concern.
    D. Evaluations provide detail about a program's strengths and weaknesses.

KEY (CORRECT ANSWERS)

#	Ans	#	Ans	#	Ans	#	Ans	#	Ans
1.	A	16.	C	31.	D	46.	B	61.	C
2.	A	17.	B	32.	C	47.	D	62.	D
3.	C	18.	A	33.	A	48.	A	63.	B
4.	A	19.	B	34.	B	49.	B	64.	B
5.	B	20.	B	35.	D	50.	C	65.	C
6.	C	21.	A	36.	C	51.	A	66.	A
7.	D	22.	A	37.	D	52.	B	67.	A
8.	A	23.	A	38.	C	53.	C	68.	B
9.	D	24.	D	39.	A	54.	B	69.	A
10.	D	25.	C	40.	C	55.	D	70.	C
11.	A	26.	C	41.	A	56.	B	71.	C
12.	A	27.	B	42.	D	57.	B	72.	B
13.	C	28.	C	43.	C	58.	A	73.	A
14.	C	29.	C	44.	A	59.	A	74.	B
15.	D	30.	C	45.	A	60.	D	75.	C

EXAMINATION SECTION
TEST 1

DIRECTIONS: Each question or incomplete statement is followed by several suggested answers or completions. Select the one that BEST answers the question or completes the statement. *PRINT THE LETTER OF THE CORRECT ANSWER IN THE SPACE AT THE RIGHT.*

1. During an assessment interview, a practitioner attempts to determine a client's "executive functioning." This means mostly the degree to which a client is able to
    I. live without stress
    II. act in a leadership role
    III. organize and implement activities
    IV. deal with multiple responsibilities

    A. I and IV
    B. II only
    C. III and IV
    D. I, II, III and IV

2. Most likely, family therapy would be the primary intervention of choice for each of the following, EXCEPT

    A. borderline personality issues
    B. individual problems related to family transitions
    C. problems in relationships
    D. problems with children

3. About _____ of today's elderly population suffer from mental health problems.

    A. 1/8
    B. 1/4
    C. 1/2
    D. 3/4

4. In interpersonal communication, responses such as ignoring a client, cutting him off in mid-sentence, changing the subject, reacting ambiguously, or being condescending can cause the client to value himself less. These types of responses are described as

    A. low-context
    B. toxic
    C. polarizing
    D. disconfirming

5. Nearly all forms of therapeutic relationships involve
    I. a suspension of moral judgment
    II. constancy of the clinician's interest no matter how disturbing the subject
    III. the practitioner allowing him/herself to be used as a transference object without the interference of counter-transference
    IV. the client's opportunity to speak the unspeakable

    A. I and II
    B. II and IV

C. III and IV
D. I, II, III and IV

6. Personality assessments are most often categorized as either 6._____

   A. verbal and performance
   B. behavioral and psychodynamic
   C. projective or objective
   D. social or vocational

7. _____ theory holds that it is a person's own unrealistic beliefs that generate a fear of failure. 7._____

   A. Systematic desensitization
   B. Empowerment
   C. Performance visualization
   D. Cognitive restructuring

8. What is the psychoanalytic term for the release of emotional energy related to unconscious conflicts? 8._____

   A. Dam-breaking
   B. Projection
   C. Catharsis
   D. Transference

9. According to the model of Rational-Emotive Behavior Therapy (REBT), which of the following would be an example of a core irrational belief? 9._____

   A. One should keep the focus on the present
   B. One must have perfect and definite self-control.
   C. No matter how bad it is, it will be over shortly.
   D. Things could always be worse.

10. Regarding professional consultation with colleagues about clients, the NASW code of ethics establishes the rule of thumb that social workers should 10._____

    A. avoid consultation in cases where the client is known to be violent
    B. disclose the least amount of information to achieve the purposes of the consultation
    C. disclose no confidential or potentially sensitive information to consultants
    D. make sure consulting professionals know as much as they do about the client before offering input into the case

11. To help female clients understand the ecosystems that affect their well-being, social work practitioners should use 11._____

    A. gender role analysis, to help women understand their relations with men
    B. stereotypes, to consider male-female interactions
    C. an androcentric knowledge base, to assess the experiences of women
    D. female biology and endocrinology, to explain emotional and behavioral responses

12. The use of psychological tests in clinical social work should be governed by the idea that
    I. clients should be involved in the test-selection process whenever possible or feasible
    II. a client should be made aware that tests are only tools, and will not provide any answers to the client's problems in and of themselves
    III. test results, and not merely scores, should always be released and explained to the client
    IV. clients' reasons for wanting tests, as well as their past experiences with tests, should be explored before selecting any assessment

    A. I and II
    B. II only
    C. II and IV
    D. I, II, III and IV

13. In Adlerian therapy, client nonverbal behaviors are often used to assess

    A. ego states
    B. self-talk
    C. hidden purposes of behaviors
    D. conflicts or discrepancies

14. In the behavioral model, maladjustment results from

    A. personality defects
    B. flawed learning
    C. heredity
    D. environmental barriers

15. Despite broad-based application and compatibility with social work values, evidence-based practice approaches are not universally accepted in clinical settings. Each of the following is a significant reason for this, EXCEPT

    A. clinician reluctance
    B. clinician unfamiliarity with empirical data collection methods
    C. lack of organizational availability
    D. client concerns

16. Which of the following is a structured personality assessment?

    A. Thematic Apperception Test (TAT)
    B. Minnesota Multiphasic Personality Inventory (MMPI)
    C. Sentence Completion Test
    D. Rorschach

17. An client must provide informed consent for psychological treatment if
    I. treatment may have positive or negative effects
    II. one treatment is not superior to another
    III. treatment may be hazardous
    IV. full cooperation is required for success of therapy

    A. I and II
    B. II only
    C. II, III and IV

D. I, II, III and IV

18. According to Sullivan, dysfunctional families seek

    A. security rather than satisfaction
    B. gratification rather than democracy
    C. power rather than cohesion
    D. avoidance rather than engagement

19. During a client interview, a practitioner wants to transition from his own preliminary comments and prompt a response from the client. Which of the following is NOT generally recognized as a gesture that would signify "turn yielding?"

    A. Talking more loudly
    B. Asking a direct question
    C. Slowing the rate of speech
    D. Terminating body movements and gazing at the client

20. Among Asian Americans, mental illness is often expressed as

    A. adjustment disorder
    B. borderline personality disorder
    C. psychosomatic complaint
    D. depression

21. In the *Diagnostic and Statistical Manual of Mental Disorders* (DSM-IV), diagnoses are a process of elimination. This means that a clinician

    I. arrives at diagnoses by eliminating differential diagnoses
    II. must adopt an attitude of skepticism when making a tentative diagnosis
    III. starts with many possible diagnostic categories, and through multiple observations eliminates each of them until only one remains
    IV. arrives at a diagnosis by determining how many symptoms the person has in common with what's published for a particular DSM diagnosis

    A. I and II
    B. I and III
    C. II and IV
    D. IV only

22. The psychoanalytic perspective holds that the infant's emergent sense of self begins in the

    A. uterus
    B. first two months of life
    C. first year of life
    D. first two years of life

23. After a client's presenting problem has been diagnosed, a social worker begins planning for service delivery. The FIRST step in this process is typically to

    A. identify services
    B. develop a plan for services
    C. conduct additional interviews and tests
    D. revisit the assessment/diagnosis phase

24. When a clinician asks his client to lie down on a couch and talk about whatever comes to mind, he is using the technique of

   A. transference
   B. catharsis
   C. free association
   D. response shaping

25. Which of the following is NOT usually part of a process recording?

   A. Recorder's feelings and reactions
   B. Observations
   C. Quotations, to the extent that they can be remembered
   D. Diagnosis

26. A mildly retarded male client lives in a resident facility and is sexually active. He has impregnated two young women at the facility, and one of the resident clinicians is recommending that the client's family consider persuading him to get a vasectomy. This case will most likely involve the ethical and legal issue of

   A. duty to warn
   B. informed consent
   C. due process
   D. confidentiality

27. Which of the following is NOT developed during infancy?

   A. Telegraphic speech
   B. Transductive reasoning
   C. Separation anxiety
   D. Object permanence

28. A client tells a practitioner: "One of the reasons I quit my job was because my boss was always pushing me. I could never say no to her. Whatever she wanted, I always gave in. I think it's hard to say no to people until I reach a point where I can't take it any more." The practitioner responds with the following summary of the client's statement: "You're discovering that you tend to give in or not do what you'd like until you become angry and break things off—not just in your working relationships, but in other relationships as well." This is an example of a summary whose purpose is to

   A. tie together multiple elements of a message
   B. review progress
   C. identify a theme
   D. regulate the pace of the session

29. Each of the following is a common form of countertransference that can occur in the treatment of clients, EXCEPT the

   A. focus on feeling liked and appreciated by the client
   B. reluctance to give advice because of a fear of creating a sense of dependence
   C. strong reaction to certain clients who evoke negative emotions in the practitioner
   D. reluctance to challenge a client because it might result in resentment or other negative feelings

30. In Baumrind's model of parenting styles, the happiest and best-behaved children usually have parents who use _____ style of parenting.

    A. permissive
    B. authoritarian
    C. disciplinarian
    D. authoritative

31. During an assessment interview, a practitioner asks a client: "In what kind of situations do you find it easier to manage or control this reaction?" The practitioner is attempting to identify

    A. secondary gains associated with the presenting problem
    B. client resources and strengths
    C. consequences of the problem
    D. antecedents to the problem

32. Interpersonal psychotherapy has proven effective in the treatment of

    A. schizophrenia
    B. depression
    C. phobias
    D. bipolar disorder

33. In the social service system, collaboration
    I. may involve community planning
    II. is achieved both formally and informally
    III. is most prominently illustrated among the work of clinic teams
    IV. increases treatment effectiveness by combining competencies

    A. I and III
    B. I, II and IV
    C. II and IV
    D. I, II, III and IV

34. Dysthymia is considered to be associated with a greater risk of suicide when it occurs in

    A. women
    B. children
    C. older men
    D. in conjunction with a personality disorder

35. A clinician suspects that a ten-year-old boy may be suffering from neglect. For children of this age, common indicators of neglect include
    I. refusal to even attempt homework assignments
    II. crying easily when hurt even slightly
    III. falling asleep in class
    IV. consistently showing up early to school

    A. I and II
    B. I, II and III
    C. III only
    D. I, II, III and

36. Minor clients-those under the age of consent-are considered to have

    A. a legal right to privacy
    B. an ethical right to privacy
    C. both an ethical and legal right to privacy
    D. deferred their right to privacy to their parents, who deserve to know the details of the intervention process

37. The use of probes is often helpful for either expanding or narrowing the parameters of discussions with clients. The FIRST step in formulating an effective probe is often to

    A. determine the purpose of the probe
    B. decide what type of question will be most helpful
    C. use a paraphrase or reflection response
    D. determine what the client needs to know or do

38. In Watson and Tellegen's map of the human emotions, the emotions that are most closely related are

    A. pleasure and pain
    B. surprise and relaxation
    C. disappointment and relief
    D. anger and fear

39. Helping a client to recognize and mobilize her own coping resources and available supportive network of friends and family is an example of the _____ effect of social support

    A. buffering
    B. transactional
    C. direct
    D. indirect

40. A working alliance with a client is said to be necessarily composed of each of the following, EXCEPT

    A. an emotional bond between client and practitioner
    B. agreement on therapeutic goals
    C. agreement on the practitioner's leadership role in planning and conducting interventions
    D. agreement on therapeutic tasks

41. Cognitive therapy has proven to be effective in the treatmqent of
    I. major depression
    II. eating disorders
    III. anxiety disorders
    IV. panic disorders

    A. I and II
    B. II only
    C. II and III
    D. I, II, III and IV

42. De-institutionalization, as it applies to mental health practices, involves the concept of the "least restrictive alternative." This concepts basically means that

    A. professionals should only commit clients who are delusional
    B. at least one less restrictive alternative must be attempted before voluntary commitment is sought
    C. practitioners should select a mode of treatment that gives them the greatest possible latitude in making decisions about a clien's future
    D. treatment should be no more intrusive or harsher than necessary in order to achieve therapeutic aims and protect clients and others from physical harm

43. Post-traumatic stress disorder falls under the category _____ disorders.

    A. dissociative
    B. mood
    C. somatoform
    D. anxiety

44. The stereotypes that lock Americans into traditional gender activities are MOST likely to be broken by

    A. equal pay for equal work
    B. greater male participation in family-oriented, nurturing activities
    C. greater female participation in institutional decision-making
    D. more stringent anti-discrimination legislation

45. _____ theories of ethics claim that certain actions are simply right or wrong as a matter of fundamental principle.

    A. Teleological
    B. Consequentialist
    C. Deontological
    D. Utilitarian

46. Which of the following is an Axis II disorder?

    A. Major Depression
    B. Separation Anxiety Disorder
    C. Mental retardation
    D. Panic Disorder

47. One of the most common dysfunctions of the nuclear family is that it can create

    A. a generation gap
    B. institutional fragmentation
    C. a breakdown of authority
    D. emotional overload

48. The frequency with which a clinical social work practitioner receives supervision should depend on each of the following, EXCEPT the

    A. level of the practitioner's training and experience
    B. worker's activities

C. expectations of the supervisor
D. agreement in theoretical perspective between supervisor and practitioner

49. _____ personality theories are based on the premise that predispositions direct the behavior of a person in a consistent pattern.

   A. Psychodynamic
   B. Behavioral
   C. Trait
   D. Humanistic

50. When a communicative response is given that matches a client's previous communication, the _____ is established.

   A. halo effect
   B. valence
   C. norm of reciprocity
   D. boundary elimination

51. Which of the following standardized assessment tools is a Likert-type self-report measure that assesses overall health or pathology in a general score?

   A. *McMaster Family Assessment Device*
   B. *Parenting Stress Index*
   C. *Family Environment Scale*
   D. *Dyadic Cohesion Scale*

52. Which of the following theories are most relevant to the humanistic-experiential model of treatment?

   A. Rational-emotive behavior therapy (REBT) and choice theory
   B. Gestalt therapy and person-centered treatment
   C. Freudian and Jungian theory
   D. Cognitive theory and behavioral theory

53. The principle that two people in a continuing relationship—such as a social worker and a client—feel a strong obligation to repay their social debts to one another is the

   A. Hawthorne effect
   B. law of empathy
   C. norm of reciprocity
   D. law of effect

54. In a therapeutic encounter, which of the following client behaviors is most likely to be interpreted as a "retroflection" by a Gestalt therapist?

   A. Not making eye contact
   B. Laughing off important things
   C. Speaking abstractly or indirectly
   D. Holding the breath

55. Verbal means of conveying empathy to a client include
    I. using verbal responses that refer to the client's feelings
    II. using verbal responses that bridge or add on to implicit client messages
    III. placing the client's presenting problems in a clinical context
    IV. explaining the client's emotions

    A. I and II
    B. I, II and III
    C. II and III
    D. I, II, III and IV

56. Conflict theorists assert that unity that is present in society is the result of

    A. consensus
    B. competition
    C. contract
    D. coercion

57. Confrontation can be a useful tool with clients who are unable or unwilling to face up to the realities of their own thoughts or feelings, but it is also a response that requires great vigilance and judiciousness on the part of the clinician. In describing a distortion or a discrepancy to a client, a clinician should NOT

    A. use a confrontation to vent frustration with a client's behaviors
    B. cite a specific example of the behavior, rather than a generalized inference
    C. avoid confronting near the end of a therapy session
    D. attempt to determine the client's willingness to change before presenting a challenge

58. In family systems theory, "first-order" change occurs only when

    A. the family's own narrative about their behavior changes
    B. the rules of the system change
    C. a feedback loop becomes evident
    D. a specific behavior in within the system changes

59. One principle of human behavior is that when people are observed, or believe someone is paying close attention, they behave differently. This phenomenon is known as

    A. role ambiguity
    B. the Peter principle
    C. self-perception bias
    D. the Hawthorne effect

60. During the service delivery process, a referral can sometimes fail to result in a positive client outcome. Which of the following is LEAST likely to be a reason for this failure?

    A. Insufficient practitioner knowledge of resources
    B. Countertransference from referring practitioner
    C. Practitioner misjudgement of client's capability to follow through with referral
    D. Practitioner insensitivity to, or misjudgement of, client needs

61. For children, the factor with the highest predictive value for social problems is 61.____
    A. ethnicity
    B. poverty
    C. education
    D. substance abuse

62. A practitioner has administered two separate standardized psychological assessments to a client. When considering the release of this assessment data to third parties, the practitioner 62.____

    A. release the data only to those competent to interpret them
    B. may release the data to anyone who asks for it
    C. should keep in mind that other practitioners can release assessment data transferred to them by the practitioner
    D. are not obligated to monitor the release of assessment data

63. Each of the following is a typical function served by the family unit, EXCEPT to 63.____

    A. provide for children's basic needs
    B. indoctrinate children in the ways of society
    C. act as the primary agent of socialization
    D. provide a uniform plan for socializing children

64. Social work supervisors who are attempting to evaluate their own questioning techniques with supervisees should be sure they 64.____

    A. ensure thorough case knowledge before moving on to questions related to intervention strategies
    B. preface individual questions with introductory statements
    C. ask questions in a general way in order to receive general answers
    D. make sure that questions related to intervention strategies and techniques are more specific that questions about diagnostic understanding

65. In its formulations, the *Diagnostic and Statistical Manual of Mental Disorders* (DSM-IV) relies on 65.____
    I. a medical model of human development
    II. an empirical array of the opinions of many diagnosticians
    III. a strengths model of human development
    IV. the opinions of a designated board of diagnosticians who share similar theoretical perspectives

    A. I and II
    B. II only
    C. II and III
    D. IV only

66. A clinician and a client are in the middle phase of a task-centered intervention. At the beginning of each session, they will 66.____

    A. establish incentives and rationales for tasks
    B. identify obstacles to task accomplishment
    C. engage in guided practice and rehearsal
    D. review problems and tasks to determine progress

67. An adolescent boy, shortly after his release from a reformatory for juvenile delinquents, commits an act of vandalism. The boy feels it is in his nature to commit such acts, because he has been identified as a "juvenile delinquent" by society. His act of vandalism is an example of

    A. primary deviance
    B. secondary deviance
    C. stigmatization
    D. a cry for help

68. What is the immediate short-term effect of a tricyclic antidepressant?

    A. Increasing the availability of serotonin and norepinephrine in synapses
    B. Dampening the CNS arousal state
    C. Reducing intracranial pressure by reducing cerebrospinal fluid
    D. Increasing available lithium in the bloodstream for absorption

69. A practitioner needs to wrap up a 50-minute session with a client in order to prepare for her next session. Of the following, the BEST closing to a session is

    A. I'm sorry this divorce has been so difficult for you. Let's pick up with that feeling next week.
    B. I see we have about ten minutes left together. Let's try to come up with some strategies that you can work on for next week.
    C. I see we have about ten minutes remaining in this session. Let's see if we can't address your drug problem to some extent before we say goodbye.
    D. It's 2:50 and my next client is in the office. Let's see if we can wrap this up together.

70. Which of the following theoretical perspectives provides a kind of bridge between psychoanalysis and family therapy?

    A. Object relations
    B. Ego identity
    C. Self psychology
    D. Family dynamism

71. When giving feedback to a client, it is usually NOT advisable to

    A. claim clear ownership of the comment
    B. be specific
    C. focus on personality traits
    D. note a behavior

72. Society typically neutralizes deviant behaviors in each of the following ways, EXCEPT by

    A. denying responsibilities
    B. denying victimhood
    C. appealing to higher loyalties
    D. denying deviant labels

73. A client, referred to a clinician, is covered by her insurer for a total of eight treatment sessions. The client is an incest victim, and the clinician believes it will take more sessions than this to help her with her problems. He decides to offer the client his services pro bono. The practitioner's decision is an illustration of the principle of

A. self-determination
B. fidelity
C. justice
D. due process

74. Each of the following is true of psychiatric inpatient care, EXCEPT that it 74.____

    A. can be combined with social systems intervention
    B. is increasingly associated with legal mandates
    C. is usually appropriate only for medical problems
    D. can often be shortened by crisis intervention

75. During an interview, a client says: "My life is really boring. There's nothing new going on 75.____
    and all my friends are away. I wish I had enough money to make something happen."
    The clinician has decided that the Adlerian approach will be most useful with this cli-
    ent. Which of the following interpretations of the above statement is most in line with
    the Adlerian approach?

    A. "You seem to be saying you don't know how to enjoy yourself without having other
       people around. Maybe recognizing this will help you learn to be more self-reliant."
    B. "Sounds as if you need excitement, friends, and money to make your life seem
       worthwhile."
    C. "It seems as if you can only be happy when you're able to play and have fun. The
       child in you seems to be in control of a good part of your life."
    D. "You seem to think things are terrible because you have no friends around now,
       and no money. Is there any proof for that? I think your feelings of boredom might
       change if you could draw a different and more logical conclusion from your circum-
       stances."

KEY (CORRECT ANSWERS)

1. C	16. B	31. B	46. C	61. B
2. A	17. D	32. B	47. D	62. A
3. B	18. A	33. D	48. D	63. D
4. D	19. A	34. B	49. C	64. A
5. D	20. C	35. D	50. C	65. A
6. C	21. B	36. B	51. A	66. D
7. D	22. B	37. C	52. B	67. B
8. C	23. D	38. D	53. C	68. A
9. B	24. C	39. A	54. D	69. B
10. B	25. D	40. C	55. A	70. A
11. A	26. B	41. D	56. D	71. C
12. D	27. B	42. D	57. A	72. D
13. C	28. C	43. D	58. D	73. C
14. B	29. B	44. C	59. D	74. C
15. B	30. D	45. C	60. B	75. B

TEST 2

DIRECTIONS: Each question or incomplete statement is followed by several suggested answers or completions. Select the one that BEST answers the question or completes the statement. *PRINT THE LETTER OF THE CORRECT ANSWER IN THE SPACE AT THE RIGHT.*

1. In which of the following cases is treatment considered to be "mandated?"   1.____
    I. The court orders a person to attend treatment sessions, with consequences for noncompliance
    II. Concerned neighbors insist that a child who is disruptive in the community be evaluated for a mental illness or disturbance
    III. Parents withhold college tuition if their child does not check into a drug rehabilitation facility
    IV. A spouse threatens to leave if a partner does not seek treatment

    A. I only
    B. I and II
    C. I, II, and III
    D. I, II, III and IV

2. Two types of psychological tests that are the most commonly used in clinical practice are   2.____

    A. cognitive/ability and personality
    B. interest surveys and vocational skills
    C. conscious and unconscious
    D. speech perception and reaction time

3. The emphasis of contemporary psychodynamic approaches to treatment tends to be   3.____

    A. interpersonal functioning
    B. repressed sexuality
    C. long-term treatment
    D. childhood events

4. A significant concept in the contemporary psychoanalytic view of families is the idea of a family as a   4.____

    A. sociological dimension
    B. group of interconnected intrapsychic systems
    C. cacophony of competing ids
    D. single organic entity focused on self-preservation

5. Assumptions associated with the practice of professional consultation include each of the following, EXCEPT   5.____

    A. Consultation may result in confirming the rightness of the clinician's current actions.
    B. The consultant has greater knowledge than the consultee in the areas of agency and worker needs.
    C. In order to work positively, consultation cannot be compelled
    D. Consultation is made more effective when the consultant provides feedback to the employer or agency about the consultee's skills..

155

6. Together, practitioner and client have identified the client's needs and corresponding services. The practitioner then turns his attention to resource selection. Typically, the paramount decision-making concern in resource selection is the

   A. capacity of the practitioner to treat the presenting problem(s)
   B. information and referral system
   C. agency's policies and procedures
   D. client's values and preferences

7. Of the following concepts, the one that most clearly is derived from the theoretical intersection between dynamic psychiatry and the social sciences is that
   I. culture influences personality
   II. role performance is an effect of personality
   III. social class will affect a person's response to stress

   A. I only
   B. I and II
   C. II and III
   D. I, II and III

8. The most prominent model for budgeting within human services organizations includes each of the following categories, EXCEPT

   A. subcontracts
   B. distribution and control
   C. recording and reporting
   D. acquisitions

9. A schizophrenic client who _____ would be considered to be at an increased risk for suicide.

   A. is female
   B. recently discharged from a hospital
   C. is older
   D. has manic symptoms

10. The distinctive quality of antipsychotic drugs is their ability to

    A. calm clients down
    B. elevate dopamine levels
    C. reduce the intensity of delusions and hallucinations
    D. reduce feelings of anxiety

11. In the *Diagnostic and Statistical Manual of Mental Disorders* (DSM-IV), a diagnosis of alcohol dependency
    I. is less severe than a diagnosis of alcohol abuse
    II. requires that the person does not have control over use
    III. requires only that the person regularly drinks to excess
    IV. requires a disruption of socio-economic functionings

    A. I and II
    B. II and IV
    C. III only
    D. III and IV

12. The FACES II is a standardized assessment tool in which members rate their families on the dimensions of

    A. conflict and cohesion
    B. cohesion and adaptability
    C. crisis-orientation and resilience
    D. adaptability and dysfunction

13. Records of client and practitioner behavior that are clinically relevant-including interventions used, client responses to treatments, the evolution of the treatment plan, and any follow-up measures taken are usually referred to as

    A. screening data
    B. progress notes
    C. baseline data
    D. assessments

14. During a session with his clinician, a 68-year-old client, who has confessed to becoming more withdrawn in recent years, describes his life as a "list of vaguely worded goals, all unachieved." Which of Erikson's stages does the client illustrate?

    A. basic trust vs. mistrust
    B. intimacy vs. isolation
    C. integrity vs. despair
    D. generativity vs. stagnation

15. The definition of psychotherapy includes each of the following characteristics, EXCEPT that it

    A. is conducted by a trained professional
    B. relies on medical treatment methods
    C. is based on psychological theory
    D. uses psychological methods

16. _____ explanation of aggression involves the process of catharsis.

    A. The social learning
    B. The frustration-aggression
    C. Freud's
    D. Jung's

17. A diagnosis of dementia requires that a clinician examine a client for

    A. aphasia
    B. alogia
    C. ataxia
    D. encephalitis

18. For Americans older than 65, isolation becomes a problem, especially for

    A. women
    B. ethnic minorities
    C. immigrants
    D. the disabled

19. A practitioner is beginning to suspect that the multiple injuries she has observed over a twelve-week period with an eight-year-old client may be the result of abuse. Because the child's family is from another culture with which the practitioner is admittedly unfamiliar, she decides not to report her suspicions to the authorities, and instead decides to address the abuse as part of her family treatment plan. The practitioner has

    A. broken the law
    B. demonstrated cultural competency
    C. shown the proper respect for the family's right to self-determination
    D. unethically shifted the focus of her intervention

19.____

20. Which of the following is a contemporary neo-Freudian form of psychotherapy that ignores unconscious motivation?

    A. Interpersonal psychotherapy
    B. Systematic desensitization
    C. Assertiveness training
    D. Social skills training

20.____

21. Human services organizations tend to have a unique set of characteristics that represent significant challenges to manager, including

    I. a mixture of private benefits for services users and public benefits for society
    II. dependence on external constituencies over which members have little control
    III. a determinate set of technologies, with predictable outcomes
    IV. core activities that involve interactive transactions between staff members and users of services

    A. I only
    B. I, II and IV
    C. III and IV
    D. I, II, III and IV

21.____

22. Which of the following refers to the elements of a person's position in society that have exceptional significance to her social identity?

    A. Role
    B. Niche markers
    C. Posting
    D. Master status

22.____

23. During a client interview, a practitioner notices a consistent discrepancy between what a client is saying and her nonverbal behaviors. Pointing out this discrepancy is an example of a response known as

    A. reflecting feeling
    B. interpretation
    C. clarification
    D. confrontation

23.____

24. Systematic desensitization and graded exposure are two techniques that are used to treat

24.____

A. bipolar disorder
B. depression
C. phobias
D. schizophrenia

25. The perspective that attributes a person's place in the society as a function of innate ability is

A. labeling theory
B. cultural transmission
C. social Darwinism
D. conflict theory

26. The Gestalt model of therapy views awareness as

A. healing
B. impossible
C. a schema
D. an inherently inhibitory process

27. The goal of a projective assessment is to

A. evaluate the way a person perceives ambiguous stimuli
B. predict a person's behavior
C. compare a person's responses to those of other persons with similar presenting problems or disorders
D. evaluate the degree to which organic factors influence a person's thinking

28. In structural family therapy, the tool used by the clinician to observe and modify problematic family patterns is the

A. family narrative
B. ecomap
C. differential diagnosis
D. enactment

29. Without the expression of warmth in the clinician/client relationship, particular strategies and helping interventions are likely to be

A. more in line with the client's expectations that with the practitioner's
B. helpful only to clients from low-context cultures
C. technically correct but therapeutically useless
D. perceived as abstract challenges by the client

30. As described by Robert Merton, typically human responses to anomie include each of the following, EXCEPT

A. rebellion
B. conformity
C. ritualism
D. recidivism

31. A clinician in object relations practice encounters a client who was abused as a child. The client believes the only way she can improve her situation is to change herself. The client is likely to solve this object-related dilemma by

   A. openly contemplating the abuse and its implications
   B. unconsciously repressing the abuse
   C. dividing the object into good and bad parts and then internalizing the bad aspects
   D. lying to the clinician about the abuse

32. Clinical scales of the Minnesota Multiphasic Personality Inventory (MMPI) include each of the following, EXCEPT the _____ scale.

   A. marital distress
   B. depression
   C. paranoia
   D. hypochondriasis

33. For legal purposes, a practitioner's "records" include

   A. audiotapes of sessions
   B. case notes
   C. appointment books
   D. intake forms

34. According to the transactional analysis model, each of the following describes the adult ego state, in transactional analysis, EXCEPT

   A. calculating
   B. instructive
   C. unemotional
   D. rational

35. Evidence suggests that the largest source of human service delivery in the area of mental health is the

   A. self-help group
   B. clergy
   C. clinician
   D. inpatient facility

36. One of the most common criticisms of diagnosis is that it

   A. is not a systematic process
   B. follows a medical model
   C. places meaningless labels on clients
   D. is subjective

37. For social workers in managerial positions who engage in program development, it is MOST important to be competent in

   A. guiding consumers in developing self-help programs
   B. organizing data in a way that increases the likelihood of gaining program support
   C. educating clients, professionals, and the community about the design and implementation of social programs

D. coordinating staff efforts in government-authorized service delivery programs

38. During the social work process, clients sometimes attempt to conceal their weaknesses by emphasizing their more desirable traits. This is an ego defense mechanism known as

    A. identification
    B. compensation
    C. denial
    D. rationalization

39. In attempting to paraphrase clients' statements, a practitioner should FIRST

    A. select an appropriate beginning or sentence stem for the paraphrase
    B. identify the emotions that are conveyed by the client's messages
    C. identify any vague or confusing parts to the message
    D. covertly restate the client's message to herself

40. The _____ model of human services organization management places the greatest value on maintaining stable and dependable procedures within the organization.

    A. internal process
    B. human relations
    C. open-system
    D. rational goal

41. Which of the following is NOT one of the major categories covered in a mental status examination?

    A. Executive functioning
    B. Impulse control
    C. Mood and affect
    D. Level of consciousness

42. Multivariate methods of data analysis include
    I. factor analysis
    II. multiple regression
    III. descriptive statistics
    IV. cross-tabulation

    A. I and II
    B. II only
    C. II, III and IV
    D. I, II, III and IV

43. The human personality

    A. appears to be organized into patterns that are observable and measurable to some degree
    B. is a product solely of social and cultural environments, and has no basis in biology
    C. involves unique characteristics, none of which are shared with others
    D. is a term used to refer to the deeper core of a person, rather than superficial aspects

44. In transactional analysis, nonverbal behaviors are often used to assess

   A. hidden and unresolved conflicts and "armoring"
   B. mixed messages
   C. ego states
   D. mistaken logic

45. A practitioner in a small rural community is considering entering a dual relationship with a client—specifically, the practitioner has a flat tire and the client owns the only tire shop in town. The practitioner should
   I. warn the client about the potential risks of adding a business association to their professional relationship
   II. accept a discounted rate for services only if it is offered by the client
   III. consult with colleagues about how to handle the dual relation ships
   IV. not enter into a dual relationship with the client under any cir cumstances

   A. I only
   B. I, II and III
   C. I and III
   D. IV only

46. According to Erving Goffman, the function of stigma is to

   A. reward those who conform
   B. diminish the importance of a behavior
   C. define a behavior as deviant
   D. punish a person for violating a norm

47. The Americans with Disabilities Act addresses each of the following, EXCEPT

   A. access of disabled persons to public and private facilities
   B. disability benefits
   C. hiring
   D. accommodation of disabled persons on the job

48. A clinician is working with a client from an ethnic group that is different from her own, and is unsure about how to address the client or even what term to use to describe his community. The best practice for working with this person would be to

   A. tentatively offer the best guess and see how it is received
   B. ask him what titles or labels are most comfortable for him
   C. adopt the terminology that is most widely used throughout the agency
   D. check the prevailing literature beforehand

49. The knowledge base of direct social work practice in health care settings is typically informed by one or more of the following models, EXCEPT the _____ model.

   A. psychiatric
   B. wellness prevention and promotion
   C. developmental
   D. behavioral

50. Generally speaking, the standard age of consent for psychotherapy is _____ years.

    A. 14
    B. 16
    C. 18
    D. 21

51. Ideologies provide
    I. practical guide for decision-making
    II. a rationale for action
    III. a way to interpret events
    IV. facts'

    A. I and II
    B. I, II and III
    C. II and III
    D. I, II, III and IV

52. The phase in case management during which the case manager must draw upon advanced clinical skills to assist the client in making use of services is known as

    A. service implementation and coordination
    B. monitoring service delivery
    C. assessment and diagnosis
    D. advocacy

53. During an assessment interview, a practitioner asks a client: "Is there anything going on with you physically–the way you eat, smoke, or sleep, for example–that affects or leads to this problem?" The practitioner is trying to identify _____ antecedents to the client's problem.

    A. behavioral
    B. affective
    C. somatic
    D. contextual

54. Ethically, a clinician should

    A. inform a client that a diagnosis can become a permanent part of a file and have ramifications in terms of insurance costs and employment
    B. inform clients that their records are the property of the clinician or the agency
    C. be willing to alter case notes if they will prove damaging to a client's case in court
    D. be available to vulnerable clients 24 hours a day

55. Because of the social stigma attached to mental illness by many Asian Americans, it is important that services be

    A. delivered by traditional helpers within the community
    B. educational and matter-of-fact
    C. presented in language that refers to the spiritual or religious
    D. disguised as social gatherings

56. Clinical social workers so NOT typically consult with

   A. administrators
   B. other professionals in different fields who are working with the same clients
   C. other mental health professionals about legal issues
   D. other mental health professionals about clinical decisions

57. In clinical practice, "obsessions" refer to

   A. psychosis
   B. behaviors
   C. ritualistic patterns
   D. thoughts

58. When a client tries to resist compliance with a suggestion or treatment by manipulating the image of the person making the recommendation (the clinician), the client is engaging in

   A. identity management
   B. altercasting
   C. negotiation
   D. non-negotiation

59. Strategic planning within a human services organization

   A. must be tailored to the organization's planning culture
   B. by its nature, affects volunteers but does not involve them in the process
   C. is an undertaking limited to top management
   D. generally requires more time than money

60. In Maslow's model, high levels of a fear of success are correlated with high

   A. affective habituation
   B. fear of failure
   C. extrinsic motivation
   D. self-esteem

61. A popular assessment tool for determining the degree of a person's intent to harm him/herself divide indicators into Level 1 through Level 4, with Level 4 being the most urgent and probably requiring hospitalization. Which of the following would be considered a Level 4 indicator?

   A. Occasional suicidal ideation, but without behavioral indicators of intent
   B. An acute episode of mental health illness requiring new medication
   C. A moderate impairment in social and occupational functioning
   D. An inability to control of the stability of one's behavior, with or without a supportive social environment

62. Because social workers are increasingly called upon to coordinate services on behalf of clients, human service organizations are encouraged to develop

   A. case management services
   B. horizontal affiliations

C. systems-of-care models
D. vertical integration

63. In Gestalt therapy, _____ occurs when a client attributes a characteristic to the outside world that truly belongs to himself.

    A. confluence
    B. retroflection
    C. projection
    D. deflection

64. When working with a client who is encountering serious economic need, the most valuable task a practitioner can perform is to

    A. help the client find a paying job
    B. verify that the client is deserving of benefits
    C. give accurate information about benefits and ensure entitlement
    D. advocate and obtain benefits for the client

65. Which of the following is NOT a component of the therapeutic relationship?

    A. Teaching/instructing
    B. Transference/countertransference
    C. Therapeutic alliance
    D. Collaboration

66. The ethical principle of _____ refers to a practitioner's acceptance of the responsibility to promote what is good for others.

    A. nonmaleficence
    B. justice
    C. beneficence
    D. autonomy

67. According to Kohlberg's theory of moral development, a child who is greatly concerned about pleasing his parents and teachers is at the _____ level of development.

    A. conventional
    B. pre-moral
    C. pre-conventional
    D. post-moral

68. The "Socratic method" is proposed by some as a technique for social work supervision. Which of the following is NOT an element of the Socratic method?

    A. Systematic questioning
    B. Inductive reasoning
    C. Utilitarian ethics
    D. Universal definitions

69. Which of the following is NOT one of the basic concepts of psychosocial therapy?

    A. Recognition of the unconscious
    B. Recognition of the nature of pathology

C. A skeptical perception of the human potential
D. Focusing on everyday living

70. A client has been released from an inpatient program for the mentally ill, but must be maintained with medication and talk therapy. Most likely, the client will make use of

    A. the local mental health center
    B. the hospital emergency room
    C. a private clinician
    D. a psychiatric nurse practitioner

71. Research suggests that homosexuality is best understood in terms of

    A. intrapsychic disposition
    B. identity formation
    C. specific genetic factors
    D. childhood sexual experience

72. The increased demand for social workers to do formal diagnosis of mental disorders has been influenced by several factors. Which of the following is NOT one of these factors?

    A. Nearly half of all Americans will have a significant mental illness in their lifetimes.
    B. Nonmedical professionals are increasingly required to serve the mentally ill as mental health services are decreased.
    C. Payers for services require a diagnosis before authorizing or reimbursing for mental health services.
    D. Generally, knowledge of the *DSM-IV* is limited to clinical professionals.

73. Which of the following is NOT an advantage associated with private practice social work?

    A. Greater consumer choice among service providers
    B. More manageable paperwork and meeting requirements
    C. Fewer incidences of conflict-of-interest situations
    D. Fewer organizational constraints

74. The Bowen family systems theory centers on the counterbalancing life forces of

    A. togetherness and individuality
    B. nature and nurturance
    C. cohesiveness and adaptability
    D. conflict and harmony

75. A clinician is working with a family in conflict. To the mother, the conflict is about the quality of interactions within the family and managing interpersonal tension and hostility. In other words, the mother sees it as a(n) _____ conflict.

    A. pseudo-
    B. ego
    C. expressive
    D. instrumental

KEY (CORRECT ANSWERS)

1. A	16. C	31. C	46. C	61. D
2. A	17. B	32. A	47. B	62. B
3. A	18. A	33. D	48. B	63. C
4. B	19. A	34. B	49. D	64. C
5. D	20. A	35. A	50. C	65. A
6. D	21. B	36. C	51. C	66. C
7. D	22. D	37. B	52. A	67. A
8. A	23. D	38. B	53. C	68. C
9. B	24. C	39. D	54. A	69. C
10. C	25. C	40. A	55. B	70. A
11. B	26. A	41. A	56. C	71. B
12. B	27. A	42. A	57. D	72. D
13. B	28. D	43. A	58. A	73. C
14. C	29. C	44. C	59. A	74. A
15. B	30. D	45. C	60. D	75. C

EXAMINATION SECTION
TEST 1

DIRECTIONS: Each question or incomplete statement is followed by several suggested answers or completions. Select the one that BEST answers the question or completes the statement. *PRINT THE LETTER OF THE CORRECT ANSWER IN THE SPACE AT THE RIGHT.*

1. In recent years, the social work profession has shifted in emphasis from concern with individual adjustment to concentration on environmental change.
   The one of the following which has NOT generally accompanied this change of emphasis is the

   A. development of new roles for social work professionals
   B. employment of non-professionals in human service organizations
   C. growth of citizen participation in social service programs
   D. determination of the community's appropriate role in relation to the agency's stage of development

   1.____

2. The reporting system known as the Social Services Information System (SSIS) is BEST described as a method of

   A. determining how direct-service staff allocate their time in relation to defined productivity measures and operating costs
   B. defining the work of a public social service agency in terms of services, elements, activities, and costs
   C. evaluating performance of staff in terms of how they allocate their time in relation to defined productivity measures
   D. determining costs for individual cases in terms of how staff allocate their time to related services, elements, and activities

   2.____

3. The one of the following which is NOT a major purpose of the Social Services Information System (SSIS) is the provision of information useful in determining

   A. trends in clientele   B. quality of service
   C. shifts in service demands   D. service priorities

   3.____

4. The system of reporting delivery of services under Goal-Oriented Social Services (GOSS) DIFFERS from the reporting requirements introduced by the 1962 Social Security amendments in that the focus of GOSS is in the

   A. objectives of specific areas of services delivery
   B. service plan for the client and the overall, long-term case purpose
   C. allocation of resources
   D. objectives set by the caseworker rather than the client

   4.____

5. In the language of social service programming, case accountability means MOST NEARLY

   A. departmental responsibility for costs of all services provided for children, adult clients, and families
   B. continuing responsibility for service to a family until the case is closed

   5.____

C. organizational autonomy for those services the particular organization provides for children, adults, and families
D. departmental responsibility to the consumer and the public for providing needed services

6. After years of controversy, family planning services are now being supported by sound fiscal backing and federal mandate.
According to current requirements, family planning services must be made available to ALL

   A. persons requesting such services
   B. persons 14 years of age and over
   C. female heads of households
   D. women of child-bearing age

7. Research studies indicate that, of the following, the basic strength of a community program sponsored by a public or voluntary agency depends MOST directly on the

   A. enlistment of support from representative minority community leaders
   B. degree of understanding by professional community organization workers of the life-style of community residents
   C. ability of community organization workers to help disadvantaged community members develop their feelings of self-worth
   D. complete control by indigenous people of decision-making and operation of the program

8. Which of the following developments would have the MOST significant impact on the current trend toward decentralization in the delivery of social services?
   A. Action by the U.S. Congress which would reduce the number of federally mandated social services
   B. Takeover by the State Department of Social Services of some aspects of the medical assistance program
   C. Participation by the Community Development Agency with the Department of Social Services in planning for community social services
   D. amendments to the Social Security Act assigning responsibility to the states for definition of services, eligibility standards, and regulations

9. When the AFDC mother's youngest child becomes eighteen, the mother is no longer eligible to receive AFDC benefits. A problem equal in magnitude to the problems of job scarcity and lack of training opportunities is the unreadiness of some of these women to move into the competitive labor market.
The one of the following which would be the MOST appropriate suggestion to help increase the motivation of AFDC mothers to become self-dependent is the establishment of

   A. cash stipends to AFDC mothers who participate in training programs
   B. therapeutic groups to help AFDC mothers develop confidence and self-esteem
   C. a food stamp bonus system for AFDC mothers who accept job offers
   D. special community-based centers for individual job counselling of AFDC mothers

10. The one of the following which is NOT generally considered to be a function of the community social worker is to

    A. act as a catalyst for the organization or community groups
    B. provide leadership in identifying community needs
    C. arrange group programs such as group counselling and consumer education
    D. give *in-depth* casework service to community residents

11. Of the following, the OLDEST original model for social work practice is

    A. group treatment
    B. milieu therapy
    C. task and situational strategy
    D. social diagnosis

12. The term *diagnosis,* as used in social work, USUALLY refers to the worker's
    A. professional assessment as to the nature of the need or the problem which the client presents
    B. identification of mental illness by investigation of its symptoms and its history
    C. recommendation as to the treatment plan for the client on the basis of his problems
    D. categorization of the individual client according to a functional classification of psycho-social problems

13. The aim of crisis intervention and treatment as a model of social work practice is to
    A. give the most help to individuals who view a crisis as a challenge rather than a threat
    B. restore the person to the level of functioning he was able to reach before the crisis occurred, and help him achieve more effective functioning if possible
    C. assess the state of crisis and the person's capacity to cope with the situation
    D. make an objective determination of the reality of the crisis in terms of the person's life situation in order to help him develop new adaptive mechanisms

14. The traditional unit of attention in social casework has been the

    A. client's environment and economic situation
    B. person-in-situation configuration
    C. opportunity systems available to the client
    D. person's ability to overcome his problems

15. The one of the following which is GENERALLY considered to be a basic purpose of the separation of income maintenance and social services is to

    A. maximize the client's choices and control over his own affairs
    B. establish more efficient methods of eligibility determination
    C. encourage community participation in the delivery of social services
    D. reduce the need for workers with college degrees and professional social work training

16. The current Federal effort to retrench on the funding of social services is accompanied by considerable debate over the merits of *hard* vs. *soft* services.
    The one of the following which can be classified as a *soft* service is

    A. child care for working mothers   C. physical therapy
    B. family planning   D. rehabilitation

17. Social work profession has developed in a pattern that is quite different from other professions in that the emphasis in social work practice has changed from _____ to _____.

    A. generalist; specialist
    B. specialist; generalist
    C. activist; reformer
    D. counselor; therapist

18. Senior citizens require a variety of services to enable them to cope effectively with physical and psychological changes and the loss of social contacts.
    Of the following services, senior citizen centers can be MOST useful for providing elderly clients with

    A. protective care
    B. vocational therapy
    C. health services and nutrition education
    D. new identifications, roles, and relationships

19. Services to alcoholics and drug abusers have been expanded to include many different types of treatment modalities. However, experts generally agree that an ESSENTIAL element of any successful treatment plan is

    A. psychoactive medication
    B. deterrent therapy
    C. individual and/or group counselling
    D. family counselling

20. Protective services in child abuse cases are now directed towards improving and strengthening positive functioning in the child's own family in order to avoid the destructive effects of separation of the child from the family. Which of the following treatment modalities would offer the GREATEST potential for success in achieving this objective?

    A. Frequent regular psychotherapy sessions for the abusing parent while the child remains at home
    B. Family counselling of the parents and siblings while the child is temporarily placed in foster care
    C. Daytime child care services for the abused child, combined with therapeutic group services for the parents
    D. Admission of the abused child to a day care center and regular psychiatric treatment of the abusing parent

21. A recent study of multi-problem families on public assistance in the city of Baltimore gives evidence that individuals and families who are most seriously in need of social services are least likely to take the initiative to ask for services.
    Of the following services, this finding has the MOST significant implications for the current public welfare policy and practice of

    A. goal-oriented social services
    B. separation of income maintenance and social services
    C. decentralization of service delivery
    D. work relief employment services

22. The State Task Force on Welfare and Social Services, known as the Scott Commission, focused PRIMARILY on the

    A. administration of financial assistance
    B. delivery of social services
    C. elimination of welfare fraud
    D. State take-over of income support operations

23. Separation of the income maintenance and social services functions originated from action by the

    A. U.S. Congress
    B. State Department of Social Services
    C. U.S. Department of Health, Education and Welfare
    D. Human Resources Administration

24. The supervisor should be familiar with many statutes, rules, and regulations for administration of care of children at public expense.
    Which of the following would be LEAST relevant to his work?

    A. Social Welfare Law
    B. Rules and Regulations of H.E.W.
    C. Rules and Regulations of the State Board and State Department of Social Services
    D. The Family Court Act of NY State

25. Assume that a supervisor is reviewing a sample of case records in order to evaluate the effectiveness of his subordinates' service to clients.
    Of the following, the BEST indication that a worker is making effective referrals of clients to other community agencies would be when the case record shows that the

    A. client has participated in the decision to make the contact with the other agency
    B. caseworker has no further contact with the other agency after the initial referral
    C. client has no further contact with the caseworker after keeping his appointment with the other agency
    D. caseworker visits the other agency before making referrals

KEY (CORRECT ANSWERS)

1.	D	11.	D
2.	A	12.	A
3.	B	13.	B
4.	B	14.	B
5.	B	15.	A
6.	B	16.	C
7.	C	17.	B
8.	D	18.	D
9.	B	19.	C
10.	D	20.	C

21. B
22. B
23. C
24. B
25. A

TEST 2

DIRECTIONS: Each question or incomplete statement is followed by several suggested answers or completions. Select the one that BEST answers the question or completes the statement. *PRINT THE LETTER OF THE CORRECT ANSWER IN THE SPACE AT THE RIGHT.*

1. Of the following, a SIGNIFICANT criticism recently made of the separation of income maintenance and social services is that services are separated without

    A. requiring periodic diagnosis of clients' problems
    B. directing clients to accept services
    C. offering referrals to private agencies
    D. making clients responsible for recognizing their needs for services

2. The MAIN source of the salaries of public assistance clients who are placed in city jobs through the Work Relief Employment Program is

    A. city capital budget funds
    B. federal appropriations
    C. state appropriations
    D. welfare funds

3. Photo ID cards, required for public assistance recipients by State regulations, were INITIALLY proposed for the purpose of

    A. locating ineligibles
    B. protecting clients
    C. recertification of clients
    D. reducing case load growth

4. A significant aspect of the general revenue sharing bill (P.L. 92-512) which has a direct impact on the expansion of social services programs is the tendency of this legislation to

    A. shift decision-making authority to states and localities and reduce federal responsibility for solutions to economic and social problems
    B. give states and localities unrestricted use of revenue-sharing funds for expenditures without considering specified priority areas
    C. give the federal government tighter control over revenue-sharing funds used to establish and expand social service programs
    D. allocate decision-making authority to states and localities on the basis of population as indicated by census figures

5. Which of the following is a present trend in community social services for the disadvantaged concurrent with the separation of income maintenance and social services?

    A. Emphasis on family functioning
    B. Lowered status of the social work professional
    C. Differential use of income maintenance staff
    D. Elimination of eligibility verification

6. The Office of the Welfare Inspector-General, which was established in response to criticism of the efficiency of state and local operations in public assistance eligibility determinations, was assigned the function of

    A. quality control of eligibility decisions
    B. registry and location of deserting parents
    C. investigation of fraud in local center operations
    D. welfare check reconciliation

7. The food stamp program, which was designed to help increase the purchasing power of low-income persons, has been only minimally used by those whom it is supposed to benefit.
   The one of the following which is NOT a plausible reason for the present underutilization of food stamps is that
   A. low-income people do not understand the program or the benefits of the bonus system
   B. the recipient's neighbors, store clerks, and casual acquaintances have the opportunity to know that they are getting government aid
   C. information about the program is channeled through institutional sources to the largest number of people who use the program
   D. participation is discouraged because of the cumbersome administrative structure of the food stamp distribution system

8. State and city public welfare officials have instituted several new administrative procedures in their efforts to insure the eligibility of the ADC caseload.
   Which of the following is NOT one of these procedures?
   A. Face-to-face recertification
   B. Photo identification cards
   C. Mandatory registration with the state employment service
   D. Mailings to verify current address and eligibility status

9. A major organizational change became effective during the seventies, when responsibility for financial aid to disabled, aged, and blind clients was transferred from the Human Resources Administration to the Social Security Administration.
   Which of the following responsibilities to DAB clients continues to be carried out by the Human Resources Administration?
   A. Eligibility certification
   B. Provision of social services
   C. Medical assistance
   D. Special grants

10. Of the following, the MOST serious problem that has developed as a result of the changeover to the Federal Supplemental Security Income program for the aged and disabled is the
    A. reduction of income for many aged recipients
    B. breakdown between income maintenance and services within the SSI formula
    C. required provision of social services to disabled recipients
    D. disqualification of alcoholics and drug addicts as *disabled* persons eligible for benefits

11. The effect of the recent increase in Social Security benefits on aged recipients of the Supplemental Security Income program has been to
    A. increase their net benefits
    B. leave their net benefits unchanged.
    C. increase benefits for those who are disabled
    D. raise their support levels

12. United States Supreme Court decisions regarding welfare rights, Jefferson vs. Hackney (1972) and Rosado vs. Wyman (1970), were IMPORTANT cases for comparison because both cases deal with the

    A. *substitute father* rule
    B. cost of living provision
    C. residence requirement
    D. mandatory home visits provision

13. The lawsuit, Wilder vs. Sugarman, alleged that the existing statutory base for the provision of child welfare services in New York City is unconstitutional. The suit sought to obtain a court order forcing the government agencies named in the petition to develop a plan for a new system of publicly supported child-welfare services to meet the present-day needs of children and families. The BASIC issue involved in this case is

    A. direct vs. purchased services for children in need of placement
    B. discrimination against black children by private adoption agencies
    C. the requirement of child placement according to race
    D. discrimination against black children in need of services

14. A recent article in a professional journal reported that narcotics addicts make up 10 percent of the welfare population, yet account for fully 50 percent of all transactions in the centers. The one of the following which is NOT a plausible reason for this situation is that

    A. services to narcotics addicts are more difficult and time-consuming than services to other clients
    B. narcotics addicts must be served by selecting a group of specially trained workers
    C. workers must devote more time to medical and psychiatric referrals for narcotics addicts
    D. necessary investigation of criminal activity of narcotics addicts is lengthy and difficult

15. The incremental approach has recently been discussed in the press as a preferable strategy for welfare reform at this period in history.
    The one of the following which is NOT an example of the incremental approach to welfare reform is the

    A. addition of a housing allowance for low-income persons and the use of this new benefit as the key to improvement of other programs
    B. provision of a work bonus to effect program reform and integration
    C. introduction of a negative income tax and a comprehensive new welfare program to replace most existing programs
    D. expansion of food stamp benefits and addition of a cost-of-living escalation provision

16. Of the following, generally the MOST crucial factor which may limit or prevent community participation in social service programs for the disadvantaged is the

    A. middle-class citizen's fear of reinforcing corrupt lifestyles
    B. taxpayers' demands for greater government economy and efficiency
    C. depersonalization and categorization of public assistance clients
    D. inherent inequality between the social work professional and the client

17. Administrators of social programs are in general agreement that public participation is a practical and necessary part of the effective implementation of social policy.
In order to ensure optimum public participation in making decisions on the size of public assistance allotments, it would be PARTICULARLY important to

   A. allow a majority of the organized welfare recipients to determine the size of the allotments
   B. achieve the proper combination of checks and balances among the various segments of the population relevant to the decision on the size of the allotments
   C. provide for ongoing, continuous decision-making on public assistance allotments by the taxpaying public who finance these payments
   D. make official liaison, concurrence, consultation, and policy-making the responsibilities of the client population

18. Effective community participation to ensure social justice for minorities does not flow automatically from more or maximum participation of individuals.
Of the following, this statement implies MOST NEARLY that

   A. effective participation requires both professional leadership and numerical strength
   B. democratic participation is not synonymous with majority rule
   C. effective participation is determined by the number of decisions made
   D. majority rule is the best means of obtaining social justice for minority groups

19. Experts generally agree that decisions on the social services to be minimally provided must be the result of city-wide centralized coordinated planning by a joint council with public, voluntary agency and community representation.
The one of the following which would NOT be a desirable result of such coordinated effort is

   A. avoidance of gaps and duplication of services
   B. universality of essential and mandated services
   C. uniformity of services at the community level
   D. minimal waste of resources

20. The one of the following elements which is MOST crucial to the success of a community social services operation is

   A. the employment of indigenous paraprofessionals
   B. operation of a day care service on the premises
   C. a carefully developed intake process
   D. centralized preliminary screening unit

21. Questions have been raised about the popular assumption that the special advantage of employing indigenous paraprofessionals in social work and mental health agencies is their similarity in background and abilities to the clients of the agency.
The BASIS for questioning this assumption is the finding that community people who serve as paraprofessionals

   A. tend to be better educated, more successful, and more upwardly mobile than their neighbors
   B. are unable to be objective about their neighbors' situation and needs because of the similarity to their own problems
   C. are more likely to be naive and to allow themselves to be manipulated by the clients
   D. tend to have inadequate education and lack of ambition and aspiration

22. The Human Resources Administration has a commitment to make extensive use of 22._____
voluntary and community-based organizations as contractors to provide services to clients.
One of the characteristics of a *voluntary*, in contrast to a *community-based* organization,
is that a *voluntary* organization is

    A. administered mainly by professionally-trained staff
    B. sponsored and staffed mainly by volunteers
    C. sponsored by community residents and staffed mainly by non-professionals
    D. established mainly by means of public funding

23. Decentralization of services into the neighborhoods has been a key feature of the organi- 23._____
zation of the Human Resources Administration during the past few years. However, the
need has recently emerged for a kind of agency which can provide services most
effectively on a city-wide, rather than a neighborhood, basis for

    A. persons recently discharged from state institutions
    B. members of other ethnic groups residing in areas largely populated by blacks
    C. middle-class residents of Human Resources Districts eligible for child welfare services
    D. narcotics addicts

24. A basic problem in the reorganization of the Department of Social Services for separation 24._____
of income maintenance and service functions has been providing access to the service
system.
Which of the following would probably be the MOST productive means of encouraging
clients to use available social services?

    A. Outreach activities by the Community Development Agency
    B. Referrals from income maintenance workers
    C. Referrals from other public and private agencies
    D. Neighborhood-based information and referral centers

25. Of the following, the MOST crucial step in clarifying long-range community strategy to 25._____
develop coordinated public and privately sponsored social services should be

    A. emphasis on functions rather than agencies
    B. definition of the functions of individual agencies
    C. limitation of the functions of a given agency
    D. community assignment of functions to each agency

KEY (CORRECT ANSWERS)

1.	A	11.	B
2.	D	12.	B
3.	B	13.	D
4.	A	14.	B
5.	A	15.	C
6.	C	16.	B
7.	C	17.	B
8.	C	18.	B
9.	B	19.	C
10.	B	20.	C

21. A
22. A
23. B
24. D
25. A

EXAMINATION SECTION
TEST 1

DIRECTIONS: Each question or incomplete statement is followed by several suggested answers or completions. Select the one that BEST answers the question or completes the statement. *PRINT THE LETTER OF THE CORRECT ANSWER IN THE SPACE AT THE RIGHT.*

1. One of the responsibilities of the supervisor is to provide top administration with information about clients and their problems that will help in the evaluation of existing policies and indicate the need for modifications. In order to fulfill this responsibility, it would be MOST essential for the supervisor to

    A. routinely forward all regularly prepared and recurrent reports from his subordinates to his immediate superior
    B. regularly review agency rules, regulations, and policies to make sure that he has sufficient knowledge to make appropriate analyses
    C. note repeated instances of failure of staff to correctly administer a policy and schedule staff conferences for corrective training
    D. analyze reports on cases submitted by subordinates in order to select relevant trend material to be forwarded to his superiors

2. You find that your division has a serious problem because of unusually long delays in filing reports and overdue approvals to private agencies under contract for services. The MOST appropriate step to take FIRST in this situation would be to

    A. request additional staff to work on reports and approvals
    B. order staff to work overtime until the backlog is eliminated
    C. impress staff with the importance of expeditious handling of reports and approvals
    D. analyze present procedures for handling reports and approvals

3. When a supervisor finds that he must communicate orally information that is significant enough to affect the entire staff, it would be MOST important to

    A. distribute a written summary of the information to his staff before discussing it orally
    B. tell his subordinate supervisors to discuss this information at individual conferences with their subordinates
    C. call a follow-up meeting of absentees as soon as they return
    D. restate and summarize the information in order to make sure that everyone understands its meaning and implications

4. Of the following, the BEST way for a supervisor to assist a subordinate who has unusually heavy work pressures is to

    A. point out that such pressures go with the job and must be tolerated
    B. suggest to him that the pressures probably result from poor handling of his workload
    C. help him to be selective in deciding on priorities during the period of pressure
    D. ask him to work overtime until the period of pressure is over

5. Leadership is a basic responsibility of the supervisor. The one of the following which would be the LEAST appropriate way to fulfill this role is for the supervisor to

    A. help staff to work up to their capacities in every possible way
    B. encourage independent judgment and actions by staff members
    C. allow staff to participate in decisions within policy limits
    D. take over certain tasks in which he is more competent than his subordinates

6. Assume that you have assigned a very difficult administrative task to one of your best subordinate supervisors, but he is reluctant to take it on because he fears that he will fail in it. It is your judgment, however, that he is quite capable of performing this task.
The one of the following which is the MOST desirous way for you to handle this situation is to

    A. reassure him that he has enough skill to perform the task and that he will not be penalized if he fails
    B. reassign the task to another supervisor who is more achievement-oriented and more confident of his skills
    C. minimize the importance of the task so that he will feel it is safe for him to attempt it
    D. stress the importance of the task and the dependence of the other staff members on his succeeding in it

7. Assume that a member of your professional staff deliberately misinterprets a new state directive because he fears that its enforcement will have an adverse effect on clients. Although you consider him to be a good supervisor and basically agree with him, you should direct him to comply. Of the following, the MOST desirable way for you to handle this situation would be to

    A. avoid a confrontation with him by transferring responsibility for carrying out the directive to another member of your staff
    B. explain to him that you are in a better position than he to assess the implications of the new directive
    C. discuss with him the basic reasons for his misinterpretation and explain why he must comply with the directive
    D. allow him to interpret the directive in his own way as long as he assumes full responsibility for his actions

8. Of the following, the MAIN reason it is important for an administrator in a large organization to properly coordinate the work delegated to subordinates is that such coordination

    A. makes it unnecessary to hold frequent staff meetings and conferences with key staff members
    B. reduces the necessity for regular evaluation of procedures and programs, production, and performance of personnel
    C. results in greater economy and stricter accountability for the organization's resources
    D. facilitates integration of the contributions of the numerous staff members who are responsible for specific parts of the total workload

9. The one of the following which would NOT be an appropriate reason for the formulation of an entirely new policy is that it would

A. serve as a positive affirmation of the agency's function and how it is to be carried out
B. give focus and direction to the work of the staff, particularly in decision-making
C. inform the public of the precise conditions under which services will be rendered
D. provide procedures which constitute uniform methods of carrying out operations

10. Of the following, it is MOST difficult to formulate policy in an organization where

    A. work assignments are narrowly specialized by units
    B. staff members have varied backgrounds and a wide range of competency
    C. units implementing the same policy are in the same geographic location
    D. staff is experienced and fully trained

11. For a supervisor to feel that he is responsible for influencing the attitudes of his staff members is GENERALLY considered

    A. *undesirable;* attitudes of adults are emotional factors which usually cannot be changed
    B. *desirable;* certain attitudes can be obstructive and should be modified in order to provide effective service to clients
    C. *undesirable;* the supervisor should be nonjudgmental and accepting of widely different attitudes and social patterns of staff members
    D. *desirable;* influencing attitudes is a teaching responsibility which the supervisor shares with the training specialist

12. The one of the following which is NOT generally a function of the higher-level supervisor is

    A. projecting the budget and obtaining financial resources
    B. providing conditions conducive to optimum employee production
    C. maintaining records and reports as a basis for accountability and evaluation
    D. evaluating program achievements and personnel effectiveness in accordance with goals and standards

13. As a supervisor in a recently decentralized services center offering multiple services, you are given responsibility for an orientation program for professional staff on the recent reorganization of the department.
    Of the following, the MOST appropriate step to take FIRST would be to

    A. organize a series of workshops for subordinate supervisors
    B. arrange a tour of the new geographic area of service
    C. review supervisors' reports, statistical data, and other relevant material
    D. develop a resource manual for staff on the reorganized center

14. Experts generally agree that the content of training sessions should be closely related to workers' practice. Of the following, the BEST method of achieving this aim is for the training conference leader to

    A. encourage group discussion of problems that concern staff in their practice
    B. develop closer working relationships with top administration
    C. coordinate with central office to obtain feedback on problems that concern staff
    D. observe workers in order to develop a pattern of problems for class discussion

15. The one of the following which is generally the MOST useful teaching tool for professional staff development is

    A. visual aids and tape recordings
    B. professional literature
    C. agency case material
    D. lectures by experts

16. The one of the following which is NOT a good reason for using group conferences as a method of supervision is to

    A. give workers a feeling of mutual support through sharing common problems
    B. save time by eliminating the need for individual conferences
    C. encourage discussion of certain problems that are not as likely to come up in individual conferences
    D. provide an opportunity for developing positive identification with the department and its programs

17. The supervisor, in his role as teacher, applies his teaching in line with his understanding of people and realizes that teaching is a highly individualized process, based on understanding of the worker as a person and as a learner.
    This statement implies MOST NEARLY that the supervisor must help the worker to

    A. overcome his biases
    B. develop his own ways of working
    C. gain confidence in his ability
    D. develop the will to work

18. Of the following, the circumstances under which it would be MOST appropriate to divide a training conference for professional staff into small workshops is when

    A. some of the trainees are not aware of the effect of their attitudes and behavior on others
    B. the trainees need to look at human relations problems from different perspectives
    C. the trainees are faced with several substantially different types of problems in their job assignments
    D. the trainees need to know how to function in many different capacities

19. Of the following, the MAIN reason why it is important to systematically evaluate a specific training program while it is in progress is to

    A. collect data that will serve as a valid basis for improving the agency's overall training program and maintaining control over its components
    B. insure that instruction by training specialists is conducted in a manner consistent with the planned design of the training program
    C. identify areas in which additional or remedial training for the training specialists can be planned and implemented
    D. provide data which are usable in effecting revisions of specific components of the training program

20. Staff development has been defined as an educational process which seeks to provide agency staff with knowledge about specific job responsibilities and to effect changes in staff attitudes and behavior patterns. Assume that you are assigned to define the educational objectives of a specific training program.
In accordance with the above concept, the MOST helpful formulation would be a statement of the

   A. purpose and goals of each training session
   B. generalized patterns of behavior to be developed in the trainees
   C. content material to be presented in the training sessions
   D. kind of behavior to be developed in the trainees and the situations in which this behavior will be applied

20.____

21. In teaching personnel under your supervision how to gather and analyze facts before attempting to solve a problem, the one of the following training methods which would be MOST effective is

   A. case study   B. role playing
   C. programmed learning   D. planned experience

21.____

22. Federal and state welfare agencies have been discussing the importance of analyzing functions traditionally included in the position of caseworker, with a view toward identifying and separating those activities to be performed by the most highly skilled personnel.
Of the following, an IMPORTANT secondary gain which can result from such differential use of staff is that

   A. supporting job assignments can be given to persons unable to meet the demands of casework, to the satisfaction of all concerned
   B. documentation will be provided on workers who are not suited for all the duties now part of the caseworker's job
   C. caseworkers with a high level of competence in working with people can be rewarded through promotion or merit increases
   D. incompetent workers can be identified and categorized as a basis for transfer or separation from the service

22.____

23. Of the following, a serious DISADVANTAGE of a performance evaluation system based on standardized evaluation factors is that such a system tends to

   A. exacerbate the anxieties of those supervisors who are apprehensive about determining what happens to another person
   B. subject the supervisor to psychological stress by emphasizing the incompatibility of his dual role as both judge and counselor
   C. create organizational conflict by encouraging personnel who wish to enhance their standing to become too aggressive in the performance of their duties
   D. lead many staff members to concentrate on measuring up in terms of the evaluation factors and to disregard other aspects of their work

23.____

24. Which of the following would contribute MOST to the achievement of conformity of staff activities and goals to the intent of agency policies and procedures?

   A. Effective communications and organizational discipline
   B. Changing nature of the underlying principles and desired purpose of the policies and procedures

24.____

C. Formulation of specific criteria for implementing the policies and procedures
D. Continuous monitoring of the essential effectiveness of agency operations

25. Job enlargement, a management device used by large organizations to counteract the adverse effects of specialization on employee performance, is LEAST likely to improve employee motivation if it is accomplished by

   A. lengthening the job cycle and adding a large number of similar tasks
   B. allowing the employee to use a greater variety of skills
   C. increasing the scope and complexity of the employee's job
   D. giving the employee more opportunities to make decisions

25.____

KEY (CORRECT ANSWERS)

1.	D	11.	B
2.	D	12.	A
3.	D	13.	A
4.	C	14.	A
5.	D	15.	C
6.	A	16.	B
7.	C	17.	B
8.	D	18.	C
9.	D	19.	A
10.	B	20.	D

21. A
22. A
23. D
24. A
25. A

TEST 2

DIRECTIONS: Each question or incomplete statement is followed by several suggested answers or completions. Select the one that BEST answers the question or completes the statement. *PRINT THE LETTER OF THE CORRECT ANSWER IN THE SPACE AT THE RIGHT.*

1. When a supervisor requires approval for case action on a higher level, the process used is known as

    A. administrative clearance
    B. going outside channels
    C. administrative consultation
    D. delegation of authority

2. In delegating authority to his subordinates, the one of the following to which a good supervisor should give PRIMARY consideration is the

    A. results expected of them
    B. amount of power to be delegated
    C. amount of responsibility to be delegated
    D. their skill in the performance of present tasks

3. Of the following, the type of decision which could be SAFELY delegated to lower-level staff without undermining basic supervisory responsibility is one which

    A. involves a commitment that can be fulfilled only over a long period of time
    B. has fairly uncertain goals and promises
    C. has the possibility of modification built into it
    D. may generate considerable resistance from those affected by it

4. Of the following, the MOST valuable contribution made by the informal organization in a large public service agency is that such an organization

    A. has goals and values which are usually consistent with and reinforce those of the formal organization
    B. is more flexible than the formal organization and more adaptable to changing conditions
    C. has a communications system which often contributes to the efficiency of the formal organization
    D. represents a sound basis on which to build the formal organizational structure

5. Of the following, the condition under which it would be MOST useful for a social services agency to develop detailed procedures is when

    A. subordinate supervisory personnel need a structure to help them develop greater independence
    B. employees have little experience or knowledge of how to perform certain assigned tasks
    C. coordination of agency activities is largely dependent upon personal contact
    D. agency activities must continually adjust to changes in local circumstances

6. Assume that a certain public agency administrator has the management philosophy that his agency's responsibility is to routinize existing operations, meet each day's problems as they arise, and resolve problems with a minimun of residual effect upon himself or his agency.
   The possibility that this official would be able to administer his agency without running into serious difficulties would be MORE likely during a period of

   A. economic change
   B. social change
   C. economic crisis
   D. social and economic stability

7. Some large organizations have adopted the practice of allowing each employee to establish his own performance goals, and then later evaluate himself in an individual conference with his immediate supervisor.
   Of the following, a DRAWBACK of this approach is that the employee

   A. may set his goals too low and rate himself too highly
   B. cannot control those variables which may improve his performance
   C. has no guidelines for improving his performance
   D. usually finds it more difficult to criticize himself than to accept criticism from others

8. Decentralization of services cannot completely eliminate the requirement of central office approval for certain case actions.
   The MOST valid reason for complaint about this requirement is that

   A. unavoidable delay created by referral to central office may cause serious problems for the client
   B. it may lower morals of supervisors who are not given the authority to take final action on urgent cases
   C. the concept of role responsibility is minimized
   D. the objective of delegated responsibility tends to be negated

9. Which of the following would be the MOST useful administrative tool for the purpose of showing the sequence of operations and staff involved?
   A(n)

   A. organization chart
   B. flow chart
   C. manual of operating procedures
   D. statistical review

10. The prevailing pattern of organization in large public agencies consists of a limited span of control and organization by function or, at lower levels, process.
    Of the following, the PRINCIPAL effect which this pattern or organization has on the management of work is that it

    A. reduces the management burden in significant ways
    B. creates a time lag between the perception of a problem and action on it
    C. makes it difficult to direct and observe employee performance
    D. facilitates the development of employees with managerial ability

11. The one of the following which would be the MOST appropriate way to reduce tensions between line and staff personnel in public service agencies is to

    A. provide in-service training that will increase the sensitivity of line and staff personnel to their respective roles
    B. assign to staff personnel the role of providing assistance only when requested by line personnel
    C. separate staff from line personnel and provide staff with its own independent reward structure
    D. give line and staff personnel equal status in making decisions

12. In determining the appropriate span of control for subordinate supervisors, which of the following principles should be followed?
    The more

    A. complex the work, the broader the effective span of control
    B. similar the jobs being supervised, the more narrow the effective span of control
    C. interdependent the jobs being supervised, the more narrow the effective span of control
    D. unpredictable the work, the broader the effective span of control

13. A method sometimes used in public service agencies to improve upward communication is to require subordinate supervisory staff to submit to top management monthly narrative reports of any problems which they deem important for consideration.
    Of the following, a MAJOR disadvantage of this method is that it may

    A. enable subordinate supervisors to avoid thinking about their problems by simply referring such matters to their superiors
    B. obscure important issues so that they are not given appropriate attention
    C. create a need for numerous staff conferences in order to handle all of the reported problems
    D. encourage some subordinate supervisors to focus on irrelevant matters and compete with each other in the length and content of their reports

14. The use of a committee as an approach to the problem of coordinating interdepartmental activities can present difficulties if the committee functions PRIMARILY as a(n)

    A. means of achieving personal objectives and goals
    B. instrument for coordinating activities that flow across departmental lines
    C. device for involving subordinate personnel in the decision-making process
    D. means of giving representation to competing interest groups

15. A study was recently made of the attitudes and perceptions of a sample of public assistance workers in nine New Jersey county welfare boards who had experienced a major organizational change and redefinition of their jobs as a result of separation of the income maintenance and social services functions. Questionnaires administered to these workers indicated that a disproportionate number of workers in the larger agencies were dissatisfied with the reorganization and their new assignments. Of the following, the MOST plausible reason for this dissatisfaction is that workers in larger agencies are

A. less likely to be known to management and to be personally disciplined if they expressed dissatisfaction with their new roles
B. less likely to have the opportunity to participate in planning a reorganization and to be given consideration for the assignments they preferred
C. given a shorter lead period to implement the change and, therefore, had insufficient time to plan the reorganization and carry it out efficiently
D. usually made up of more older members who have had routinized their work according to habit and find it more difficult to adjust to change

16. An article which recently appeared in a professional journal presents a proposal for participatory leadership in which the goal of supervision would be development of subordinates' self-reliance, with the premise that each staff member is held accountable for his own performance. The one of the following which would NOT be a desirable outcome of this type of supervision is the

   A. necessity for subordinates to critically examine their performance
   B. development by some subordinates of skills not possessed by the supervisor
   C. establishment of a quality control unit for sample checking and identification of errors
   D. relaxation of demands made on the supervisor

17. The *management by objectives* concept is a major development in the administration of human services organizations. The purpose of this approach is to establish a system for

   A. reduction of waiting time
   B. planning and controlling work output
   C. consolidation of organizational units
   D. work measurement

18. Assume that you encounter a serious administrative problem in implementing a new program. After consulting with members of your staff individually, you come up with several alternate solutions.
    Of the following, the procedure which would be MOST appropriate for evaluating the relative merits of each solution would be to

   A. try all of them on a limited experimental basis
   B. break the problem down into its component parts and analyze the effect of each solution on each component in terms of costs and benefits
   C. break the problem down into its component parts, eliminate all intangibles, and measure the effect of the tangible aspects of each solution on each component in terms of costs and benefits
   D. bring the matter before your weekly staff conference, discuss the relative merits of each alternate solution, and then choose the one favored by the majority of the conference

19. When establishing planning objectives for a service program under your supervision, the one of the following principles which should be followed is that objectives

   A. are rarely verifiable if they are qualitative
   B. should be few in number and of equal importance
   C. should cover as many of the activities of the program as possible
   D. should be set in the light of assumptions about future funding

20. Assume that you have been assigned responsibility for coordinating various aspects of the case aide program in a community social services center.
    Which of the following administrative concepts would NOT be applicable to this assignment?

    A. Functional job analysis
    B. Peer group supervision
    C. Differential use of staff
    D. Systems design

21. Good administrative practice includes the use of outside consultants as effective technique in achieving agency objectives.
    However, the one of the following which would NOT be an appropriate role for the consultant is

    A. provision of technical or professional expertise not otherwise available in the agency
    B. administrative direction of a new program activity
    C. facilitating coordination and communication among agency staff
    D. objective measurement of the effectiveness of agency services

22. Of the following, the MOST common fault of recent research projects attempting to measure the effectiveness of social programs has been their

    A. questionable methodology
    B. inaccurate findings
    C. unrealistic expectations
    D. lack of objectivity

23. One of the most difficult tasks of supervision in a modern public agency is teaching workers to cope with the hostile reactions of clients.
    In order to help the disconcerted worker analyze and understand a client's hostile behavior, the supervisor should FIRST

    A. encourage the worker to identify with the client's frustrations and deprivations
    B. give the worker a chance to express and accept his feelings about the client
    C. ask the worker to review his knowledge of the client and his circumstances
    D. explain to the worker that the client's anger is not directed at the worker personally

24. Determination of the level of participation, or how much of the public should participate in a given project, is a vital step in community organization.
    In order to make this determination, the FIRST action that should be taken is to

    A. develop the participants
    B. fix the goals of the project
    C. evaluate community interest in the project
    D. enlist the cooperation of community leaders

25. The one of the following which would be the MOST critical factor for successful operation of a decentralized system of social programs and services is

    A. periodic review and evaluation of services delivered at the community level
    B. transfer of decision-making authority to the community level wherever feasible
    C. participation of indigenous non-professionals in service delivery
    D. formulation of quantitative plans for dealing with community problems wherever feasible

KEY (CORRECT ANSWERS)

1. A
2. A
3. C
4. C
5. B

6. D
7. A
8. A
9. B
10. B

11. A
12. C
13. D
14. A
15. B

16. D
17. B
18. C
19. D
20. B

21. B
22. C
23. B
24. B
25. B

EXAMINATION SECTION
TEST 1

DIRECTIONS: Each question or incomplete statement is followed by several suggested answers or completions. Select the one that BEST answers the question or completes the statement. *PRINT THE LETTER OF THE CORRECT ANSWER IN THE SPACE AT THE RIGHT.*

1. A supervisor should consider a social worker to be skilled in diagnosis if, of the following, the worker excels in

    A. categorizing behavior, personality, and social problems in syndrome classes using a standardized nomenclature
    B. relating diagnoses to a theoretical system such as Freudian, Adlerian, Rogerian, etc.
    C. describing the person, problem, and setting as related to the casework situation
    D. determining the genesis of the problems for which the client seeks help

2. The one of the following which is the BASIC difference between the function of a supervisor and the function of a consultant in a large social agency is that the supervisor

    A. is a permanent staff member, while the consultant is a person brought in from the outside
    B. trains young and experienced workers, while the consultant trains those who no longer need supervision
    C. has administrative responsibility for agency operation, while the consultant has no direct administrative responsibility
    D. has a personal relationship with the worker, while the consultant provides administrative controls for evaluating the supervisor

3. Experts in social work supervision have stated that the role of the supervisor should be *authoritative* rather than *authoritarian.*
Of the following, this means MOST NEARLY that the supervisor's authority should come from

    A. his superior skill and competence
    B. his ability to exercise democratic control
    C. responsibility delegated through administrative channels
    D. differences in role perception of the worker and the supervisor

4. Assume that a supervisor who finds himself immobilized in the face of a difficult problem complains because his subordinates are confused and indecisive.
Of the following, it is MOST probable that the supervisor

    A. needs to give more guidance to his subordinates so that they will be able to make decisions within their sphere of responsibility
    B. is projecting his own state of mind on to his subordinates and is venting his feelings of frustration on their incompetence
    C. requires professional help for a personality problem which may make him unsuited for supervisory responsibility
    D. should arrange for his subordinates to get special training in decision-making within their areas of responsibility

5. A supervisor in a large agency with a recent graduate of a school of social work on his staff should be aware that the one of the following which is a common problem of the new professional worker is a tendency to

   A. interpret agency rules and regulations literally because of the desire for supervisory approval
   B. feel frustrated because agency rules and regulations prevent him from making independent decisions based on his professional training
   C. make independent decisions without calling upon the supervisor for expert advice and guidance
   D. protect himself from situations of stress by working with his clients in a routine, uninspired manner

6. Assume that your agency has a serious shortage of professional staff. However, an analysis of the daily tasks of professional social workers reveals that many of the tasks performed are of a clerical or administrative nature.
   Of the following, the MOST appropriate step to take FIRST in order to alleviate the shortage is to

   A. hire indigenous paraprofessionals from the community to take over part of the job load
   B. assign clerical and administrative staff to take over these non-professional tasks
   C. survey professional social workers in order to determine whether some of these clerical or administrative tasks are superfluous
   D. determine how many additional professional social workers are needed and arrange for recruitment in accordance with requirements

7. Experts have made a distinction between the formal and the informal organization of a large agency.
   Of the following, the informal organization has been described as

   A. dysfunctional due to its inevitable conflict with the basic objectives of the agency
   B. those levels of the agency which are separate from the administrative units which have direct responsibility for policy formulation
   C. including only those positions within the agency which have no direct responsibility for its service delivery function
   D. those relationships and channels of communication that resourceful employees develop and use in order to get the work done

8. The term *bureaucracy* has invidious implications for the general public. To the social scientist, however, *bureaucracy* is a technical term for a large, complex organization.
   Of the following, according to the social scientist, a *bureaucracy* is structured on rational principles and characterized by

   A. a democratic system in which each person has maximum freedom to make his own decisions
   B. a strict and well-defined hierarchy of authority functioning on the basis of clear-cut chain of command principles
   C. the assignment of independent responsibility to administrative and professional personnel responsible for delivery of services
   D. equal accessibility of all personnel within program units of the agency to personnel at the level where decisions are made

9. In the hierarchical administrative organization which is characteristic of a large agency, levels of authority emanate from the top downward.
Of the following, this structure has a tendency toward

   A. decreasing opportunities for staff participation in areas beyond their immediately circumscribed responsibilities
   B. easing the communications flow between departmental lines at the lower levels of the hierarchy
   C. permitting the flow of communication from the top downward, but not from the bottom upward
   D. structural flexibility which adapts readily to changing demands upon the organization

10. Of the following, adherence to *democratic* principles in the administration of a large agency means MOST NEARLY

    A. the feeling of all employees that they are participating in planning and policy making
    B. an equal voice for all employees in planning and policy making
    C. relevant participation of all employees according to their special competence
    D. friendliness, regardless of rank, among all employees at all levels

11. The one of the following which is the MOST important reason that all social workers who work in large agencies should be well-oriented to the administrative process is that they will

    A. be better qualified to participate in planning, decision-making, and formulation of policies
    B. be more sensitive to the needs of extra-agency components in the agency administrative system
    C. have a greater capacity to contribute to the agency and to accept their responsibilities within the system of cooperative effort
    D. be qualified for appointment to positions which do not include direct involvement in service

12. By virtue of training and orientation, social workers are well aware of personality traits that enhance or diminish administrative competence. Social agencies are becoming increasingly conscious, however, of the importance of understanding the effects of different forms of agency organization and structure, not only in relation to staff performance but also in relation to the service the agency performs.
Of the following, this statement means MOST NEARLY that

    A. administrative difficulties can be analyzed and resolved, not only in terms of personality shortcomings of given individuals but also in terms of organizational arrangements
    B. such factors in agency organization as size, physical arrangements, and organizational roles can be more important than personality traits of administrators in influencing effective delivery of services
    C. agency organization and structure can have a significant effect on staff performance
    D. social workers should give more emphasis to the importance of understanding the effects of agency organization and structure, rather than personality traits

13. According to the task-centered concept of administrative organization, attention is focused on the problem or task at hand, involving all persons who may have a contribution to make, regardless of their professional status or rank in the organization.
Of the following, the MOST probable result of such an approach to agency administration would be to

    A. increase delegation of responsibility from the top downward
    B. increase promotion opportunities for non-professionals
    C. enhance the opportunities for staff to participate in policy formulations
    D. interfere with hierarchical distribution of authority from the top downward

14. The one of the following which CORRECTLY describes the change of focus in social work today is:

    A. New psychological studies and research on human behavior have resulted in increased emphasis on personality problems and the need to change individual dependency patterns
    B. The psychoanalytic orientation and the emphasis on personality problems are being challenged by social science perspectives which stress the environmental causes of individual maladjustment
    C. Emphasis on giving clients supportive assistance with personal problems and on changing individual behavior patterns has shifted to heightened attention to decreasing dependency through required work programs
    D. Sociological studies and other research in the social sciences have resulted in a new emphasis on changing family life and substituting communal ways of living for obsolete institutions

15. The one of the following which is an important distinction between the profession of social work and many other professions is that

    A. there is a basic conflict between social workers' professional interests and the interests of the agency in which they are employed
    B. there is little activity by social workers in the direction of private practice
    C. the claim for recognition of social work as a profession arose when it was practiced mainly within administrative organizations
    D. social workers have a tendency to move from private practice to practice within administrative organizations

16. As the supervisor for the After Hours Emergency Child Care Services, you have been asked by a group of home aides whether they could go out in pairs to areas of the city where they feel uneasy and where some of them have had unpleasant experiences. They point out that caseworkers have approval for this although they usually visit these neighborhoods during daytime hours, while home aides are in the field at all hours of the night. Of the following, your BEST response would be to

    A. remind the home aides that they knew the working conditions when they were hired
    B. question the statement that caseworkers have approval to go in the field in pairs
    C. sympathize with the home aides' fears and agree that their work presents many challenges
    D. indicate that you will consider each such request on an individual basis so that all possible protective measures can be taken

17. At a meeting of your supervisory staff, several supervisors inform you that they lack staff to provide coverage for all service requests. Some units are more overburdened than others because some kinds of service requests are more numerous. A group of caseworkers have suggested to their supervisors that all service requests be distributed throughout the units, instead of continuing the present system of sending requests to specialized units.
Of the following, your BEST immediate response to this proposal would be to

    A. indicate that assignment of work is not a decision to be made by casework staff, but that you will forward the suggestion to your supervisor
    B. point out that, although you have made this serious situation known at higher levels, you do not have the authority to reorganize your units in the manner suggested
    C. ask the supervisors to submit more factual data on volume, distribution of cases, and staff available, along with their recommendations as to the feasibility of the caseworkers' proposal
    D. draft a memo to your supervisor stating that staff shortages are now so serious that caseworkers cannot cover all service requests, and ask for instructions

18. An institution or group home is usually the BEST placement for

    A. children who are committed by the court because of neglect or abuse by their parents
    B. adolescents and school-age children who have temporarily lost their ability to relate to parent substitutes
    C. pre-school age children whose parents cannot care for them temporarily
    D. children who have difficulty relating to their peers

19. Foster homes must be periodically re-examined as a requirement for continued licensing.
Of the following, the MOST important reason for this requirement is that

    A. homes that have been used for many years tend to deteriorate and may need to be closed
    B. child welfare workers often do not see the foster fathers at any other time
    C. foster parents may become overwhelmed by too many placements and may desire to have their homes closed
    D. changes in the composition and competence of a foster family should be evaluated and reported regularly

20. A child welfare agency can USUALLY expect that new foster parents who have children of their own will

    A. take on the role of foster parents with very little difficulty
    B. need more help than childless couples in adjusting to their new roles
    C. need to have their responsibilities to their foster children clearly differentiated from their responsibilities to their own children
    D. have a good understanding of the needs of foster children and adjust quickly to the agency's role in providing care for them

21. When a young child makes repeated attempts to break through the reasonable limits which his foster parents have set on his behavior, it is PROBABLY a sign that

    A. the foster parents are not punishing him appropriately for his misbehavior
    B. he does not respect parental authority

C. he is testing whether his foster parents care enough about him to discipline him
D. the foster parents should be more lenient with him

22. Adoptive parents should be provided with factual information about the child's natural parents MAINLY

   A. in order to be able to answer his questions about his natural parents
   B. because they would try to obtain this information anyway
   C. so that they can be prevented from worrying about the child's background
   D. to encourage them to tell the child about his natural parents

23. Foster parents are usually responsible for transporting and accompanying their foster children to various appointments arranged by the child welfare worker.
When a foster parent informs the worker that he is unable to keep a specific appointment, the worker should

   A. accompany the child to the appointment himself
   B. insist that the foster parent keep the appointment
   C. reschedule the appointment for a time more convenient for the foster parent
   D. evaluate whether cancellation of the appointment would be harmful, and act accordingly

24. After spending several months in a congregate shelter, John is to be placed in a foster home with his younger siblings. However, the discharge physical reveals that he needs a tonsillectomy.
In this situation, the child welfare worker should FIRST

   A. ask the shelter to arrange for John's tonsillectomy and postpone the placement until after the operation
   B. ask the doctor if he considers the tonsillectomy to be urgent so the worker can decide whether or not to postpone the placement
   C. arrange for the tonsillectomy at once and have John hospitalized
   D. tell the prospective foster mother about the need for the tonsillectomy so she can decide when the surgery should be done

25. An eight-month-old baby, born with withdrawal symptoms and abandoned by her drug-addicted mother, is being made ready for placement in a foster home.
In this situation, the child welfare worker should

   A. not tell the prospective foster parents about the natural mother's drug addiction so that they won't become unduly worried
   B. tell the prospective foster parents about the natural mother's addiction but assure them that the child has been treated and cured
   C. inform the prospective foster parents of the child's background, explain that she may have a convulsion, and tell them what to do if this should happen
   D. not tell the prospective foster parents about the child's background unless they ask

KEY (CORRECT ANSWERS)

1. C
2. C
3. A
4. B
5. B

6. B
7. D
8. B
9. A
10. C

11. C
12. A
13. C
14. B
15. C

16. D
17. C
18. B
19. D
20. C

21. C
22. A
23. D
24. B
25. C

TEST 2

DIRECTIONS: Each question or incomplete statement is followed by several suggested answers or completions. Select the one that BEST answers the question or completes the statement. *PRINT THE LETTER OF THE CORRECT ANSWER IN THE SPACE AT THE RIGHT.*

1. Of the following, the BEST placement for a twelve-year-old boy who has been diagnosed as having a severe behavior disorder would probably be in a(n)   1._____

   A. small group home which is programmed to offer a permissive living atmosphere and home instruction from the State Department of Education
   B. institution geared to treat pre-delinquent children
   C. foster home where his acting out behavior would be understood and accepted
   D. institution where his behavior would be controlled through routines, discipline, and relationships with adults and peers

2. In planning services for a young woman expecting an out-of-wedlock child, the child welfare worker should be PRIMARILY concerned with   2._____

   A. obtaining as much information as possible about the young woman's ethnic background and health history
   B. determining how the young woman's family is reacting to the situation and whether they will help plan for the unborn child
   C. making up a list of suitable adoption agencies to which the young woman can be referred
   D. providing the young woman with information about all the various arrangements she can make for her unborn child

3. A foster mother who has been caring for two retarded preschool children, and receiving a special board rate for the foster care, has become very tired. Her doctor has told her that she needs a vacation, and she so informs the child welfare worker. However, she does not wish to give up caring for the children.
   Of the following, the BEST approach for the worker to take is to   3._____

   A. recognize the foster mother's need for a vacation and make temporary arrangements for the care of the children
   B. remind the foster mother that she is receiving a special board rate which should be enough to provide her with babysitting relief
   C. find a new facility for the children since the foster mother's health is apparently failing as a result of taking care of the children
   D. try to determine if there is another reason for the foster mother's exhaustion

4. In planning for 18-month-old twins, one who appears to be developing normally and one who is functioning below normal and has many physical problems, the child welfare worker should place the GREATEST emphasis on   4._____

   A. placing them in one foster home since research has shown that a symbiotic relationship exists between twins
   B. placing them separately since it would be psychologically harmful for the *normal* twin to live with his *abnormal* sibling

C. finding an institution that has a specially trained staff for taking care of handicapped children but also accepts *normal* children so that the twins could remain together
D. finding an appropriate placement for each child according to his needs, realizing that meeting their individual needs is more important than their twin-ship

5. A mother has had all five of her children in placement since she was hospitalized for mental illness three years ago. The hospital has now discharged her, and she is receiving follow-up treatment in an after-care clinic where she receives her medication. She wants her children back, and the clinic approves. The private agency, however, feels that the mother is not ready and also reports that the children do not want to go home.
Of the following, the BEST course of action for you, as a supervisor, to take is to

   A. recommend that the children be returned to their mother as soon as possible since the clinic approves
   B. keep the children in placement until the private agency feels that the mother is ready to cope with them and that they want to go back to her
   C. refer the case to your psychiatric consultant and be guided by his recommendation
   D. confer with representatives of the private agency and the clinic to determine if and when the children should be returned, and how to prepare the mother and children for eventual reunion

6. A child welfare worker in one of your units reports that a mother with whom she is working claims that the school is discriminating against her children because she is a welfare recipient. Her children have a history of truancy and poor school achievement. The child welfare worker feels that the mother's assessment of the situation has some validity.
Of the following, the BEST course of action for you to suggest to your worker is to

   A. support the mother's defense of her children and report the alleged discrimination on the part of the school to the Board of Education
   B. inquire further into the reasons for the children's truancy and poor achievement with the children, the mother, and school officials
   C. explore with the mother her feelings about receiving public assistance and encourage her to find a job so she won't need assistance
   D. disengage herself from her close involvement in this case since she has stopped being objective

7. It is standard practice, in providing service to children in their own homes, for the child welfare worker to work directly with the child when

   A. it is determined that his parents have no emotional problem
   B. his problems are primarily in the school and community
   C. he needs help in coping with his living situation and in accepting parental limitations
   D. his parents do not speak English and the worker needs an interpreter

8. Which one of the following statements regarding the provision of services to children in their own homes is CORRECT?

   A. The caretaking parent is the primary client.
   B. Services for the child under six are generally provided through the parents.
   C. The way the home is kept is of primary importance in evaluating the case.
   D. The most pertinent service is the one given directly to the child.

9. Of the following, the MOST important problem in the development of group day care services for infants is that this service

   A. requires many safeguards to protect the child's physical health and emotional development
   B. costs too much for the parents or the community to support
   C. cannot be licensed by the Board of Health or State Department of Social Services
   D. is looked upon by the community with disfavor because people, in general, feel that mothers should stay home with infants

10. A child welfare worker should offer day care services

    A. to every mother on her caseload
    B. to mothers on her caseload who have the necessary motivation and strength to work but must provide for the care of their children during the day
    C. only to those mothers on her caseload who are already working and could take their children out of placement if day care services were available
    D. only to parents who have several children and are receiving supplementary assis-

11. The one of the following which is an important, although not the primary, function of a homemaker, from the point of view of the child welfare agency, is to

    tance which could be cut off if the mother went to work
    A. interpret foster care services to the family
    B. provide the family with counseling services, as needed, in relation to the problems the homemaker encounters in her work with the family
    C. provide the child welfare worker with additional information about the family which might not be obtained otherwise, and which could be used in further planning with the family
    D. help the mother to understand her feelings of inadequacy as a parent and to face reality

12. A mother who is legally married to someone not the father of her illegitimate child wants to surrender the child legally for adoption. Her husband does not know about the child. The child welfare worker should advise her that she may have difficulty in legally surrendering the child unless she

    A. signs a surrender and swears her husband is not the child's father
    B. informs her husband about the child and can obtain his written denial of paternity
    C. tells the court the child's real father abandoned her and the child
    D. can prove that she and her husband cannot care for the child properly

13. In planning for the placement of a ten-year-old child in foster care, it is standard practice for the child welfare worker to

    A. make the decision with the parents, without including the child in the planning
    B. enlist the child's participation to the fullest extent possible, depending on his level of maturity
    C. have the parents take responsibility for preparing the child for placement
    D. help the child to accept the agency's and his parents' decision since he cannot do anything about it

14. Of the following, the MOST important reason that child welfare agencies should place more emphasis upon early case finding is in order to

    A. help more families obtain needed public assistance
    B. offer families more extensive diagnostic evaluation
    C. prevent separation of children from their parents
    D. provide more extensive referral services

15. If a parent accused of child neglect refuses protective service, the caseworker should inform him that

    A. he does not have the right to refuse protective service since this service is mandatory
    B. the child will be removed from the home as soon as a foster home can be found
    C. the problem may be referred to the jurisdiction of the Family Court as the result of his refusal
    D. any further complaints of child neglect against him will be investigated by the agency and reported to the police if substantiated

16. As a supervisor, you are asked to work on a committee which is planning for the appropriate use of case aides in family and child welfare programs.
    Of the following, the one which would be the LEAST appropriate assignment for a case aide is

    A. determining, as a result of interviewing the client, the best solution to his family problems
    B. helping a parent to attend an important school meeting by caring for his children at home during the meeting
    C. finding and suggesting recipes to make a client's medically required diet more appetizing and palatable
    D. visiting an overburdened parent's home in order to suggest how to divide some of the home chores among the children

17. As a Supervisor II, you observe that the two case aides assigned to your area, who attend school parttime, are not given many work assignments. You discuss this situation with the Supervisors I, who state that it is too time-consuming to design appropriate tasks for the case aides since they are not available for a full day's work. The Supervisors I express their willingness to have the case aides do their school assignments in the office.
    Of the following, your BEST response would be that the

    A. Supervisors I should see to it that the case aides do not do homework in the office because it would give the clients a bad impression
    B. Supervisors I must assign appropriate tasks to case aides so that the agency and its clients may derive the maximum benefit from their time on the job
    C. agency has great confidence in the use of parapro-fessionals
    D. schools are able to adjust their schedules for case aides and that Supervisors I should be able to do the same

18. As a supervisor, you are asked to help obtain assistance for a group of residents of your geographic area who have taken a number of unrelated children into their homes and are caring for them at their own expense.
Of the following, the MOST accurate information you can give this group is:

   A. There is no legal basis for meeting their requests
   B. Home Relief is not available as a means of providing for some of the cost of a child's care in a non-related home
   C. An ADC grant can be made for child care to friends of the child's parents who are now supporting the child
   D. They can apply to the Bureau of Child Welfare for certification as foster parents for these children and for payment of foster home boarding care rates

19. Mr. and Mrs. A are requesting the discharge from foster care of Mary, their eight-year-old daughter, who was placed voluntarily six weeks ago after the child told her teacher that Mr. A *bothered* her. Although Mary had given an elaborate account of this alleged sexual molestation, both parents denied that such an incident occurred, but requested placement as a way of relieving the tension in the home.
As the supervisor asked to participate in the decision about the parent's request for Mary's discharge from placement, your MAIN consideration should be

   A. the dynamics involved in differentiating between a child's fantasy and reality
   B. Mary's feelings about returning home to her family
   C. the factors that went into the earlier decision for placement
   D. that cases of alleged sexual molestation can be handled by court action only

20. As a supervisor on call for consultation on decisions to be made by the emergency night child welfare staff, you are asked to approve by telephone the discharge of a seven-year-old boy to his father. The boy had been admitted to a city children's shelter when his mother, who was separated from his father, died suddenly during surgery.
Of the following pieces of information supplied by the child welfare worker over the phone, which is the LEAST relevant to your decision? The

   A. father and child know each other
   B. child is in reasonably good health
   C. father has arranged with his mother to look after his son while he is at work
   D. father does not know whether the mother had initiated divorce proceedings

21. As a supervisor in the foster home program, you receive a request for a change of case worker from a foster mother who is caring for four adolescents. The mother complains that the case worker spends too much time with the children when he visits. In a conference with you, the Supervisor I, who had worked with this foster home until his recent promotion, states his belief that his positive relationship with the foster mother is more important than her relationship with the present case worker. He, therefore, wants to keep the foster home within his unit but assign it to a different case worker. He is concerned that any other course of action might result in the foster mother's request for removal of the children from her home.
Your conference with the Supervisor I on this situation should focus on the

   A. difficulty involved in securing homes for four adolescents
   B. rights of foster parents to request removal of foster children

C. rights of foster parents to request a different case worker
D. way in which the Supervisor I sees his enabling role

22. As the supervisor for the After Hours Emergency Child Care Services, you recognize, while reviewing the reports of the previous night's activities, the name of a five-year-old boy who had been reported as a runaway two weeks earlier. The current report again indicates that the police found the child wandering in the street at 3:00 A.M. about six blocks from his grandmother's house, where he has been living for the past six months. The current report also indicates that the grandmother arrived at the police station and took the boy home before any action was taken by the Emergency Child Care staff. Of the following, the LEAST valid focus for your next group conference with your staff in discussing this case would be to

    A. stress the advisability of placement of children referred for the second time in a two-week period
    B. discuss critical indices of potential difficulties that may be present when a five-year-old child is a chronic runaway
    C. review indices for referring emergency situations that are overtly resolved after hours to the regular unit the next day
    D. develop a workshop on how to interview children

23. As a Supervisor II in a Protective Services section, you are reviewing a case record forwarded to you by the Supervisor I of one of your units, to show you how promptly his case workers have been making field visits on new referrals. In this case, the case worker visited the home within an hour after receipt of an anonymous report of neglect of an infant. The record stated that the worker was impressed by the mother's politeness and the cleanliness of the home, that the allegation of neglect was false, and that no follow-up was indicated.
Of the following, your MAIN emphasis in reviewing this case material should be on

    A. determining how the case worker interpreted to the mother the reason for his visit
    B. finding out whether the baby was seen during the case worker's visit to the home
    C. planning to compliment the Supervisor I on having helped his caseworkers to make field visits promptly
    D. determining whether or not the record shows that the anonymous complaint was actually disproved

24. As a Supervisor II in an adoption program, you notice that the Supervisor I of one of your units presents about four times as many atypical situations for your review and approval as the Supervisor I of any other unit under your supervision.
Of the following, the BEST step for you take FIRST in order to evaluate the significance of this observation would be to

    A. recognize that, because many children are hard to place, no family that offers to adopt a child should be eliminated
    B. accept the fact that all atypical situations should be reviewed carefully because adoption policies are changing rapidly
    C. analyze the handling of all the studies initiated within this unit during a specific time span in order to determine if appropriate action has been taken in every case
    D. become aware that the supervisors of the other units are probably rejecting atypical situations without bringing them to your attention

25. As a supervisor, you read at night a newspaper report on a serious fire in an apartment building in your work area in which a number of children suffered from severe burns and smoke inhalation, and were admitted to X Hospital. The next morning, the MOST appropriate action for the district office to take would be to

    A. explore whether or not X Hospital sees evidence of abuse or neglect of any of the children hospitalized and, if so, whether the hospital plans to refer the children and families to the Bureau of Child Welfare
    B. initiate steps for referral for re-housing
    C. send a worker to the area to determine how or if he can be of help
    D. send a worker to the hospital to offer family and child welfare services

25.____

KEY (CORRECT ANSWERS)

1.	D	11.	C
2.	D	12.	B
3.	A	13.	B
4.	D	14.	C
5.	D	15.	C
6.	B	16.	A
7.	C	17.	B
8.	B	18.	D
9.	A	19.	C
10.	B	20.	D

21.	D
22.	A
23.	D
24.	C
25.	A

TEST 3

DIRECTIONS: Each question or incomplete statement is followed by several suggested answers or completions. Select the one that BEST answers the question or completes the statement. *PRINT THE LETTER OF THE CORRECT ANSWER IN THE SPACE AT THE RIGHT.*

1. Of the following, the MOST important influence on the personality development of a child during the first year is the

    A. family as a whole
    B. mother
    C. way his siblings react to him
    D. relationship between the parents

    1.____

2. Of the following, the terms which is GENERALLY applied to the situation in which an infant in foster care has insufficient interaction with a substitute mother is

    A. maternal rejection
    B. mothering complex
    C. maternal deprivation
    D. interaction deficiency

    2.____

3. When a foster child exhibits nonconforming behavior, it is MOST important for the foster parents to be able to

    A. ignore this behavior since this is the child's way of expressing his emotional needs
    B. accept and condone this behavior as an expression of the child's insecurity
    C. use punishment and reward to force the child to conform
    D. accept this behavior without condoning it, while trying to meet the child's emotional needs

    3.____

4. Separation of the infant from his mother can be a traumatic experience.
The amount of emotional damage to the infant and the consequent effects on his personality depend MAINLY on the

    A. quality and consistency of the substitute mothering he receives
    B. reasons for and duration of the separation
    C. kind of preparation for separation the infant receives
    D. degree of the mother's acceptance of the placement

    4.____

5. Research studies of language development in young children have shown that

    A. the multiple mothering of children in a large family retards language development
    B. language retardation in otherwise normal children is usually related to inadequate language stimulation
    C. language retardation is always associated with slow motor development
    D. children are usually slow in learning to talk when more than one language is spoken in the home

    5.____

6. The two MOST important influences on the cultural development of a seven-year-old child are the

    A. home and peer group
    B. school and peer group
    C. home and school
    D. home and church

    6.____

7. In our culture, a child gains his sense of identity MAINLY from

   A. knowledge about and experience with his parents and extended family
   B. association with members of his own ethnic group
   C. a study of the historical and ethnic factors in this culture
   D. association with his peers

8. A child who has grown up in foster care may want to talk about his natural parents, although he has never known them.
   Of the following, the BEST way for a child welfare worker to deal with this situation is to

   A. help the child to forget that he is a foster child and to relate to his foster parents as though they were his natural parents
   B. encourage the child to express his feelings and fantasies about his natural parents so that the worker can help his understand these feelings and fantasies
   C. set up a psychiatric interview for the child to determine if he is making a satisfactory adjustment to his foster child status
   D. tell the child that he can look for his natural parents when he is older

9. Of the following, the MOST important reason that those responsible for the care of a child in placement should never depreciate the child's natural parents or the home from which he came is that the

   A. child's self-esteem depends on how he feels about his natural parents and his previous experiences
   B. natural parents may have been incapable of being adequate parents
   C. child may feel that the substitute parents are jealous of his natural parents
   D. child will be forced into the position of defending his natural parents and will resent the substitute parents

10. The Children's Appercception Test (CAT) is a commonly used protective test for preschool children in which the child

    A. has an opportunity to express his fantasies and moods through drawing and painting
    B. tells a story about pictures that are shown to him
    C. completes an unfinished story
    D. is given a variety of toys and is placed in a make-believe play situation

11. Sickle cell anemia is a blood disease MOST commonly found in children whose parents are

    A. Caucasian   B. interracial
    C. Black or Latin American   D. Oriental

12. Schizophrenia in children USUALLY becomes manifest

    A. during the latency period
    B. during adolescence only
    C. when the mother has a history of schizophrenia
    D. during early childhood or adolescence

13. Although day care was originally established mainly as a social service for working mothers, it has been found that

    A. day care can also be an educational experience for a child and help in the development of peer relationships
    B. most working mothers would prefer to leave their children with friends or relatives rather than at a day care center
    C. it would be economically feasible to make day care centers available to all mothers in the community
    D. working mothers of physically and mentally handicapped children do not benefit from day care facilities

14. In deciding on which day care center to recommend to a working mother, the MOST important of the following considerations is the

    A. educational background of the staff
    B. ratio of staff to children
    C. director of the center
    D. physical plant and recreational facilities

15. During the past few years, dramatic and serious incidents of child abuse have resulted in

    A. the passage of legislation in all states requiring medical and other designated personnel to report incidents of abuse
    B. the proliferation of child care agencies dealing with child abuse cases only
    C. a tightening of restrictions in most states on eligibility for public assistance of parents who abuse their children
    D. a slight decline in the number of child neglect cases reported to authorities and a slight increase in the number of child abuse cases reported

16. Of the following alternatives, the one which is LEAST available to the Black unwed mother in planning for her child is

    A. adoption
    B. temporary care in a small group home
    C. foster family care
    D. dependence upon her family

Questions 17-19.

DIRECTIONS: Questions 17 through 19 are to be answered by matching each of the persons listed in Column I with the field in which the person is an authority, as stated in Column II.

COLUMN I

17. Lauretta Bender

18. Fritz Redl

19. Gisela Konopka

COLUMN II

A. Group work
B. Homefinding
C. Day care
D. Acting out, emotionally disturbed children and adolescents
E. Childhood schizophrenia

20. As a supervisor in the Division of Interagency Relationships, you become aware that a particular voluntary child-caring agency often reports discharges of children from foster care either on the date the discharge plan is to be implemented or shortly after the discharge has taken place. Your staff informs you that such late discharge reports are forwarded most frequently when the discharge plans indicate a need for intensive supportive help. The BEST approach for you to take would be to meet with

    A. your team and tell them to disapprove all such discharges in the future
    B. your team and tell them to take all appropriate clerical action as quickly as possible
    C. your immediate supervisor to inform him that a particular agency is making unsound discharges
    D. representatives of the voluntary child-caring agency to discuss the subject of discharge practice

21. As a supervisor, you are representing the Bureau of Child Welfare on a committee that meets bi-monthly to plan for the needs of retarded children. You note that the comments of the parents of retardates are warmly accepted at each session, but are never incorporated into the minutes or included in recommendations for follow-up action.
Of the following, the BEST approach for you to take would be to

    A. report this discrepancy to your immediate supervisor
    B. attempt to maneuver the group so that the parents of retardates will be encouraged to make more comments at committee meetings
    C. raise a question at the next regular meeting about the discrepancy you have found in the recording of participation by parents
    D. talk to several parents after the next meeting to find out if they object to the manner in which minutes are recorded

22. As a Supervisor II, you note that your staff appears to make minimal use of community resources to meet client needs. When you discuss this at a staff meeting, you meet a great deal of resistance from both the Supervisors I and the case workers, who say: *You are not out there.*
Of the following, your BEST response in this situation would be to

    A. refer to an article you have read about how workers can involve themselves in the community
    B. ask for volunteers for a committee to explore possible resources in the community they serve
    C. ask the group to give examples of their use of community resources
    D. ask the group to describe their experiences in seeking out community resources

23. As a supervisor, you are invited as an expert consultant to meet with a community group discussing child day care needs. At the meeting, one parent urges the establishment of group care for infants in her apartment building, where there are about ten infants between the ages of three and twelve months.
Of the following, the FIRST suggestion you should make concerning this proposal is that

    A. those parents in the building who are interested in infant care attend a meeting to discuss the specific needs of his own infant and what his expectations of group care are

B. the group invite an expert on infant development to its next meeting for the purpose of outlining a possible infant group care program
C. the community group insure that pediatric consultation would be available to the persons providing the infant group care
D. one parent contact the landlord of the apartment building to inquire about regulations or stipulations for use of an apartment or other building facility for an infant group care program

24. Of the following, the MOST desirable pattern to utilize in community planning of child welfare services is to

    A. leave each agency in the community free to develop those services which its constituency feels strongly about and wishes to support
    B. have each agency in the community assigned a particular function by the state licensing authority in line with community need
    C. consult a central planning body, representative of all agencies in the community, when any agency is considering developing a new service or dropping an old one
    D. merge all agencies in the community providing like services, in order to reduce administrative expenses

25. It is recognized that very young children should not remain in hospitals after the condition for which they were admitted is under control and can be managed outside the hospital setting.
Of the following, the BEST method for preventing well children from remaining in hospitals longer than necessary is for

    A. hospital policy to provide for referral of children to the Bureau of Child Welfare when the hospital staff believe parents may not be able to take their children home as soon as they are medically well
    B. hospital social service departments to prepare social histories on children hospitalized, focusing especially on children *at risk*
    C. the public child welfare agency to receive on a regular basis lists of children remaining in hospitals
    D. hospitals to send to child caring agencies lists of children not discharged, although medically well

KEY (CORRECT ANSWERS)

1. B
2. C
3. D
4. A
5. B

6. C
7. A
8. B
9. A
10. B

11. C
12. D
13. A
14. B
15. A

16. A
17. E
18. D
19. A
20. D

21. C
22. D
23. A
24. C
25. A

EXAMINATION SECTION
TEST 1

DIRECTIONS: Each question or incomplete statement is followed by several suggested answers or completions. Select the one that BEST answers the question or completes the statement. *PRINT THE LETTER OF THE CORRECT ANSWER IN THE SPACE AT THE RIGHT.*

1. The term *first-line supervisor* refers to the lowest level of supervision in an organization. A dilemma faced by the first-line supervisor is that he represents

    A. management
    B. labor
    C. management and labor
    D. neither management nor labor

2. Management experts generally consider it advisable to give instructions orally, even though these instructions may later be put in writing for permanent reference.
The MAIN reason for this advice is that

    A. employees sometimes misplace written instructions
    B. explanations can be made in accordance with individual needs
    C. written instructions tend to be unclear and ambiguous
    D. employees resent being given instructions in writing

3. Of the following, the BEST reason why a supervisor should NOT delegate a certain job to a subordinate is that

    A. he does not have any subordinate who can develop the skills needed to do the job
    B. it is easier and quicker to do it himself
    C. he knows it will be done correctly if he does it himself
    D. he enjoys doing it himself

4. Of the following, the step which the supervisor should take FIRST in handling a complaint from a member of his staff is to

    A. gather background information relevant to the complaint
    B. establish tentative solutions or answers to the complaint
    C. determine the nature of the complaint as clearly and as fully as possible
    D. make a determination as to whether the complaint is valid

5. Before a supervisor delegates one of the duties which he normally performs to a member of his staff, the FIRST thing he should do is

    A. determine the long-range purpose of the job
    B. determine exactly what tasks the job involves
    C. decide how long it takes him to do the job
    D. decide to whom he will assign the job

6. When an employee is not sure of the intent of a policy statement, it is usually BEST for him to consult

    A. a fellow worker
    B. a member of the planning staff
    C. his supervisor
    D. the manual of procedures

7. The MOST appropriate time for a supervisor to have a discussion with an employee who has violated an agency policy is

   A. as soon as possible after the violation has occurred
   B. after a cooling-off period has elapsed
   C. the day after the violation occurred
   D. during the next staff meeting

8. Of the following, the MOST appropriate use of staff conferences is to enable the supervisor to

   A. inform staff of the latest administrative policies
   B. obtain the benefits of collective thinking about a problem
   C. let staff know that he is aware of violations of personnel policies
   D. give dissatisfied employees a chance to voice their grievances

9. Of the following, a term used to describe how a supervisor may determine whether he is communicating effectively with his staff is called

   A. backlash   B. feedback
   C. implementation   D. delegation

10. False rumors about unpleasant possibilities such as employee cutbacks can do serious damage to morale. Most rumors of this kind in large organizations and public agencies are caused by

    A. over-permissiveness and general laxity of supervision
    B. a breakdown in communication between management and employees
    C. employees who distort the facts for their own purposes
    D. newspaper articles planted by special interest groups

11. Of the following, staff meetings are LEAST likely to be productive when

    A. only four or five people are present
    B. the chairman conducts the meeting in a formal manner
    C. discussion is kept to a minimum
    D. private discussions are not allowed

12. The one of the following persons who USUALLY would be classified as belonging to middle management is the

    A. senior clerk   B. agency head
    C. bureau director   D. deputy commissioner

13. Of the following, the BEST way for a person to develop competence as an interviewer is to

    A. attend lectures on interviewing techniques
    B. practice with employees on the job
    C. conduct interviews under the supervision of an experienced instructor
    D. attend a training course in counselling

14. Of the following, the type of employee who would PROBABLY expect to be given the most authority to use independent judgment is the

    A. chemical engineer
    B. clerical worker
    C. bookkeeper
    D. registered nurse

15. Assume that you are asked to study and report on employee turnover in several agency units which vary widely as to total number of employees and the number of employees involved in turnover.
    In order to present an accurate picture of turnover, your report should show, with regard to persons leaving, both actual numbers and

    A. central tendencies
    B. percentages
    C. raw data
    D. rounded totals

16. Many employees tend to resist a reorganization because they feel that their status and security are threatened. Of the following, the BEST way to make it easier for employees to accept the changes necessitated by reorganization is to

    A. introduce many changes at the same time
    B. give them a chance to participate in evaluating proposed changes
    C. keep the changes secret until they are put into effect
    D. have staff people who have had little contact with the affected employees initiate the changes

17. The MOST important reason for investigating every accident on the job is to

    A. find out who was responsible for the accident
    B. determine the organization's legal liability for the accident
    C. correct the conditions or actions which caused the accident
    D. discipline the employee who caused the accident

18. Research studies indicate that an important difference between high-production and low-production supervisors lies in their manner of handling mistakes.
    When subordinates make mistakes, the high-production supervisor PROBABLY would

    A. concentrate on fixing responsibility and determining the subordinate's excuse for the mistake
    B. take over the assignment himself in order to avoid recurrence of the mistake
    C. look upon the mistake as an opportunity to provide training
    D. give the assignment to a subordinate who is not likely to repeat the mistake

19. The use of statistical controls is generally considered to be one of management's most effective means of determining what is happening at the operating level of an agency.
    Of the following, statistical controls are LEAST useful for

    A. furthering coordination
    B. measuring morale
    C. setting standards
    D. pinpointing responsibility

20. A basic problem of the supervisor is how to motivate employees. One approach is to *internalize* motivation by providing opportunities for employees to derive satisfaction from the work itself.
    Of the following, internalized motivation would be the LEAST effective approach where the employee

    A. enjoys autonomy because of the nature of the job
    B. accepts the organization's objectives
    C. makes the job his central life focus
    D. does a routine or assembly line job

20.____

KEY (CORRECT ANSWERS)

1.	C	11.	C
2.	B	12.	C
3.	A	13.	C
4.	C	14.	A
5.	B	15.	B
6.	C	16.	B
7.	A	17.	C
8.	B	18.	C
9.	B	19.	B
10.	B	20.	D

TEST 2

DIRECTIONS: Each question or incomplete statement is followed by several suggested answers or completions. Select the one that BEST answers the question or completes the statement. *PRINT THE LETTER OF THE CORRECT ANSWER IN THE SPACE AT THE RIGHT.*

1. Of the following, the BEST time for a supervisor to give advice about a job-related problem which a subordinate has brought up during an interview is USUALLY after the

    A. subordinate has told him all the facts
    B. supervisor has determined the employee's unconscious motives for bringing up the problem
    C. employee has submitted a written report on the problem
    D. supervisor has discussed the problem with his superior

2. Of the following, the situation in which a supervisor would have to make the GREATEST effort in order to communicate effectively with his subordinates would occur when

    A. there is a large gap between the supervisor's background and experience and that of his subordinates
    B. the subordinates have already learned about the information through informal channels
    C. the subordinates have completed their education much more recently than the supervisor
    D. the supervisor has been with the organization for a much shorter time than most of his subordinates

3. Of the following, the factor which would be MOST critical in influencing whether subordinates accept or resent a supervisor's authority is the

    A. manner in which the supervisor uses his authority
    B. frequency with which the supervisor ignores minor violations of rules
    C. degree of delegation to subordinates by the supervisor
    D. cultural attitudes of individual subordinates toward authority

4. In which one of the following situations would employees be MOST likely to accept temporarily difficult working conditions without excessive complaining?

    A. The organization has a strict policy of disciplinary action against uncooperative employees.
    B. Employees do not have the right to take part in *job actions* or strikes.
    C. An atmosphere of mutual trust and good human relations exists between subordinates and managerial personnel.
    D. Relationships between subordinates and managerial personnel are strictly businesslike.

5. Assume that an agency has been reorganized into integrated work teams. Instead of assigning employees performing the same task to a single unit, such as a typing pool, those performing different but interdependent parts of an activity are put into the same work group.
   Of the following, the MOST probable result of such a reorganization would be to

    A. permit more efficient work scheduling
    B. achieve greater economy
    C. decrease training costs
    D. improve employee job satisfaction

217

6. The need for identification with a work group has been found to be one of the most powerful on-the-job motivations.
   Of the following, the employee who is LEAST likely to have a strong attachment to his work group is one who

   A. is at the very bottom of the organization's promotional ladder
   B. belongs to a small department
   C. works with others of similar background and interests
   D. has worked for the organization for a considerable period of time

7. According to many management experts, the one of the following situations which would be the MOST significant indication that employees of an organization are dissatisfied with their supervisors and feel that they are being treated unfairly is one in which

   A. employees submit a large number of work-related suggestions
   B. many employees are unproductive and seem to be continually loafing on the job
   C. union membership has recently increased
   D. turnover is low in spite of a comparatively good labor market

8. A supervisor who has informal, friendly relationships with his subordinates is conducting himself

   A. *appropriately;* good informal relationships set the stage for better communication between the supervisor and subordinates on work-related problems
   B. *inappropriately;* subordinates who have informal relationships with their supervisor are not likely to accept his authority
   C. *appropriately;* friendly relationships between the supervisor and his subordinates will create a true feeling of equality between them
   D. *inappropriately;* subordinates are likely to become suspicious of insincerity and fearful of being manipulated

9. Specialization is a commonly-used method of increasing productivity and efficiency in a large organization. Task specialization means that separate and comparatively simple parts of a more complex job are performed by different employees.
   Of the following, this type of specialization probably would NOT

   A. reduce training costs
   B. permit the use of more specialized equipment
   C. simplify the development of job controls
   D. give most employees a greater sense of accomplishment

10. Some management experts who have studied informal communication patterns in large organizations believe that the office grapevine is an effective means of communication.
    Of the following, an IMPORTANT function performed by the grapevine is to

    A. permit feedback and spread information faster than most formal communication systems
    B. give employees important information from reliable sources
    C. permit management to identify rumor-mongers and troublemakers
    D. bring informal leaders to the attention of management

11. Recent studies of morale and productivity tend to show that 11.____

    A. the correlation between morale and productivity is rather low
    B. high morale is associated with high productivity
    C. low morale is associated with high productivity
    D. low morale is associated with low productivity

12. Research studies have indicated that teamwork among employees is MOST likely to result in higher productivity in a situation where 12.____

    A. employees accept as legitimate management's demands for higher productivity
    B. management strongly encourages the workers' demands spirit
    C. employees are unified for the purpose of protecting themselves against management's demands
    D. management does not encourage employees to make independent decisions

13. The relationship between boredom on the job and fatigue is CORRECTLY stated as follows: 13.____

    A. Boredom usually results in increased fatigue
    B. A worker usually becomes bored when he expends a minimum of physical energy
    C. Fatigue usually results in boredom
    D. A worker who is bored does not usually become fatigued

14. The *halo effect* can PROPERLY be suspected of harming supervisor-subordinate relationships when the supervisor 14.____

    A. does not discriminate between the good and poor work of an employee considered by him to be generally superior
    B. expects his subordinates to treat him in an impersonal and formal manner
    C. hesitates to discipline employees because of an extreme need for them to like him
    D. is unable to gain his employees' confidence because he cannot shed his reputation for being hardboiled and unfair

15. It is generally considered that the best interview is the one in which the interviewer talks less than the person interviewed.
    The one of the following which is an EFFECTIVE device to encourage the other person to talk during the interview is for the interviewer to 15.____

    A. summarize the feelings the person has expressed, omitting details and incidentals
    B. keep silent and show no indication of his reaction to what the person is saying
    C. clearly show his approval or disapproval of what the person is saying
    D. talk to the person in terms of concepts rather than specifics

16. Studies of groups of workers doing the same job under the same conditions have shown that there are always a few workers who have more accidents than the rest. The one of the following which is LEAST likely to be a finding of such studies is that those who have the MOST accidents PROBABLY are 16.____

    A. middle-aged
    B. poorly adjusted to work
    C. inexperienced at the job
    D. less efficient than other workers

17. Work measurement has been defined as *the determination of the proper amount of time and effort required for the effective performance of a specific task.*
Of the following, the factor which would be LEAST relevant in studying an operation by means of work measurement is whether the operation is

    A. repetitive with constant standards of quality
    B. compensated for at a prevailing rate of pay
    C. routine in nature and relatively easy to perform
    D. performed in large volume

18. Of the following, *participative management* can be defined BEST as a method in which

    A. subordinates have formed groups for the purpose of gaining participation in the decisions of management
    B. management makes a practice of encouraging subordinates as a group to discuss and participate in decisions on a wide variety of work-related problems
    C. managerial employees are given varied assignments on a rotating basis
    D. management gives all employees the opportunity to participate in major policy decisions

19. *Internalized motivation* has been described as a method of motivating employees by enabling them to derive satisfaction through doing the job itself. This approach to motivating employees would require management to

    A. assume that most employees like work and enjoy doing a good job
    B. encourage competition among employees for promotions and higher salaries
    C. emphasize improved fringe benefits and conditions of work
    D. consider employee needs to be more important than organizational needs

20. If a supervisor should find that he must issue an order his subordinates will probably resist, it is advisable for the supervisor to FIRST

    A. discuss the order with his subordinates and give them an opportunity to ask questions and make objections
    B. issue the order without comment and discourage discussion and objections by his subordinates
    C. inform his subordinates that he does not agree with the order he is going to give them, but must carry out the decisions of higher authority
    D. inform his subordinates that he will take disciplinary action against those who resist carrying out the order he will present to them

21. When a supervisor finds that his subordinates differ considerably in the amount of attention and guidance they require of him, it would be MOST advisable for the supervisor to

    A. adjust his supervisory practices according to individual needs
    B. give an equal amount of attention and guidance to each subordinate in order to be fair
    C. give less responsibility to subordinates who seek assistance
    D. permit employees who prefer independence to work strictly on their own

22. Connecting lines on an organization chart represent liaes of

    A. management quality controls
    B. work flow
    C. authority and responsibility
    D. fiscal accountability

23. *General supervision* has been defined as a method in which the supervisor makes assignments in broad, general terms and gives considerable autonomy to subordinates, in accordance with their knowledge and abilities.
    A supervisor who uses this method is LEAST likely to

    A. do different work from that of subordinates
    B. concentrate on long-range problems
    C. exert excessive pressure on subordinates
    D. devote considerable effort to training subordinates

24. Of the following, the MOST important reason why a supervisor should be cautious about giving subordinates advice about personal problems is that the

    A. subordinate may blame him if the advice turns out to be misleading
    B. supervisor should not discuss personal problems with subordinates on office time
    C. subordinate may lose confidence in his ability to perform on the job
    D. supervisor may not know enough to give helpful advice

25. Professional or technical consultants may be used MOST appropriately by a human services agency to

    A. direct staff conferences centered around programs
    B. give advice regarding the quality of service or the effectiveness of plans
    C. supervise implementation of programs they have developed
    D. direct the in-service training program

KEY (CORRECT ANSWERS)

1.	A	11.	A
2.	A	12.	A
3.	A	13.	A
4.	C	14.	A
5.	D	15.	A
6.	A	16.	A
7.	B	17.	B
8.	A	18.	B
9.	D	19.	A
10.	A	20.	A

21. A
22. C
23. C
24. D
25. B

EXAMINATION SECTION
TEST 1

DIRECTIONS: Each question or incomplete statement is followed by several suggested answers or completions. Select the one that BEST answers the question or completes the statement. *PRINT THE LETTER OF THE CORRECT ANSWER IN THE SPACE AT THE RIGHT.*

1. It is generally accepted that, of the following, the MOST important medium for developing integration and continuity in learning on the job is
    A. day-to-day experience on the job
    B. the supervisory conference
    C. the staff meeting
    D. the professional seminar

    1.____

2. Assume that you find that one of your workers is over-identifying with a particular client.
    Of the following, the MOST appropriate step for you to take FIRST in dealing with this situation is to
    A. transfer the cases to another worker
    B. inform the worker that he cannot give satisfactory service if he over-identifies with a client
    C. interview the client yourself to determine his feelings about his relationship with the worker
    D. arrange a conference with the worker to discuss the reasons for her over-identification with this client

    2.____

3. The one of the following which is the MOST likely reason why a newly-appointed supervisor would have a tendency to interfere actively in a relationship between one of his workers and a client is that the supervisor
    A. has unresolved feelings about relinquishing the role of worker, and has not yet accepted his role as supervisor
    B. must give direct assistance in the situation because the worker cannot handle it
    C. is attempting to share with his worker the knowledge and skill which he has developed in direct practice
    D. has not realized that immediate responsibility for work with clients has been delegated to others

    3.____

4. A worker who has a tendency to resist authority and supervision can be helped MOST effectively if, of the following, the supervisor
    A. behaves in a strict and impersonal manner so that the worker will accept his authority as a supervisor
    B. modifies the relationship so that he will be less authoritarian and threatening to the worker
    C. gives the worker a simple, matter-of-fact interpretation of the supervisory relationship and has an understanding acceptance of the worker's response
    D. temporarily establishes a peer relationship with the worker in order to overcome his resistance

    4.____

5. Before interviewing a newly-appointed worker for the first time, of the following, it is DESIRABLE for the supervisor to
   A. learn as much as he can about the worker's background and interests in order to eliminate the routine of asking questions and eliciting answers
   B. review the job information to be covered in order to make it easier to be impersonal and keep to the business at hand
   C. send the worker orientation material about the agency and the job and ask him to study it before the interview
   D. review available information about the worker in order to find an area of shared experience to serve as a *taking off* point for getting acquainted

6. In interviewing a new worker, of the following, it is IMPORTANT for the supervisor to
   A. give direction to the progress of the interview and maintain a leadership role throughout
   B. allow the worker to take the initiative in order to give him full scope for freedom of expression
   C. maintain a non-directional approach so that the worker will reveal his true attitudes and feelings
   D. avoid interrupting the worker, even though he seems to want to do all the talking

7. When a new worker, during his first few days, shows such symptoms of insecurity as *stage fright*, helpless immobility, or extreme talkativeness, of the following, it would be MOST helpful for the supervisor to
   A. start the worker out on some activity in which he is relatively secure
   B. ignore the symptoms and allow the worker to *sink or swim* on his own
   C. have a conference with the worker and interpret to him the reasons for his feelings of insecurity
   D. consider the probability that this worker may not be suited for a profession which requires skill in interpersonal relationships

8. Of the following, the MOST desirable method of minimizing workers' dependence on the supervisor and encouraging self-dependence is to
   A. hold group instead of individual supervisory conferences at regular intervals
   B. schedule individual supervisory conferences only in response to the workers' obvious need for guidance
   C. plan for progressive exposure to other opportunities for learning afforded by the agency and the community
   D. allow workers to learn by trial and error rather than by direct supervisory guidance

9. Of the following, it would NOT be appropriate for the supervisor to use early supervisory conferences with the new workers as a means of
   A. giving him direct practical help in order to get going on the job
   B. estimating the level of his native abilities, professional skills and experience
   C. getting clues as to his characteristic ways of learning in a new situation
   D. assessing his potential for future supervisory responsibility

10. Without careful planning by the supervisor for orientation of the new worker, an informal system of orientation by co-workers inevitably develops.
Such an informal system of orientation is USUALLY
    A. *beneficial*, because many new workers learn more readily when instructed by their peers
    B. *harmful*, because informal orientation by an undesignated co-worker can lead a new worker astray instead of helping him
    C. *beneficial*, because assumption by subordinates of responsibility for orientation will free the supervisor for other urgent work
    D. *harmful*, because such informal orientation by a co-worker will tend to destroy the authority of the supervisor

11. Of the following, the BEST way for a supervisor to assist a subordinate who has unusual work pressures is to
    A. relieve him of some of his cases until the pressures subside
    B. help him to decide which cases should be given the most attention during the period of pressure, and how to provide coverage for less urgent cases
    C. inform him that he must learn to tolerate and adjust to such pressures
    D. point out that he should learn to understand the causes of the pressures, which probably resulted from his own deficiencies

12. Many supervisors have a tendency to use case records mainly for the purpose of analysis of the workers' skill or evaluation of their performance.
Of the following, a PROBABLE result of this practice is that
    A. workers are likely to tie-in recording with supervisory evaluation of their work, without giving proper emphasis to their importance in improving service to clients
    B. the worker is likely to devote an inordinate amount of time to case records at the expense of his clients
    C. the records are likely to be too lengthy and detailed, limiting their value for other important purposes
    D. the records are likely to be of little value for administrative and research purposes

13. A common obstacle to adequate recording in a large social work agency is the fact that many workers consider recording to be a time-consuming chore.
In order to obtain the cooperation of staff in keeping proper records, of the following, it is MOST important for an agency to provide
    A. indisputable evidence of the intelligent use of records as tools in formulating policy and improving service
    B. a system of checks and controls to assure that workers are preparing adequate and timely records
    C. adequate clerical services and mechanical equipment for recording
    D. sufficient time for recording in the organization of every job

14. The one of the following which is NOT a purpose of keeping case records in an agency is
    A. planning
    B. research
    C. training
    D. job classification

15. When a supervisor is reviewing the records of a worker, of the following, he should plan to read
    A. records of new cases only, following up each interview selectively
    B. the total caseload, in order to determine which aspects of the worker's performance should be examined
    C. those records which the worker has brought to the supervisor's attention because of the need for help
    D. a block of records selected according to the worker's need for help, and some records selected at random

16. The one of the following which is the PRIMARY purpose of the regular staff meeting in an agency is
    A. initiation of action in order to get the agency's work done
    B. staff training and development
    C. program and policy determination
    D. communication of new policies and procedures

17. Of the following, group supervision in an agency is intended as a means of
    A. strengthening the total supervisory process
    B. shifting the focus of supervision from the individual to the group
    C. saving costs in terms of time and manpower
    D. influencing policy through group interaction

18. The supervisor's job brings him closer to such limiting factors in the operation of an agency as faulty administrative structure, shortage of funds and lack of facilities, inadequacies in personnel practices, community pressures, and excessive workload.
    For the supervisor to make a practice of communicating to his subordinates his feelings of frustration about such limitations in the work setting would be
    A. *appropriate*, because the worker will be more understanding of the supervisor's burdens and frustrations
    B. *inappropriate*, because the climate created will block rather than further the purposes of supervision
    C. *appropriate*, because such communication will create a more democratic climate between the worker and the supervisor
    D. *inappropriate*, because the supervisor must support and condone agency policies and practices in the presence of subordinates

19. A suggestion has been made that the teaching and administrative functions of supervision should be separated, so that the supervisor responsible for teaching would not be responsible for evaluation of the same workers.
    The one of the following which is the MOST important reason for this point of view is that
    A. elements that confer on the supervisor a position of authority and power unduly threaten the learning situation
    B. teaching skill and administrative ability do not usually go together

C. a supervisor who has been responsible for training a worker is likely to be prejudiced in his favor
D. performance evaluation and total job accountability should be two separate functions

20. In reviewing a worker's cases in preparation for a periodic evaluation, you note that she has done a uniformly good job with certain types of cases and poor work with other types of cases.
    Of the following, the BEST approach for you to take in this situation is to
    A. bring this to the worker's attention, find out why she favors certain types of clients, and discuss ways in which she can improve her service to all clients
    B. bring this to the worker's attention and suggest that she may need professional counseling, as she seems to be blocked in working with certain types of cases
    C. assign to her mainly those cases which she handles best and transfer the types of cases which she handles poorly to another worker
    D. accept the fact that a worker cannot be expected to give uniformly good service to all clients, and take no further action

20.____

KEY (CORRECT ANSWERS)

1.	B	11.	B
2.	D	12.	A
3.	A	13.	A
4.	C	14.	D
5.	D	15.	D
6.	A	16.	A
7.	A	17.	A
8.	C	18.	B
9.	D	19.	A
10.	B	20.	A

TEST 2

DIRECTIONS: Each question or incomplete statement is followed by several suggested answers or completions. Select the one that BEST answers the question or completes the statement. *PRINT THE LETTER OF THE CORRECT ANSWER IN THE SPACE AT THE RIGHT.*

1. Of the following, the choice of method to be used in the supervisory process should be influenced MOST by the
    A. number and type of cases carried by each worker
    B. emotional maturity of the worker
    C. number of workers supervised and their past experience
    D. subject matter to be learned and the long-range goals of supervision

    1.____

2. In an evaluation conference with a worker, the BEST approach for the supervisor to take is to
    A. help the worker to identify his strengths as a basis for working on his weaknesses
    B. identify the worker's weaknesses and help him overcome them
    C. allow the worker to identify his weaknesses first and then suggest ways of overcoming them
    D. discuss the worker's weaknesses but emphasize his strengths

    2.____

3. Assume that a worker is discouraged about the progress of his work and feels that it is futile to attempt to cope with many of his cases.
    Of the following, it would be BEST for the supervisor to
    A. suggest to the worker that such feelings are inappropriate for a professional worker
    B. tell the worker that he must seek professional help in order to overcome these feelings
    C. reduce the worker's caseload and give him cases that are less complex
    D. review with the worker several of his cases in which there were obvious accomplishments

    3.____

4. The supervisor is responsible for providing the worker with the following means of support, with the EXCEPTION of
    A. interest and advice on his personal problems
    B. instruction on community resources
    C. inspiration for carrying out the work of the agency
    D. understanding his strengths and limitations

    4.____

5. When a worker frequently takes the initiative in asking questions and discussing problems during a supervisory conference, this is PROBABLY an indication that the
    A. supervisor is not sufficiently interested in the work
    B. conference is a positive learning experience for the worker
    C. worker is hostile and resists supervision
    D. supervisor's position of authority is in question

    5.____

6. When a supervisor finds that one of his workers cannot accept criticism, of the following, it would be BEST for the supervisor to
    A. have the worker transferred to another supervisor
    B. warn the worker of disciplinary proceedings unless his attitude changes
    C. have the worker suspended after explaining the reason
    D. explore with the worker his attitude toward authority

7. Of the following, the condition which the inexperienced worker is LEAST likely to be aware of, without the guidance of the supervisor, is
    A. when he is successful in helping a client
    B. when he is not making progress in helping a client
    C. that he has a personal bias toward certain clients
    D. that he feels insecure because of lack of experience

8. The supervisor should provide an inexperienced worker with controls as well as freedom MAINLY because controls will
    A. enable him to set up his own controls sooner
    B. put him in a situation which is closer to the realities of life
    C. help him to use authority in handling a casework problem
    D. give him a feeling of security and lay the foundation for future self-direction

9. A result of the use of summarized case recording by the worker is that it
    A. gives the supervisor more responsibility for selecting cases to discuss in conference
    B. makes more time available for other activities
    C. lowers the morale of many workers
    D. decreases discussion of cases by the worker and the supervisor

10. The distinction between the role of professional workers and the role of auxiliary or sub-professional workers in an agency is based upon the
    A. position within the agency hierarchy
    B. amount of close supervision given
    C. emergent nature of tasks assigned
    D. functions performed

11. Of the following, the MOST important source of learning for the worker should be
    A. departmental directives and professional literature
    B. his co-workers in the agency
    C. the content of in-service training courses
    D. the clients in his caseload

12. A client is MOST likely to feel that he is receiving acceptance and understanding if the social worker
    A. gets detailed information about the client's problem
    B. demonstrates that he realistically understands the client's problem
    C. has an intellectual understanding of the client's problem
    D. offers the client assurance of assistance

13. A client will be MORE encouraged to speak freely about his problems if the worker
    A. avoids asking too many questions
    B. asks leading rather than pointed questions
    C. suggests possible answers
    D. identifies with the client

14. A client would be MOST likely to be able to accept help in a time of crisis and need if the worker
    A. explains agency policy to him
    B. responds immediately to the client's need
    C. explains why help cannot be given immediately
    D. reaches out to help the client establish his rightful claim for assistance

15. It is a generally accepted principle that the worker should interpret for himself what the client is saying, but usually should not pass his interpretation on to the client because the client
    A. will become hostile to the worker
    B. should arrive at his own conclusions at his own pace
    C. must request the interpretation first
    D. usually wants facts, rather than the worker's interpretation

16. In evaluating the client's capacity to cope with his problems, it is MOST important for the worker to assess his ability to
    A. form close relationships
    B. ask for help
    C. express his hostility
    D. verbalize his difficulties

17. When a worker finds that he disagrees strongly with an agency policy, it is DESIRABLE for him to
    A. share his feelings about the policy with his client
    B. understand fully why he has such strong feelings about the policy
    C. refer cases involving the policy to his supervisor
    D. refuse to give help in cases involving the policy

18. Which of the following practices is BEST for a supervisor to use when assigning work to his staff?
    A. Give workers with seniority the most difficult jobs
    B. Assign all unimportant work to the slower workers
    C. Permit each employee to pick the job he prefers
    D. Make assignments based on the workers' abilities

19. In which of the following instances is a supervisor MOST justified in giving commands to people under his supervision?
    When
    A. they delay in following instructions which have been given to them clearly
    B. they become relaxed and slow about work, and he wants to speed up their production
    C. he must direct them in an emergency situation
    D. he is instructing them on jobs that are unfamiliar to them

20. Which of the following supervisory actions or attitudes is MOST likely to result in getting subordinates to try to do as much work as possible for a supervisor?
    He
    A. shows that his most important interest is in schedules and production goals
    B. consistently pressures his staff to get the work out
    C. never fails to let them know he is in charge
    D. considers their abilities and needs while requiring that production goals be met

20.____

KEY (CORRECT ANSWERS)

1.	D	11.	D
2.	A	12.	B
3.	D	13.	D
4.	A	14.	D
5.	B	15.	B
6.	D	16.	A
7.	C	17.	B
8.	D	18.	D
9.	B	19.	C
10.	D	20.	D

TEST 3

DIRECTIONS: Each question or incomplete statement is followed by several suggested answers or completions. Select the one that BEST answers the question or completes the statement. *PRINT THE LETTER OF THE CORRECT ANSWER IN THE SPACE AT THE RIGHT.*

1. One of your workers comes to you and complains in an angry manner about your having chosen him for some particular assignment. In your opinion, the subject of the complaint is trivial land unimportant, but it seems to be quite important to your worker.
   The BEST of the following actions for you to take in this situation is to
   A. allow the worker to continue talking until he has calmed down and then explain the reasons for your having chosen him for that particular assignment
   B. warn the worker to moderate his tone of voice at once because he is bordering on insubordination
   C. tell the worker in a friendly tone that he is making a tremendous fuss over an extremely minor matter
   D. point out to the worker that you are his immediate supervisor and that you are running the unit in accordance with official policy

   1.____

2. The one of the following which is the LEAST desirable action for an assistant supervisor to take in disciplining a subordinate for an infraction of the rules is to
   A. caution him against repetition of the infraction, even if it is minor
   B. point out his progress in applying the rules at the same time that you reprimand him
   C. be as specific as possible in reprimanding him for rule infractions
   D. allow a cooling-off period to elapse before reprimanding him

   2.____

3. A training program for workers assigned to the intake section should include actual practice in simulated interviews under simulated conditions.
   The one of the following educational principles which is the CHIEF justification for this statement is that
   A. the workers will remember what they see better and longer than what they read or hear
   B. the workers will learn more effectively by actually doing the act themselves than they would learn from watching others do it
   C. the conduct of simulated interviews once or twice will enable them to cope with the real situation with little difficulty
   D. a training program must employ methods of a practical nature if the workers are to find anything of lasting value in it

   3.____

4. In order for a supervisor to employ the system of democratic leadership in his supervision, it would generally be BEST for him to
   A. allow his subordinates to assist in deciding on methods of work performance and job assignments but only in those areas where decisions have not been made on higher administrative levels

   4.____

B. allow his subordinates to decide how to do the required work, interposing his authority when work is not completed on schedule or is improperly completed
C. attempt to make assignments of work to individuals only of the type which they enjoy doing
D. maintain control over job assignment and work production, but allow the subordinates to select methods of work and internal conditions of work at democratically conducted staff conferences

5. In a unit in which supervision has been considered quite effective, it has become necessary to press for above-normal production for a limited period to achieve a required goal.
The one of the following which is a LEAST likely result of this pressure is that
   A. there will be more *griping* by employees
   B. some workers will do both more and better work than has been normal for them
   C. there will be an enhanced feeling of group unity
   D. there will be increased absenteeism

6. For a supervisor to encourage competitive feelings among his staff is
   A. *advisable*, chiefly because the workers will perform more efficiently when they have proper motivation
   B. *inadvisable*, chiefly because the workers will not perform well under the pressure of competition
   C. *advisable*, chiefly because the workers will have a greater incentive to perform their job properly
   D. *inadvisable*, chiefly because the workers may focus their attention on areas where they excel and neglect other essential aspects of the job

7. In selecting jobs to be assigned to a new worker, the supervisor should assign those jobs which
   A. give the worker the greatest variety of experience
   B. offer the worker the greatest opportunity to achieve concrete results
   C. present the worker with the greatest stimulation because of their interesting nature
   D. require the least amount of contact with outside agencies

8. A supervisor should avoid a detailed discussion of a worker-client interview with a new worker before the worker has fully recorded the interview CHIEFLY because such a discussion might
   A. cover matters which are already fully covered and explained in the written record
   B. make the worker forget some important deal learned during the interview
   C. color the recording according to the worker's reaction to his supervisor's opinions
   D. minimize the worker's feeling of having reached a decision independently

9. Some supervisors encourage their worker to submit a list of their questions about specific jobs or their comments about problems they wish to discuss in advance of the worker-supervisor conference.
   This practice is
   A. *desirable*, chiefly because it helps to stimulate and focus the worker's thinking about his caseload
   B. *undesirable*, chiefly because it will stifle the worker's free expression of his problems and attitudes
   C. *desirable*, chiefly because it will allow the conference to move along more smoothly and quickly
   D. *undesirable*, chiefly because it will restrict the scope of the conference and the variety of jobs discussed

9.____

10. An alert supervisor hears a worker apparently giving the wrong information to a client and immediately reprimands him severely.
    For the supervisor to reprimand the worker at his point is poor CHIEFLY because
    A. instruction must precede correct performance
    B. oral reprimands are less effective than written reprimands
    C. the worker was given no opportunity to explain his reasons for what he did
    D. more effective training can be obtained by discussing the errors with a group of workers

10.____

11. The one of the following circumstances when it would generally be MOST proper for a supervisor to do a job himself rather than to train a subordinate to do the job is when it is
    A. a job which the supervisor enjoys doing and does well
    B. not a very time-consuming job but an important one
    C. difficult to train another to do the job, yet is not difficult for the supervisor to do
    D. unlikely that this or any similar job will have to be done again at any future time

11.____

12. Effective training of subordinates requires that the supervisor understand certain facts about learning and forgetting processes.
    Among these is the fact that people GENERALLY
    A. forget what they learned at a much greater rate during the first day than during subsequent periods
    B. both learn and forget at a relatively constant rate and this rate is dependent upon their general intellectual capacity
    C. learn at a relatively constant rate except for periods of assimilation when the quantity of retained learning decreases while information is becoming firmly fixed in the mind
    D. learn very slowly at first when introduced to a new topic, after which there is a great increase in the rate of learning

12.____

13. It has been suggested that a subordinate who likes his superior will tend to do better work than one who does not.
    According to the MOST widely held current theories of supervision, this suggestion is a
    A. *bad* one, since personal relationships tend to interfere with proper professional relationships
    B. *bad* one, since the strongest motivating factors are fear and uncertainty
    C. *good* one, since liking one's superior is a motivating factor for good work performance
    D. *good* one, since liking one's supervisor is the most important factor in employee performance

14. One factor which might be given consideration in deciding upon the optimum span of control of a supervisor over his immediate subordinates is the position of the supervisor in the hierarchy of the organization.
    It is generally considered proper that the number of subordinates immediately supervised by a higher, upper echelon supervisor _____ the number supervised by lower level supervisors.
    A. is unrelated to and tends to form no pattern with
    B. should be about the same as
    C. should be larger than
    D. should be smaller than

15. The one of the following instances when it is MOST important for an upper level supervisor to follow the chain of command is when he is
    A. communicating decisions
    B. communicating information
    C. receiving suggestions
    D. seeking information

16. At the end of his probationary period, a supervisor should be considered potentially valuable in his position if he shows
    A. awareness of his areas of strength and weakness, identification with the administration of the department, and ability to learn under supervision
    B. skill in work, supervision, and administration, and a friendly democratic approach to the staff
    C. knowledge of departmental policies and procedures and ability to carry them out, ability to use authority, and ability to direct the work of the staff
    D. an identification with the department, acceptance of responsibility, and ability to give help to the individuals who are to be supervised

17. Good supervision is selective because
    A. it is not necessary to direct all the activities of the person
    B. a supervisor would never have time to know the whole caseload of a worker
    C. workers resent too much help from a supervisor
    D. too much reading is a waste of valuable time

18. An important administrative problem is how precisely to define the limits of authority that is delegated to subordinate supervisors.
Such definition of limits of authority should be
    A. as precise as possible and practicable in all areas
    B. as precise as possible and practicable in areas of function, but should allow considerable flexibility in the area of personnel management
    C. as precise as possible and practicable in the area
    D. of personnel management, but should allow considerable flexibility in the areas of function
    E. in general terms so as to allow considerable flexibility both in the areas of function and in the areas of personnel management

19. Experts in the field of personnel relations feel that it is generally a bad practice for subordinate employees to become aware of pending or contemplated changes in policy or organizational set-up via the *grapevine* CHIEFLY because
    A. evidence that one or more responsible officials have proved untrustworthy will undermine confidence in the agency
    B. the information disseminated by this method is seldom entirely accurate and generally spreads needless unrest among the subordinate staff
    C. the subordinate staff may conclude that the administration feels the staff cannot be trusted with the true information
    D. the subordinate staff may conclude that the administration lacks the courage to make an unpopular announcement through official channels

20. Supervision is subject to many interpretations, depending on the area in which it functions.
Of the following, the statement which represents the MOST appropriate meaning of supervision as it is known in social work practice is that it
    A. is a leadership process for the development of new leaders
    B. is an educational and administrative process aimed at teaching personnel the goal of improved service to the client
    C. is an activity aimed chiefly at insuring that workers will adhere to all agency directives
    D. provides the opportunity for administration to secure staff reaction to agency policies

21. A supervisor may utilize various methods in the supervisory process.
The one of the following upon which sound supervisory practice rests in the selection of supervisory techniques is
    A. an estimate of the worker arrived at through current and past evaluation of performance as well as through worker's participation
    B. the previous supervisor's evaluation and recommendation
    C. the worker's expression of his personal preference for certain types of experience
    D. the amount of time available to supervisor and supervisee

22. It is the practice of some supervisors, when they believe that it would be desirable for a subordinate to take a particular action in a case, to inform the subordinate of this in the form of a suggestion rather than in the form of a direct order.
In general, this method of getting a subordinate to take the desired action is
   A. *inadvisable*; it may create in the mind of the subordinate the impression that the supervisor is uncertain about the efficacy of her plan and is trying to avoid whatever responsibility she may have in resolving the case
   B. *advisable*; it provides the subordinate with the maximum opportunity to use her own judgment in handling the case
   C. *inadvisable*; it provides the subordinate with no clear-cut direction and, therefore, is likely to leave her with a feeling of uncertainty and frustration
   D. *advisable*; it presents the supervisor's view in a manner which will be most likely to evoke the subordinate's cooperation

23. A veteran supervisor noticed that one of her workers of average ability had begun developing some bad work habits, becoming especially careless in her recordkeeping. After reprimand from the supervisor, the investigator corrected her errors and has been doing satisfactory work since then.
For the supervisor to keep referring to this period of poor work during her weekly conferences with this employee would generally be considered poor personnel practice CHIEFLY because
   A. praise rather than criticism is generally the best method to use in improving the work of an unsatisfactory worker
   B. the supervisor cannot know whether the employee's errors will follow an established pattern
   C. the fault which evoked the original negative criticism no longer exists
   D. this would tend to frustrate the worker by making her strive overly hard to reach a level of productivity which is beyond her ability to achieve

24. Assume that you are now a supervisor in a specific unit. Two experienced investigators in your unit, both of whom do above average work, have for some time not gotten along with each other for personal reasons Their attitude toward one another has suddenly become hostile and noisy disagreement has taken place in the office.
The BEST action for you to take FIRST in this situation is to
   A. transfer one of the two investigators to another unit where contact with the other investigator will be unnecessary
   B. discuss the problem with the two investigators together, insisting that they confide in you and tell you the cause of their mutual antagonism
   C. confer with the two investigators separately, pointing out to each the need to adopt an adult professional attitude with respect to their on-the-job relations
   D. advise the two investigators that should the situation grow worse, disciplinary action will be considered

25. It has long been recognized that relationships exist between worker morale and working conditions.
The one of the following which BEST clarifies these existing relationships is that morale is
   A. affected for better or worse in direct relationship to the magnitude of the changes in working conditions for better or worse
   B. better when working conditions are better
   C. little affected by working conditions so long as the working conditions do not approach the intolerable
   D. more affected by the degree of interest shown in providing good working conditions than by the actual conditions and may, perversely, be highest when working conditions are worst

25.____

KEY (CORRECT ANSWERS)

1.	A		11.	D
2.	D		12.	A
3.	B		13.	C
4.	A		14.	D
5.	D		15.	A
6.	D		16.	D
7.	B		17.	A
8.	C		18.	A
9.	A		19.	B
10.	C		20.	B

21. A
22. D
23. C
24. C
25. D

EXAMINATION SECTION
TEST 1

DIRECTIONS: Each question or incomplete statement is followed by several suggested answers or completions. Select the one that BEST answers the question or completes the statement. *PRINT THE LETTER OF THE CORRECT ANSWER IN THE SPACE AT THE RIGHT.*

1. A specialist is meeting with a panel of local community leaders to determine their perceptions about the effectiveness of a recent outreach program. The leaders seem unresponsive to the specialist's questions, looking at the floor or each other without directly answering the specialist's questions.
   One strategy that might work to elicit the desired information would be to
   A. try to discern the hidden meaning of their silence
   B. adopt a mildly confrontational tone and remind them of what's at stake in the community
   C. keep asking open-ended questions and wait patiently for responses
   D. tell them to come back when they're ready to tell you their opinions

2. Each of the following statements about maintaining a community's attention is true, EXCEPT:
   A. The more challenging it is to pay attention to a message, the more likely it is that it will be attended to
   B. Listeners will be more motivated to pay attention if a speech is personally meaningful
   C. People will be more likely to attend if a speaker pauses to suggest natural transitions in a speech
   D. Listeners will attend to messages that stand out

3. Each of the following is a key strategy to integrative bargaining among community members in conflict, EXCEPT
   A. focusing on positions, rather than interests
   B. separating the people from the problem
   C. aiming for an outcome based on an objectively identified standard
   D. using active listening skills, such as rephrasing and questioning

4. Which of the following is NOT one of the major variables to take into account when considering a community needs assessment?
   A. State of program development   B. Resources available
   C. Demographics   D. Community attitudes

5. Which of the following groups would probably be formed specifically for, or be involved in, the purpose of addressing a specific unmet community need?
   A. An existing consumer group
   B. A council of community representatives
   C. A committee
   D. An existing community organization

6. If a public outreach campaign designed to mobilize a community fails, the MOST likely reason for this failure is that the campaign
   A. was not specific about what it wanted people to do
   B. was overly serious and did not appeal to people's sense of humor
   C. offered no incentive for the audience to make a change
   D. did not use language that appealed to the audience's emotions

7. Nationwide, the rate of involvement of elderly people in community-based programs demonstrates that they are
   A. under-served when compared to other age groups
   B. served at about the same rate as other age groups
   C. over-served when compared to other age groups
   D. hardly served at all

8. In projecting the likelihood of an education program's success, a domestic violence specialist identifies every single event that must occur to complete the project. The specialist then arranges these events in sequential order and allocates time requirements for each. Finally, the total time is calculated and a model showing all their events and timelines is charted.
   The specialist has used
   A. a PERT chart   B. a simulation
   C. a Markov model   D. the critical path method

9. When working with members of a predominantly African-American community, specialists from other cultural backgrounds should be aware that African-Americans tend to express thoughts and feelings through descriptions of
   A. physically tangible sensations   B. problems to be analyzed
   C. corresponding analogies   D. spiritual issues

10. Local nonprofessionals should be considered useful to a specialist who is looking to undertake a community outreach or educational initiative.
    Which of the following is LEAST likely to be a characteristic or role demonstrated by these community members?
    A. Undertaking support functions at the agency
    B. Serving as a communication channel between the agency and clients
    C. Encouraging greater agency acceptance and credibility within the community
    D. Helping the agency to accomplish meaningful change

11. In working with Native American groups or clients, it is important to recognize that the GREATEST health problem facing their communities today is
    A. domestic violence   B. depression and suicide
    C. alcoholism   D. tuberculosis

12. A specialist is facilitating a cooperative conflict resolution session between community members who have different opinions about what kinds of intervention services should be offered by the local adult protective services agency.
    Which of the following is NOT a guideline that should be followed in this process?
    A. Early in the negotiations, ask each party to name the issues on which they will positively not yield.
    B. Try to get the parties to view the issue from other points of view, beside the two or three conflicting ones.
    C. Have each side volunteer what it would be willing to do to resolve the conflict.
    D. At the end of the session, draw up a formal agreement with agreed-upon actions for both parties.

13. A specialist wants to evaluate the effectiveness of a local women's shelter. The shelter has suffered from lax participation, given the number of women who have been abused in the surrounding area. The specialist wants to speak with the women in the community who did not follow up on referrals to the shelter, and begins by visiting some of these women. After gaining the trust of these women, the specialist asks for the names of women they know who might be in need of help with a domestic violence situation.
    The specialist's approach in this case is _____ sampling.
    A. maximum variation   B. snowball
    C. convenience   D. typical case

14. When it comes to perceiving messages, people typically DON'T
    A. tend to simplify causal connections and sometimes even seek a single cause to explain what may be a highly complex effect
    B. tend to perceive messages independently of a categorical framework, especially if the message may be distorted by such an interpretation
    C. have a predisposition toward accepting any pattern that a speaker offers to explain seemingly unconnected facts
    D. tend to interpret things in the way they are viewed by their reference group

15. The elder members of Native American communities, regardless of kinship, are MOST commonly referred to as
    A. the ancients   B. father or mother
    C. grandfather or grandmother D. chiefs

16. Each of the following is typically an objective of community mobilization, EXCEPT:
    A. To convince existing community resources to alter their services or work together to address an unmet need
    B. To gather and distribute information to consumers and agencies about unmet needs

C. To publicize existing community resources and make them more accessible
D. To bring an unmet community need to public attention in order to achieve acceptance of and support for fulfilling the need

17. Research in community outreach shows that women often build friendships through shared positive feelings, whereas men often build friendships through
    A. metacommunication
    B. catharsis
    C. impression management
    D. shared activities

17.____

18. Typically, the FIRST step in a community-needs assessment is to
    A. identify community's strengths
    B. explore the nature of the neighborhood
    C. get to know the area and its residents
    D. talk to people in the community

18.____

19. Most public relations experts agree that _____ exposure(s) to a message is the minimum just to get the message noticed. If the aim of a public outreach campaign is action or a change in behavior, the agency budget must plan for more exposures.
    A. one   B. two   C. three   D. four

19.____

20. In the program development/community liaison model of community work and public outreach, the PRIMARY constituency is considered to be
    A. community representatives and the service agency board or administrators
    B. elected officials, social agencies, and interagency organizations
    C. marginalized or oppressed population groups in a city or region
    D. residents of a neighborhood, parish or rural county

20.____

21. Social or interpersonal problems in many African-American communities have their roots in
    A. personality deficits
    B. unresolved family conflicts
    C. poor communication
    D. external stressors

21.____

22. A public outreach campaign should
    I. focus on short-term, measurable goals, rather than ultimate outcomes
    II. try to alter entrenched attitudes within a short time, with powerfully worded messages
    III. proceed in steps or phases, each of which lays out a mechanism that leads to the desired effect
    IV. ignore causes that led to a problem, and instead focus on solutions

    The CORRECT answer is:
    A. I and II   B. II and III   C. III only   D. I, II, III and IV

22.____

23. Research findings indicate that in listing preferences for helping professional attributes, individuals from culturally diverse groups are MOST likely to consider _____ as more important than _____.
    A. personality similarity; either race/ethnic similarity or attitude similarity
    B. therapist experience; any kind of similarity
    C. race/ethnic similarity; attitude similarity
    D. attitude similarity; race/ethnic similarity

24. Each of the following is considered to be an objective of community organization EXCEPT
    A. effecting changes in the distribution of decision-making power
    B. helping people develop and strengthen the traits of self-direction and cooperation
    C. effecting and maintaining the balance between needs and resources in a community
    D. helping people deal with their problems by developing alternative behaviors

25. A specialist is helping the adult protective services agency to design a public outreach campaign. The topic to be addressed is complex, public understanding is low, and most professionals at the agency feel that having more complete information might change the opinions of community members. Which method of pre-campaign research is probably MOST appropriate?
    A. Deliberative polling
    B. Attitude scales
    C. Surveys or questionnaires
    D. Focus groups

KEY (CORRECT ANSWERS)

1.	C		11.	C
2.	A		12.	A
3.	A		13.	B
4.	C		14.	B
5.	C		15.	C
6.	A		16.	B
7.	A		17.	D
8.	D		18.	B
9.	C		19.	C
10.	A		20.	A

21. D
22. C
23. D
24. D
25. A

TEST 2

DIRECTIONS: Each question or incomplete statement is followed by several suggested answers or completions. Select the one that BEST answers the question or completes the statement. *PRINT THE LETTER OF THE CORRECT ANSWER IN THE SPACE AT THE RIGHT.*

1. A specialist has been called in to resolve a dispute between two community leaders who have been arguing about the level of service needed within the community. The discussion has been going on for several hours when the specialist arrives, and both people seem to be upset.
After calming the two down and getting each of them to agree on a statement of the problem, the specialist should ask each person to
   A. summarize his or her argument in three main points
   B. explain why he or she became so upset
   C. clearly state, in objective terms, the position of the other in a form that meets with the other's approval
   D. identify the best alternative outcome, other than their presumed ideal

   1.____

2. In evaluating the impact of a public outreach campaign, the _____ model can be used early in the campaign to address first impressions.
   A. exposure or advertising
   B. expert interview
   C. impact monitoring or process
   D. experimental or quasi-experimental

   2.____

3. When trying to motivate an older population to take action on a community problem, it is helpful to remember that older people
   A. are more self-reliant in their decision-making than other members of the same family
   B. often need more time to decide than younger people
   C. are more likely than younger people to view community problems self-referentially
   D. tend to take a pragmatic, rather than philosophical, view of life

   3.____

4. The method of group or community decision-making that is normally MOST time-consuming is
   A. majority opinion   B. consensus
   C. expert opinion   D. authority rule

   4.____

5. A local adult protective services agency has identified one of the goals of its recent public outreach campaign to be the mobilization of activists.
The campaign should probably
   A. target neutral audiences
   B. home in on supporters
   C. stick to purely factual information
   D. try to persuade community fence-sitters

   5.____

6. Research of Native American youths' perceptions of family concerns for their well-being has generally found that these youths
    A. have a high degree of uncertainty about their families' feelings toward them
    B. believe their families don't care about them
    C. believe that their mothers care a great deal about them, but their fathers don't
    D. believe their families care a great deal about them

7. A domestic violence specialist is developing a new outreach program for the local community. The specialist has defined the target problem, set program goals, and planned the actions that will take place as a result of the program. Most likely, the next step will be to
    A. evaluate the resources available to achieve program goals
    B. define and sequence the steps that will be taken to achieve program goals
    C. determine how the program will be evaluated
    D. decide how the program will operate

8. Elder: *I'm so glad to have someone to talk to, someone who really understands my problem.*
   Specialist: *It is nice to be able to talk to someone who will listen.*
   Elder: *That's for sure.*
   In the above exchange, what listening skill is evident in the underlined statement?
    A. Verbatim response
    B. Paraphrasing
    C. Advising
    D. Evaluation

9. Which of the following activities is involved in the specialist's task of mobilizing?
    A. Meeting individuals in the community with problems and assisting them in finding help
    B. Identifying unmet community needs
    C. Speaking out against an unjust policy or procedure
    D. Developing new services or linking presently available services to meet community needs

10. The preliminary research associated with a public outreach campaign should FIRST be aimed at determining
    A. the budget
    B. the message's ultimate audience
    C. what media to use
    D. the short-term behavioral goals of the campaign

11. A specialist in a low-income community wants to plan programs that will deal with the influence of unemployment on domestic disturbances. The specialist needs to know not only how many unemployed people are in the community now, but also how many people will be unemployed at any particular tie in the future, and how those numbers will vary given certain conditions.

Probably the BEST way to trace employment rates over time and within differing conditions is through the use of
- A. the critical path
- B. linear programming
- C. difference equations
- D. the Markov model

12. Generally, public outreach programs—whatever their stated goal—should
    I. create a sense of urgency about a problem
    II. decline to identify opponents of the issue or idea
    III. propose concrete, easily understandable solutions
    IV. urge a specific action

    The CORRECT answer is:
    A. I only   B. I, III and IV   C. II and III   D. I, II, III and IV

13. Which of the following methods of community needs assessment relies to the GREATEST degree on existing public records?
    - A. Social indicators
    - B. Field study
    - C. Rates under treatment
    - D. Key informant

14. During an interview with a Native American client, a specialist is careful to maintain close and nearly constant eye contact.
    The client is MOST likely to interpret this as a(n)
    - A. show of high concern
    - B. sign of disrespect
    - C. uncomfortable assumption of intimacy
    - D. attempt to intimidate

15. The BEST strategy for addressing an audience that is known to be captive, or even hostile, is to
    - A. refer to experiences in common
    - B. flatter the audience
    - C. joke about things in or near the audience
    - D. plead for fairness

16. Integrative conflict resolution is characterized by
    - A. an overriding concern to maximize joint outcomes
    - B. one side's interests opposing the other's
    - C. a fixed and limited amount of resources to be divided, so that the more one group gets, the less another gets
    - D. manipulation and withholding information as negotiation strategies

17. A specialist wants to learn how to interact with the members of a largely Latino community in a more culturally sensitive way.
    Which of the following is NOT a guideline for interacting with members of a Latino community?
    - A. Efforts to foster independence and self-reliance may be interpreted by many Latinos as a lack of concern for others.
    - B. Efforts to deal one-on-one with an adolescent client may serve to alienate the parents, especially the mother.

C. A nonverbal gesture, such as lowering the eyes, is interpreted by many Latinos as a sign of respect and deference to authority.
D. In much of Latino culture, the focus of control for problems tends to be much more external than internal.

18. Each of the following is a supporting assumption of community organization, EXCEPT:
    A. Democracy requires cooperative participation.
    B. In order for communities to change, it is necessary for each individual in the community to be willing to change.
    C. Communities often need help with organization and planning.
    D. Holistic approaches work better than fragmented or ad-hoc programs.

19. Helping professionals often have difficulty to bring community resources together to fulfill unmet community needs.
    Which of the following is NOT usually a reason for this?
    A. Some community groups resist assistance when it is offered.
    B. Few community groups make their needs known.
    C. Community resources frequently change the type of services they offer.
    D. Often, community resources prefer to work alone.

20. When dealing with groups or populations of elderly clients, specialists should be mindful that about _____ of the nation's elderly suffer from mental health problems.
    A. a tenth   B. a quarter   C. a third   D. half

21. In an African-American community, a specialist from another culture should recognize that church participation, for most African-Americans, is viewed as a
    A. method for maintaining control and communicating competency
    B. way of depersonalizing problems or troubles
    C. way to divert attention away from problems
    D. means of cathartic emotional release

22. Adult protective service programs supported by state statutes protect elderly people from abuse and neglect under the doctrine of
    A. parens patriae   B. habeas corpus
    C. in loco parentis   D. volenti non fit injuria

23. In terms of public outreach, which of the following statements about an audience is NOT generally true?
    A. The more heterogeneous the audience, the more necessary it will be to use specific examples and appeals to certain types of people.
    B. The smaller the audience, the more likely that its members will share assumptions and values.
    C. When the speaker does not know the status of an audience, it is best to assume that they are captive rather than voluntary.
    D. The larger an audience, the more formal a presentation is likely to be.

24. A specialist often spends time in the places frequented by community residents. She listens carefully to what residents seem most concerned about, and engages many in conversations, asking them how they see the problems in the community. During these conversations, she makes mental notes about whether the statements of the problems are the same things that are mentioned in their conversations. From these conversations, the worker determines what she thinks the unmet needs of the community are.
Which of the key issues in identifying unmet needs has the worker neglected to address?
    A. The different points of view regarding the issues, and whether there is any common ground
    B. Whether the stated problems and conversations with community residents reflect the same concerns
    C. How community residents define the issues
    D. What the residents talk about with one another in a community

25. Which of the following political styles should be used to promote an issue that could become controversial if it is perceived to involve major reforms?
    A. High-conflict, polarized
    B. High-conflict, consensual
    C. Moderate conflict, compromise-oriented
    D. Low-conflict, technical

KEY (CORRECT ANSWERS)

1.	C	11.	D
2.	A	12.	B
3.	B	13.	A
4.	B	14.	B
5.	B	15.	A
6.	D	16.	A
7.	A	17.	D
8.	B	18.	B
9.	D	19.	C
10.	B	20.	B

21. D
22. A
23. A
24. A
25. D

REPORT WRITING

EXAMINATION SECTION

TEST 1

DIRECTIONS: Each question or incomplete statement is followed by several suggested answers or completions. Select the one that BEST answers the question or completes the statement. *PRINT THE LETTER OF THE CORRECT ANSWER IN THE SPACE AT THE RIGHT.*

Questions 1-3.

DIRECTIONS: Questions 1 to 3 are based on the following example of a report. The report consists of ten numbered sentences, some of which are *not* consistent with the principles of good report writing.

(1) On the evening of February 24, Roscoe and Leroy, two members of the "Red Devils," were entering with a bottle of wine in their hands. (2) It was unusually good wine for these boys to buy, (3) I told them to give me the bottle and they refused, and added that they wouldn't let anyone "put them out." (4) I told them they were entitled to have a good time, but they could not do it the way they wanted; there were certain rules they had to observe. (5) At this point, Roscoe said he had seen me box at camp and suggested that Leroy not accept my offer. (6) Then I said firmly that the admission fee did not give them the authority to tell me what to do. (7) I also told them that, if they thought I would fight them over such a matter, they were sadly mistaken. (8) I added, however, that we could go to the gym right now and settle it another way if they wished. (9) Leroy immediately said that he was sorry, he had not understood the rules, and he did not want his quarter back. (10) On the other hand, they would not give up their bottle either, so they left the premises.

1. Only material that is relevant to the main thought of a report should be included. Which of the following sentences from the report contains material which is LEAST relevant to this report? Sentence
 "A. 2   B. 3   C. 8   D. 9

1.____

2. A good report should be arranged in logical order. Which of the following sentences from the report does NOT appear in its proper sequence in the report? Sentence
 A. 3   B. 5   C. 7   D. 9

2.____

3. Reports should include all essential information. Of the following, the MOST important fact that is *missing* from this report is:
 A. Who was involved in the incident   B. How the incident was resolved
 C. When the incident took place   D. Where the incident took place

3.____

4. The MOST serious of the following faults *commonly* found in explanatory reports is
 A. the use of slang terms   B. excessive details
 C. personal bias   D. redundancy

4.____

5. In reviewing a report he has prepared to submit to his superiors, a supervisor finds that his paragraphs are a typewritten page long and decides to make some revisions.
   Of the following, the MOST important question he should ask about each paragraph is
   A. Are the words too lengthy?
   B. Is the idea under discussion too abstract?
   C. Is more than one central thought being expressed?
   D. Are the sentences too long?

   5.____

6. The summary or findings of a long management report intended for the typical manager should, *generally*, appear _____ the report.
   A. at the very beginning of	B. at the end of
   C. throughout	D. in the middle of

   6.____

7. In preparing a report that includes several tables, if not otherwise instructed, the typist should MOST properly include a list of tables
   A. in the introductory part of the report
   B. at the end of each chapter in the body of the report
   C. in the supplementary part of the report as an appendix
   D. in the supplementary part of the report as a part of the index

   7.____

8. When typing a preliminary draft of a report, the one of the following which you should *generally* NOT do is to
   A. erase typing errors and deletions rather than "X"ing them out
   B. leave plenty of room at the top, bottom, and sides of each page
   C. make only the number of copies that you are asked to make
   D. type double or triple space

   8.____

9. When you determine the methods of emphasis you will use in typing the titles, headings and subheadings of a report, the one of the following which it is MOST important to keep in mind is that
   A. all headings of the same rank should be typed in the same way
   B. all headings should be typed in the single style which is most pleasing to the eye
   C. headings should not take up more than one-third of the page width
   D. only one method should be used for all headings, whatever their rank

   9.____

10. The one of the following ways in which inter-office memoranda *differ* from long formal reports is that they, *generally*,
    A. are written as if the reader is familiar with the vocabulary and technical background of the writer
    B. do not have a "subject line" which describes the major topic covered in the text
    C. include a listing of reference materials which support the memo writer's conclusions
    D. require that a letter of transmittal be attached

    10.____

11. It is *preferable* to print information on a field report rather than write it out longhand MAINLY because
    A. printing takes less time to write than writing long hand
    B. printing is usually easier to read than longhand writing
    C. longhand writing on field reports is not acceptable in court cases
    D. printing occupies less space on a report than longhand writing

12. Of the following characteristics of a written report, the one that is MOST important is its
    A. length   B. accuracy   C. organization   D. grammar

13. A written report to your superior contains many spelling errors.
    Of the following statements relating to spelling errors, the one that is MOST NEARLY correct is that
    A. this is unimportant as long as the meaning of the report is clear
    B. readers of the report will ignore the many spelling errors
    C. readers of the report will get a poor opinion of the writer of the report
    D. spelling errors are unimportant as long as the grammar is correct

14. Written reports to your superior should have the same general arrangement and layout.
    The BEST reason for this requirement is that the
    A. report will be more accurate
    B. report will be more complete
    C. person who reads the report will know what the subject of the report is
    D. person who reads the report will know where to look for information in the report

15. The first paragraph of a report usually contains detailed information on the subject of the report.
    Of the following, the BEST reason for this requirement is to enable the
    A. reader to quickly find the subject of the report
    B. typist to immediately determine the subject of the report so that she will understand what she is typing
    C. clerk to determine to whom copies of the report will be needed
    D. typist to quickly determine how many copies of the report will be needed

16. Of the following statements concerning reports, the one which is LEAST valid is:
    A. A case report should contain factual material to support conclusions made
    B. An extremely detailed report may be of less value than a brief report giving the essential facts
    C. Highly technical language should be avoided as far as possible in preparing a report to be used at a court trial
    D. The position of the important facts in a report does not influence the emphasis placed on them by the reader

17. Suppose that you realize that you have made an error in a report that has been forwarded to another unit. You know that this error is not likely to be discovered for some time.
Of the following, the MOST advisable course of action for you to take is to
    A. approach the supervisor of the other unit on an informal basis, and ask him to correct the error
    B. say nothing about it since most likely one error will not invalidate the entire report
    C. tell your supervisor immediately that you have made an error so that it may be corrected, if necessary
    D. wait until the error is discovered and then admit that you had made it

18. In a report, words in a sentence must be arranged properly to make sure that the intended meaning of the sentence is clear.
The sentence below that does NOT make sense because a clause has been separated from the word on which its meaning depends is:
    A. To be a good writer, clarity is necessary.
    B. To be a good writer, you must write clearly.
    C. You must write clearly to be a good writer.
    D. Clarity is necessary to good writing.

19. The use of a graph to show statistical data in a report is *superior* to a table because it
    A. emphasizes approximations
    B. emphasizes facts and relationships more dramatically
    C. presents data more accurately
    D. is easily understood by the average reader

20. Of the following, the degree of formality required of a written report is, MOST likely to depend on the
    A. subject matter of the report
    B. frequency of its occurrence
    C. amount of time available for its preparation
    D. audience for whom the report is intended

Questions 21-25.

DIRECTIONS: Questions 21 through 25 consist of sets of four sentences lettered A, B, C, and D. For each question, choose the sentence which is grammatically and stylistically MOST appropriate for use in a formal written report.

21. A. It is recommended, therefore, that the impasse panel hearings are to be convened on September 30.
    B. It is therefore recommended that the impasse panel hearings be convened on September 30.
    C. Therefore, it is recommended to convene the impasse panel hearings on September 30.
    D. It is recommended that the impasse panel hearings therefore should be convened on September 30.

22.
- A. Penalties have been assessed for violating the Taylor Law by several unions.
- B. When they violated provisions of the Taylor Law, several unions were later penalized.
- C. Several unions have been penalized for violating provisions of the Taylor Law.
- D. Several unions' violating provisions of the Taylor Law resulted in them being penalized.

22.____

23.
- A. The number of disputes settled through mediation has increased significantly over the past two years.
- B. The number of disputes settled through mediation are increasing significantly over two-year periods.
- C. Over the past two years, through mediation, the number of disputes settled increased significantly.
- D. There is a significant increase over the past two years of the number of disputes settled through mediation.

23.____

24.
- A. The union members will vote to determine if the contract is to be approved.
- B. It is not yet known whether the union members will ratify the proposed contract.
- C. When the union members vote, that will determine the new contract.
- D. Whether the union members will ratify the proposed contract, it is not yet known.

24.____

25.
- A. The parties agreed to an increase in fringe benefits in return for greater work productivity.
- B. Greater productivity was agreed to be provided in return for increased fringe benefits.
- C. Productivity and fringe benefits are interrelated; the higher the former, the more the latter grows.
- D. The contract now provides that the amount of fringe benefits will depend upon the level of output by the workers.

25.____

KEY (CORRECT ANSWERS)

1.	A		11.	B
2.	B		12.	B
3.	D		13.	C
4.	C		14.	D
5.	C		15.	A
6.	A		16.	D
7.	A		17.	C
8.	A		18.	A
9.	A		19.	B
10.	A		20.	D

21. B
22. C
23. A
24. B
25. A

TEST 2

DIRECTIONS: Each question or incomplete statement is followed by several suggested answers or completions. Select the one that BEST answers the question or completes the statement. *PRINT THE LETTER OF THE CORRECT ANSWER IN THE SPACE AT THE RIGHT.*

Questions 1-4.

DIRECTIONS: Questions 1 through 4 are to be answered on the basis of the following report which was prepared by a supervisor for inclusion in his agency's annual report.

Line #

1 On Oct. 13, I was assigned to study the salaries paid
2 to clerical employees in various titles by the city and by
3 private industry in the area.
4 In order to get the data I needed, I called Mr. Johnson at
5 the Bureau of the Budget and the payroll officers at X Corp.-
6 a brokerage house, Y Co. –an insurance company, and Z Inc. –
7 a publishing firm. None of them was available and I had to call
8 all of them again the next day.
9 When I finally got the information I needed, I drew up a
10 chart, which is attached. Note that not all of the companies I
11 contacted employed people at all the different levels used in the
12 city service.
13 The conclusions I draw from analyzing this information is
14 as follows: The city's entry-level salary is about average for
15 the region; middle-level salaries are generally higher in the
16 city government than in private industry; but salaries at the
17 highest levels in private industry are better than city em-
18 ployees' pay.

1. Which of the following criticisms about the style in which this report is written is MOST valid?   1._____
   A. It is too informal.
   B. It is too concise.
   C. It is too choppy.
   D. The syntax is too complex.

2. Judging from the statements made in the report, the method followed by this employee in performing his research was   2._____
   A. *good*; he contacted a representative sample of businesses in the area
   B. *poor*; he should have drawn more definite conclusions
   C. *good*; he was persistent in collecting information
   D. *poor*; he did not make a thorough study

3. One sentence in this report contains a grammatical error. This sentence *begins* on line number   3._____
   A. 4   B. 7   C. 10   D. 13

4. The type of information given in this report which should be presented in footnotes or in an appendix, is the
   A. purpose of the study
   B. specifics about the businesses contacted
   C. reference to the chart
   D. conclusions drawn by the author

5. Of the following, a DISTINGUISHING characteristic of a written report intended for the head of your agency as compared to a report prepared for a lower-echilon staff member is that the report for the agency head should, *usually*, include
   A. considerably more detail, especially statistical data
   B. the essential details in an abbreviated form
   C. all available source material
   D. an annotated bibliography

6. Assume that you are asked to write a lengthy report for use by the administrator of your agency, the subject of which is "The Impact of Proposed New Data Processing Operations on Line Personnel" in your agency. You decide that the *most* appropriate type of report for you to prepare is an analytical report, including recommendations.
   The MAIN reason for your decision is that
   A. the subject of the report is extremely complex
   B. large sums of money are involved
   C. the report is being prepared for the administrator
   D. you intend to include charts and graphs

7. Assume that you are preparing a report based on a survey dealing with the attitudes of employees in Division X regarding proposed new changes in compensating employees for working overtime. Three percent of the respondents to the survey voluntarily offer an unfavorable opinion on the method of assigning overtime work, a question not specifically asked of the employees. On the basis of this information, the MOST appropriate and significant of the following comments for you to make in the report with regard to employees' attitudes on assigning overtime work is that
   A. an insignificant percentage of employees dislike the method of assigning overtime work
   B. three percent of the employees in Division X dislike the method of assigning overtime work
   C. three percent of the sample selected for the survey voiced an unfavorable opinion on the method of assigning overtime work
   D. some employees voluntarily voiced negative feelings about the method of assigning overtime work, making it impossible to determine the extent of this attitude

8. Assume that you have been asked to prepare a narrative summary of the monthly reports submitted by employees in your division.
   In preparing your summary of this month's reports, the FIRST step to take is to
   A. read through the reports, noting their general content and any unusual features
   B. decide how many typewritten pages your summary should contain
   C. make a written summary of each separate report, so that you will not have to go back to the original reports again
   D. ask each employee which points he would prefer to see emphasized in your summary

8._____

9. Assume that an administrative officer is writing a brief report to his superior outlining the advantages of matrix organization.
   Of the following, it would be INCORRECT to state that
   A. in matrix organization, a project is emphasized by designating one individual as the focal point for all matters pertaining to it
   B. utilization of manpower can be flexible in matrix organization because reservoir of specialists is maintained in the line operations
   C. the usual line-staff management is generally reversed in matrix organization
   D. in matrix organization, responsiveness to project needs is generally faster due to establishing needed communication lines and decision points

9._____

10. Written reports dealing with inspections of work and installations SHOULD be
    A. as long and detailed as practicable
    B. phrased with personal interpretations
    C. limited to the important facts of the inspection
    D. technically phrased to create an impression on superiors

10._____

11. It is important to use definite, exact words in preparing a descriptive report and to avoid, as much as possible, nouns that have vague meanings and, possibly, a different meaning for the reader than for the author.
    Which of the following sentences contains only nouns that are *definite* and *exact*?
    A. The free enterprise system should be vigorously encouraged in the United States.
    B. Arley Swopes climbed Mount Everest three times last year.
    C. Beauty is a characteristic of all the women at the party.
    D. Gil Noble asserts that he is a real democrat.

11._____

12. One way of shortening n unnecessarily long report is to reduce sentence length by eliminating the use of several words where a single one that does not alter the meaning will do.
    Which of the following sentences CANNOT be shortened without losing some of its information content?
    A. After being polished, the steel ball bearings ran at maximum speed.
    B. After the close of the war, John Taylor was made the recipient of a pension.
    C. In this day and age, you can call anyone up on the telephone.
    D. She is attractive in appearance, but she is a rather selfish person.

12._____

13. Employees are required to submit written reports of all unusual occurrences promptly.
    The BEST reason for such promptness is that the
    A. report may be too long if made at one's convenience
    C. report will tend to be more accurate as to facts
    D. employee is likely to make a better report under pressure

14. In making a report, it is poor practice to erase information on the report in order to make a change because
    A. there may be a question of what was changed and why it was changed
    B. you are likely to erase through the paper and tear the report
    C. the report will no longer look neat and presentable
    D. the duplicate copies will be smudged

15. The one of the following which BEST describes a periodic report is that it
    A. provides a record of accomplishments for a given time span and a comparison with similar time spans in the past
    B. covers the progress made in a project that has been postponed
    C. integrates, summarizes, and, perhaps, interprets published data on technical or scientific material
    D. describes a decision, advocates a policy or action, and presents facts in support of the writer's position

16. The PRIMARY purpose of including pictorial illustrations in a formal report is *usually* to
    A. amplify information which has been adequately treated verbally
    B. present details that are difficult to describe verbally
    C. provide the reader with a pleasant, momentary distraction
    D. present supplementary information incidental to the main ideas developed in the report

KEY (CORRECT ANSWERS)

1.	A		6.	A
2.	D		7.	D
3.	D		8.	A
4.	B		9.	C
5.	B		10.	C

11. B.
12. A.
13. C
14. A.
15. A.
16 B.

EXAMINATION SECTION
TEST 1

DIRECTIONS: Each sentence contains one error in spelling, diction, or grammar which may be corrected by changing one word. Underline the faulty word and write your correction in the first column opposite the sentence. Then, in the second column, write C if the sentence is correctly punctuated, F if the sentence has faulty punctuation. Make the necessary change in punctuation in the typed sentence.

		CORRECTION	PUNCTUATION
1.	Neither of the books, which Miss Smith suggested, are available at the library.		
2.	Many a typist writing in haste has mispelled "benefited."		
3.	Mr. Ames, together with his two sons, attend church every Sunday; their regularity, in fact, is almost unbelievable.		
4.	Although I agree with you on most subjects, I differ from you on this question.		
5.	My new duties are different than my former ones, however, I infer from your comments that I am giving satisfaction.		
6.	ABC, a local textile firm, is employing two of our students—Mary and I.		
7.	Which of your friends writes to you most often Edith or Anne?		
8.	The new of Ann and John getting married came as a complete surprise to us.		
9.	Rachel, Mary, and Mrs. Mason, have all announced that their going to the meeting.		
10.	The supervisor, who gave the report, referred to data which has been collected in the file.		
11.	If I was in your place—and I'm sorry I'm not—I'd do just what you plan to do in this matter.		

12. Miss Jones, the Supervisor of Files, has said said that we have less folders in use than we should have.

13. The E Company which is now located on Seventh Avenue, will build their new office building on Fifth Avenue.

14. It was Lee and me, not you and she, who planned this meeting.

15. I expect everyone but me to have their plans finished by Thursday, mine will keep me busy until next week.

16. The Committee, having arrived at it's decision, adjourned the meeting.

17. A young woman, together with three cats, a dog, and a parakeet, live in a nearby apartment.

18. One of the typists or bookkeepers, must have dropped their cigarette on the floor.

19. Three plural possessives which give many people trouble are: ladies' boys', and thiefs'.

20. Neither Mrs. Blake nor her daughter has swam in the ocean all summer; though each is a good swimmer.

21. The boys and the girls go in the building through separate entrances.

22. The lawyer advised his client to accept the altared contract, but the suggestion was ignored.

23. Occasionally a series of tests are given for the benefit of personnel, who seek promotion.

24. Don't anyone here know the correct date?

25. A new, well-planned, sketch lead us to our own office.

KEY (CORRECT ANSWERS)

CORRECTION	PUNCTUATION
1. Underline are; replace by is	1. F (remove commas (,) after books and after suggested)
2. Underline mispelled; replace by misspelled	2. C
3. Underline attend; replace by attends	3. C
4. Underline from; replace by with	4. C
5. Underline than; replace by from	5. F (remove comma (,) after ones; replace by semicolon (;)
6. Underline I; replace by me	6. C
7. Underline most; replace by more	7. F (add comma (,) after often)
8. Underline John; replace by John's	8. C
9. Underline their; replace by they're	9. F (remove comma (,) after Mason)
10. Underline has; replace by have	10. F (remove comma (,) after supervisor and after report)
11. Underline was; replace by were	11. C
12. Underline less; replace by fewer	12. C
13. Underline their; replace by its	13. F (place comma (,) after Company)
14. Underline me; replace by I	14. C
15. Underline their; replace by his	15. F (remove comma (,) after Thursday; replace by semicolon (;))
16. Underline it's; replace by its	16. C
17. Underline live; replace by lives	17. C
18. Underline their; replace by his	18. F (remove comma (,) after bookkeepers)
19. Underline thiefs'; replace by thieves'	19. F (place comma (,) after ladies')

4 (#1)

20.	Underline swam; replace by swum	20.	F (remove semicolon (;) after summer; replace by comma (,))
21.	Underline in; replace by into	21.	C
22.	Underline altared; replace by altered	22.	C
23.	Underline are; replace by is	23.	F (remove comma (,) after personnel)
24	Underline Don't; replace by Doesn't	24.	C
25.	Underline lead; replace by led	25.	F (remove comma (,) after well-planned)

TEST 2

DIRECTIONS: Each sentence contains one error in spelling, diction, or grammar which may be corrected by changing one word. Underline the faulty word and write your correction in the first column opposite the sentence. Then, in the second column, write C if the sentence is correctly punctuated, F if the sentence has faulty punctuation. Make the necessary change in punctuation in the typed sentence.

		CORRECTION	PUNCTUATION
1.	The girls have gone to the meeting, their papers laying about the desk.	_____	_____
2.	There seems to be more people here than I expected, but others are still arriving.	_____	_____
3.	The reason I went home yesterday was because I was ill; I am glad to say, that I am better now.	_____	_____
4.	I saw on the bulletin board where the meeting, scheduled for tomorrow, has been postponed.	_____	_____
5.	Will the new regulations have any affect upon our routine?	_____	_____
6.	Each of today's reports, according to this statement, have been filled in duplicate.	_____	_____
7.	In order to avoid embarassment, we must keep this matter in confidence, between you and me.	_____	_____
8.	Miss X called Ellen and I to her office, because we were to be commended for punctuality.	_____	_____
9.	The officer has occasionally objected to my boss parking his car in front of the office.	_____	_____
10.	The girl dresses well, furthermore, she looks irresistable.	_____	_____
11.	American business, if we may believe the <u>Wall Street Journal</u>, operate on the principal of free competition.	_____	_____

263

2 (#2)

12. The fine climate and the beautiful scenery of New York State, attracts tourists from all over the country.

13. Stenographers, who have trouble with spelling often refer to the dictionary continuously.

14. I was amazed—you know this without me telling you—when I heard the news about you.

15. The records show that most every employee has made suggestions for work improvement.

16. The traffic signal changed, as they past the corner.

17. John said that he did not know if he would accept the invitation or not, but I think he will.

18. I do not know as I can persuade her to see the matter in this light, however, I will try,

19. I thought the weather looked some better this morning; the newspaper, however, says we may expect another hot, humid day.

20. The employment manager eliminated her from consideration because of Ethel being under eighteen.

21. Every one of the girls, who were lucky enough to see the parade, have been giving a glowing account of it,

22. Mary Jones's brother is taller than her, although he is only thirteen years old.

23. When the news report came in everyone in the room was quietly reading to themselves.

24. The thing visitors to New York first notice is the heighth of the buildings.

25. Whom do you expect to see if not Charles and I.

KEY (CORRECT ANSWERS)

CORRECTION

1. Underline laying; replace by lying
2. Underline seems; replace by seem
3. Underline was; replace by is
4. Underline where; replace by that
5. Underline affect; replace by effect
6. Underline have; replace by has
7. Underline embarassment; replace by embarrassment
8. Underline I; replace by me
9. Underline boss; replace by boss's
10. Underline irresistable; replace by irresistible
11. Underline principal; replace by principle
12. Underline attracts; replace by attract
13. Underline continuously; replace by continually
14. Underline me; replace by my
15. Underline most; replace by almost
16. Underline past; replace by passed
17. Underline if; replace by whether
18. Underline as; replace by whether
19. Underline some; replace by somewhat

PUNCTUATION

1. C
2. C
3. F (remove comma (,) after say)
4. F (remove commas (,) after meeting and after tomorrow)
5. C
6. C
7. F (remove comma (,) after confidence)
8. F (remove comma (,) after office)
9. F (remove commas (,) after has and after occasionally)
10. F (remove comma (,) after well; replace by semicolon (;))
11. C
12. F (remove comma) (,) after State)
13. F (place commas (,) after Stenographers and after spelling)
14. C
15. C
16. F (remove comma (,) after changed)
17. C
18. F (remove comma (,) after light; replace by semicolon (;))
19. C

4 (#2)

20. Underline Ethel; replace by Ethel's
21. Underline have; replace by has

22. Underline her; replace by she
23. Underline themselves; replace by himself

24. Underline heighth; replace by height
25. Underline I; replace by me

20. C
21. F (remove commas (,) after girls and after parade)

22. F (remove comma (,) after her she)
23. F (place comma (,) after came in)

24. C
25. F (place question mark (?) after I (me))

———

WRITTEN ENGLISH EXPRESSION EXAMINATION SECTION
TEST 1

DIRECTIONS: The following questions are designed to test your knowledge of grammar, sentence structure, correct usage, and punctuation. In each group there is one sentence that contains no errors. Select the letter of the CORRECT sentence. *PRINT THE LETTER OF THE CORRECT ANSWER IN THE SPACE AT THE RIGHT.*

1.   A. A low ceiling is when the atmospheric conditions make flying inadvisable.
    B. They couldn't tell who the card was from.
    C. No one but you and I are to help him.
    D. What kind of a teacher would you like to be?
    E. To him fall the duties of foster parent.

1.____

2.   A. They couldn't tell whom the cable was from.
    B. We like these better than those kind.
    C. It is a test of you more than I.
    D. The person in charge being him, there can be no change in policy.
    E. Chicago is larger than any city in Illinois.

2.____

3.   A. Do as we do for the celebration.
    B. Do either of you care to join us?
    C. A child's food requirements differ from the adult.
    D. A large family including two uncles and four grandparents live at the hotel.
    E. Due to bad weather, the game was postponed.

3.____

4.   A. If they would have done that they might have succeeded.
    B. Neither the hot days or the humid nights annoy our Southern visitor.
    C. Some people do not gain favor because they are kind of tactless.
    D. No sooner had the turning point come than a new issue arose.
    E. I wish that I was in Florida now.

4.____

5.   A. We haven't hardly enough tine.
    B. Immigration is when people come into a foreign country to live.
    C. After each side gave their version, the affair was over with.
    D. Every one of the cars were tagged by the police.
    E. He either will fail in his attempt or will seek other employment.

5.____

6.   A. They can't seem to see it when I explain the theory.
    B. It is difficult to find the genuine signature between all those submitted.
    C. She can't understand why they don't remember who to give the letter to
    D. Every man and woman in America is interested in his tax bill.
    E. Honor as well as profit are to be gained by these studies.

6.____

7. A. He arrived safe.
    B. I do not have any faith in John running for office.
    C. The musicians began to play tunefully and keeping the proper tempo indicated for the selection.
    D. Mary's maid of honor bought the kind of an outfit suitable for an afternoon wedding.
    E. If you would have studied the problem carefully you would have found the solution more quickly.

8. A. The new plant is to be electric lighted.
    B. The reason the speaker was offended was that the audience was inattentive.
    C. There appears to be conditions that govern his behavior.
    D. Either of the men are influential enough to control the situation.
    E. The gallery with all its pictures were destroyed.

9. A. If you would have listened more carefully, you would have heard your name called.
    B. Did you inquire if your brother were returning soon?
    C. We are likely to have rain before nightfall.
    D. Let's you and I plan next summer's vacation together.
    E. The man whom I thought was my friend deceived me.

10. A. There's a man and his wife waiting for the doctor since early this morning.
    B. The owner of the market with his assistants is applying the most modern principles of merchandise display.
    C. Every one of the players on both of the competing teams were awarded a gold watch.
    D. The records of the trial indicated that, even before attaining manhood, the murderer's parents were both dead.
    E. We had no sooner entered the room when the bell rang.

11. A. Why don't you start the play like I told you?
    B. I didn't find the construction of the second house much different from that of the first one I saw.
    C. "When", inquired the child, "Will we begin celebrating my birthday?"
    D. There isn't nothing left to do but not to see him anymore.
    E. There goes the last piece of cake and the last spoonful of ice cream.

12. A. The child could find neither the shoe or the stocking.
    B. The musicians began to play tunefully and keeping the proper tempo indicated for the selection.
    C. The amount of curious people who turned out for Opening Night was beyond calculation.
    D. I fully expected that the children would be at their desks and to find them ready to begin work,
    E. "Indeed," mused the poll-taker, "the winning candidate is much happier than I."

13.
    A. Just as you said, I find myself gaining weight.
    B. A teacher should leave the capable pupils engage in creative activities.
    C. The teacher spoke continually during the entire lesson, which, of course, was poor procedure.
    D. We saw him steal into the room, pick up the letter, and tear it's contents to shreds.
    E. It is so dark that I can't hardly see.

13.____

14.
    A. The new schedule of working hours and rates was satisfactory to both employees and employer.
    B. Many common people feel keenly about the injustices of Power Politics.
    C. Mr. and Mrs. Burns felt that their grandchild was awfully cute when he waved good-bye.
    D. The tallest of the twins was also the most intelligent,
    E. Please come here and try and help me finish this piece of work.

14.____

15.
    A. My younger brother insists that he is as tall as me.
    B. Suffering from a severe headache all day, one dose of the prescribed medicine relieved me,
    C. "Please let my brothers and I help you with your packages," said Frank to Mrs. Powers.
    D. Every one of the rooms we visited had displays of pupils' work in them.
    E. Do you intend bringing most of the refreshments yourself?

15.____

16.
    A. The telephone linesmen, working steadily at their task during the severe storm, the telephones soon began to ring again.
    B. Meat, as well as fruits and vegetables, is considered essential to a proper diet.
    C. He looked like a real good boxer that night in the ring.
    D. The man has worked steadily for fifteen years before he decided to open his own business.
    E. The winters were hard and dreary, nothing could live without shelter.

16.____

17.
    A. No one can foretell when I will have another opportunity like that one again.
    B. The last group of paintings shown appear really to have captured the most modern techniques,
    C. We searched high and low, both in the attic and cellar, but were unsuccessful in locating mementos.
    D. None of the guests was able to give the rules of the game accurately.
    E. When you go to the library tomorrow, please bring this book to the librarian in the reference room.

17.____

18.
    A. After the debate, every one of the speakers realized that, given another chance, he could have done better.
    B. The reason given by the physician for the patient's trouble was because of his poor eating habits.
    C. The fog was so thick that the driver couldn't hardly see more than ten feet ahead.
    D. I suggest that you present the medal to who you think best.
    E. I don't approve of him going along.

18.____

19. A. A decision made by a man without much deliberation is sometimes no different than a slow one.
    B. By the time Mr. Brown's son will graduate Dental School, he will be twenty-six years of age.
    C. Who did you predict would win the election?
    D. The auctioneer had less stamps to sell this year than last year.
    E. Being that he is occupied, I shall not disturb him.

    19._____

20. A. Having pranced into the arena with little grace and unsteady hoof for the jumps ahead, the driver reined his horse.
    B. Once the dog wagged it's tail, you knew it was a friendly animal.
    C. Like a great many artists, his life was a tragedy.
    D. When asked to choose corn, cabbage, or potatoes, the diner selected the latter.
    E. The record of the winning team was among the most noteworthy of the season.

    20._____

21. A. The maid wasn't so small that she couldn't reach the top window for cleaning.
    B. Many people feel that powdered coffee produces a really good flavor.
    C. Would you mind me trying that coat on for size?
    D. This chair looks much different than the chair we selected in the store.
    E. I wish that he would have talked to me about the lesson before he presented it.

    21._____

22. A. After trying unsuccessfully to land a job in the city, Will located in the country on a farm.
    B. On the last attempt, the pole-vaulter came nearly to getting hurt.
    C. The observance of Armistice Day throughout the world offers an opportunity to reflect on the horrors of war.
    D. Outside of the mistakes in spelling, the child's letter was a very good one.
    E. The annual income of New York is far greater than Florida.

    22._____

23. A. Scissors is always dangerous for a child to handle.
    B. I assure you that I will not yield to pressure to sell my interest.
    C. Ask him if he has recall of the incident which took place at our first meeting.
    D. The manager felt like as not to order his usher-captain to surrender his uniform.
    E. Everyone on the boat said their prayers when the storm grew worse.

    23._____

24. A. The mother of the bride climaxed the occasion by exclaiming, "I want my children should be happy forever."
    B. We read in the papers where the prospects for peace are improving.
    C. "Can I share the cab with you?" was frequently heard during the period of gas rationing.
    D. The man was enamored with his friend"s sister.
    E. Had the police suspected the ruse, they would have taken proper precautions.

    24._____

25. A. The teacher admonished the other students neither to speak to John, nor should they annoy him.
    B. Fortunately we had been told that there was but one service station in that area.
    C. An usher seldom rises above a theatre manager.
    D. The epic, "Gone With the Wind," is supposed to have taken place during the Civil War Era.
    E. Now that she has been graduated she should be encouraged to make her own choice as to the career she is to follow.

    25._____

KEY (CORRECT ANSWERS)

1.	E		11.	B
2.	A		12.	E
3.	A		13.	A
4.	D		14.	A
5.	E		15.	E
6.	D		16.	B
7.	A		17.	D
8.	B		18.	A
9.	C		19.	C
10.	B		20.	E

21. B
22. C
23. B
24. E
25. B

TEST 2

DIRECTIONS: The following questions are designed to test your knowledge of grammar, sentence structure, correct usage, and punctuation. In each group, there is one sentence that contains no errors. Select the letter of the CORRECT sentence. *PRINT THE LETTER OF THE CORRECT ANSWER IN THE SPACE AT THE RIGHT.*

1.
   A. Shall you be at home, let us say, on Sunday at two o'clock?
   B. We see Mr. Lewis take his car out of the garage daily, newly polished always.
   C. We have no place to keep our rubbers, only in the hall closet.
   D. Isn't it true what you told me about the best way to prepare for an examination?
   E. Mathematics is among my favorite subjects.

   1.____

2.
   A. The host thought the guests were of the hungry kinds so he prepared much food.
   B. The museum is often visited by students who are fond of early inventions, and especially patent attorneys.
   C. I rose to nominate the man who most of us felt was the most diligent worker in the group.
   D. The child was sent to the store to purchase a bottle of milk, and brought home fresh rolls, too.
   E. Hidden away in the closet, I found the long-lost purse.

   2.____

3.
   A. The garden tool was sent to be sharpened, and a new handle to be put on.
   B. At the end of her vacation, Joan came home with little money, but which systematic thrift soon overcame.
   C. We people have opportunities to show the rest of the world how real democracy functions.
   D. The guide paddled along, then fell in a reverie which he related the history of the region.
   E. No sooner had the curtain dropped when the audience shouted its approval in chorus.

   3.____

4.
   A. The data you need is to be made available shortly.
   B. The first few strokes of the brush were enough to convince me that Tom could paint much better than me.
   C. We inquired if we could see the owner of the store, after we waited for one hour.
   D. The highly-strung parent was aggravated by the slightest noise that the baby made.
   E. We should have investigated the cause of the noise by bringing the car to a halt.

   4.____

5.
   A. The police, investigating the crime, were successful in discovering only one possibly valuable clue.
   B. Due to an unexpected change in plans, the violin soloist did not perform.
   C. Besides being awarded a Bachelor's degree at college, the scientist has since received many honorary degrees.
   D. The data offered in advance of the recent Presidential election seems to have possessed elements of inaccuracy.
   E. I don't believe your the only one who has been asked to come here.

   5.____

6. A. I don't quite see that I will be able to completely finish the job in time.
    B. By my statement, I infer that you are guilty of the offense as charged.
    C. Wasn't it strange that they wouldn't let no one see the body?
    D. I hope that this is the kind of rolls you requested me to buy.
    E. The storekeeper distributed cigars as bonuses between his many customers.

    6.____

7. A. He said he preferred the climate of Florida to California.
    B. Because of the excessive heat, a great amount of fruit juice was drunk by the guests.
    C. This week's dramatic presentation was neither as lively nor as entertaining as last week.
    D. The fashion expert believed that no one could develop new creations more successfully than him.
    E. A collection of Dicken's works is a "must" for every library.

    7.____

8. A. There was such a large amount of books on the floor that I couldn't find a place for my rocking chair.
    B. Walking up the rickety stairs, the bottle slipped from his hands and smashed.
    C. The reason they granted his request was because he had a good record.
    D. Little Tommy was proud that the teacher always asked him to bring messages to the office.
    E. That kind of orange is grown only in Florida.

    8.____

9. A. The new mayor is a resident of this city for thirty years.
    B. Do you mean to imply that had he not missed that shot he would have won?
    C. Next term I shall be studying French and history.
    D. I read in last night's paper where the sales tax is going to be abolished.
    E. In order to prevent breakage, she placed a sheet of paper between each of the plates when she packed them.

    9.____

10. A. To have children vie against one another is psychologically unsound.
    B. Would anyone else care to discuss his baby?
    C. He was interested and aware of the problem.
    D. I sure would like to discover if he is motivating the lesson properly.
    E. The cloth was first lain on a flat surface; then it was pressed with a hot iron.

    10.____

11. A. She graduated Barnard College twenty-five years ago.
    B. He studied the violin since he was seven.
    C. She is not so diligent a researcher as her classmate.
    D. He discovered that the new data corresponds with the facts disclosed by Werner.
    E. How could he enjoy the television program; the dog was barking and the baby was crying.

    11.____

12. A. You have three alternatives: law, dentistry, or teaching.
    B. If I would have worked harder, I would have accomplished my purpose.
    C. He affected a rapid change of pace and his opponents were outdistanced.
    D. He looked prosperous, although he had been unemployed for a year.
    E. The engine not only furnishes power but light and heat as well.

    12.____

13. A. The children shared one anothers toys and seemed quite happy.
    B. They lay in the sun for many hours, getting tanned.
    C. The reproduction arrived, and had been hung in the living room.
    D. First begin by calling the roll.
    E. Tell me where you hid it; no one shall ever find it.

13.____

14. A. Deliver these things to whomever arrives first.
    B. Everybody but she and me is going to the conference.
    C. If the number of patrons is small, we can serve them.
    D. When each of the contestants find their book, the debate may begin.
    E. Some people, farmers in particular, lament the substitution of butter by margarine.

14.____

15. A. After his illness, he stood in the country three weeks.
    B. If you wish to effect a change, submit your suggestions.
    C. It is silly to leave children play with knives.
    D. Play a trick on her by spilling water down her neck.
    E. There was such a crowd of people at the crossing we couldn't hardly get on the bus.

15.____

16. A. This is a time when all of us must show our faith and devotion to our country.
    B. Either you or I are certain to be elected president of the new club.
    C. The interpellation of the Minister of Finance forced him to explain his policies.
    D. After hoisting the anchor and removing the binnacle, the ship was ready to set sail.
    E. Please bring me a drink of cold water from the refrigerator.

16.____

17. A. Mistakes in English, when due to carelessness or haste, can easily be rectified.
    B. Mr. Jones is one of those persons who will try to keep a promise and usually does.
    C. Being very disturbed by what he had heard, Fred decided to postpone his decision.
    D. There is a telephone at the other end of the corridor which is constantly in use.
    E. In his teaching, he always kept the childrens' interests and needs in mind.

17.____

18. A. The lazy pupil, of course, will tend to write the minimum amount of words acceptable.
    B. His success as a political leader consisted mainly of his ability to utter platitudes in a firm and convincing manner.
    C. To be cognizant of current affairs, a person must not only read newspapers and magazines but also recent books by recognized authorities.
    D. Although we intended to have gone fishing, the sudden outbreak of a storm caused us to change our plans.
    E. It is the colleges that must take the responsibility for encouraging greater flexibility in the high-school curriculum.

18.____

19. A. "I am sorry," he said, "but John's answer was 'No'."
    B. A spirited argument followed between those who favored and opposed Marie's expulsion from the club.
    C. Whether a forward child should be humored or punished often depends upon the circumstances.
    D. Excessive alcoholism is certainly not conducive with efficient performance of one's work.
    E. Stroking his beard thoughtfully, an idea suddenly came to him.

20. A. "Take care, my children," he said sadly, "lest you not be deceived."
    B. Those continuous telephone calls are preventing Betty from completing her homework.
    C. They dug deep into the earth at the spot indicated on the map, but they found nothing.
    D. We petted and cozened the little girl until she finally stopped weeping.
    E. There was, in the mail, an inquiry for a house by a young couple with two or three bedrooms.

21. A. Please fill in the required information on the application form and return same by April 15.
    B. Tom was sitting there idly, watching the clouds scud across the sky.
    C. We started for home so that our parents would not suspect that anything out of the ordinary took place.
    D. The sudden abatement from the storm enabled the ladies to resume their journey.
    E. Each of the twelve members were agreed that the accused man was innocent.

22. A. The number of gifted students not continuing their education beyond secondary school present a nationwide problem.
    B. A man's animadversions against those he considers his enemies are usually reflections of his own inadequacies.
    C. The alembic of his fevered imagination produced some of the greatest romantic poetry of his era.
    D. The first case of smallpox dates back more than 3000 years and has gone unchecked until recently.
    E. He promised to go irregardless of the rain or snow.

23. A. The child picked up several of the coracles, which he had seen glittering in the sand, and brought them to his mother.
    B. He muttered in dejected tones – and no one contradicted him – "We have failed."
    C. A girl whom I believed to be she waved cheerily to me from a passing automobile.
    D. We discovered that she was a former resident of our own neighborhood who eloped some years ago with a milkman.
    E. It looks now like he will not be promoted after all.

24.
 A. Mary is the kind of a person on whom you can depend in any emergency.
 B. I am sure that either applicant can fill the job you offer competently and efficiently.
 C. Although we searched the entire room, the scissors was not to be found.
 D. Being that you are here, we can proceed with the discussion.
 E. In spite of our warning whistle, the huge ship continued to sail athwart our course.

24.____

25.
 A. The salaries earned by college graduates vary as much if not more than those earned by high school graduates.
 B. The apothegms that he felt to be so witty were all too often either trite or platitudinous.
 C. She read the letter carefully, took out one of the pages, and tore it into small pieces.
 D. A young man, who hopes to succeed, must be diligent in his work and alert to his opportunities.
 E. No one should plan a long journey for pleasure in these days.

25.____

KEY (CORRECT ANSWERS)

1. A
2. C
3. C
4. E
5. A

6. D
7. B
8. E
9. B
10. B

11. C
12. D
13. E
14. C
15. B

16. C
17. A
18. E
19. C
20. C

21. B
22. C
23. B
24. E
25. B

WRITTEN ENGLISH EXPRESSION
EXAMINATION SECTION
TEST 1

DIRECTIONS: The following questions are designed to test your knowledge of grammar, sentence structure, correct usage, and punctuation. In each group, there is one sentence that contains an error. Select the letter of the INCORRECT sentence. *PRINT THE LETTER OF THE CORRECT ANSWER IN THE SPACE AT THE RIGHT.*

1. A. All things considered, he did unusually well.
    B. The poor boy takes everything too seriously.
    C. Our club sent two delegates, Ruth and I, to Oswego.
    D. I like him better than her.
    E. His eccentricities continually made good newspaper copy.

    1.____

2. A. If we except Benton, no one in the club foresaw the changes.
    B. The two-year-old rosebushes are loaded with buds—and beetles!
    C. Though the pitcher had been broken by the cat, Teena was furious.
    D. Virginia got the cake recipe off of her grandmother.
    E. Neither one of the twins was able to get a summer vacation.

    2.____

3. A. "What do you wish?" he asked, "may I help you?"
    B. Whose gloves are these?
    C. Has he drink all the orange juice?
    D. It was he who spoke to the manager of the store.
    E. Mary prefers this kind of evening dress.

    3.____

4. A. Charles himself said it before the assembled peers of the realm.
    B. The wind stirred the rose petals laying on the floor.
    C. The storm beat hard on the frozen windowpanes.
    D. Worn out by the days of exposure and storm, the sailor clung pitifully to the puny raft.
    E. The day afterward he thought more kindly of the matter.

    4.____

5. A. Between you and me, I think Henry is wrong.
    B. This is the more interesting of the two books.
    C. This is the most carefully written letter of all.
    D. During the opening course I read not only four plays but also three historical novels.
    E. This assortment of candies, nuts, and fruits are excellent.

    5.____

6. A. According to your report card, you are not so clever as he.
    B. If he had kept his eyes open, he would not have fallen into that trap.
    C. We were certain that the horse had broken it's leg.
    D. The troop of scouts and the leader are headed for the North Woods.
    E. I knew it to be him by the knock at the door.

    6.____

7. A. Being one of the earliest spring flowers, we welcome the crocus.
    B. The cold running water became colder as time sped on.
    C. Those boys need not have stood in line for lunch.
    D. Can you, my friend, donate ten dollars to the cause?
    E. Because it's a borrowed umbrella, return it in the morning.

8. A. If Walter would have planted earlier in the spring, the rosebushes would have survived.
    B. The flowers smell overpoweringly sweet.
    C. There are three *e*'s in dependent.
    D. May I be excused at the end of the test?
    E. Carl has three brothers-in-law.

9. A. We have bought neither the lumber nor the tools for the job.
    B. Jefferson was re-elected despite certain powerful opposition.
    C. The Misses Jackson were invited to the dance.
    D. The letter is neither theirs nor yours.
    E. The retail price for those items are far beyond the wholesale quotations.

10. A. To find peace of mind is to gain treasure beyond price.
    B. Fred is cheerful, carefree; his brother is morose.
    C. Whoever fails to understand the strategic importance of the Arctic fails to understand modern geography.
    D. They came promptly at 8 o'clock on August 7, 2020, without prior notification.
    E. Every one tried their best to guess the answer, but no one succeeded.

11. A. Is this hers or theirs?
    B. Having been recognized, Frank took the floor.
    C. Alex invited Sue; Paul, Marion; and Dan, Helen.
    D. If I were able to do the task, you can be sure that I'd do it.
    E. Stamp collecting, or philately as it is otherwise called is truly an international hobby.

12. A. He has proved himself to be reliable.
    B. The fisherman had arisen before the sun.
    C. By the time the truck arrived, I had put out the blaze.
    D. The doctor with his colleagues were engaged in consultation.
    E. I chose to try out a new method, but in spite of my efforts it failed.

13. A. He has drunk too much iced tea.
    B. I appreciated him doing that job for me.
    C. The royal family fled, but they were retaken.
    D. The secretary and the treasurer were both present on Friday,
    E. Iago protested his honesty, yet he continued to plot against Desdemona.

14. A. The family were all together at Easter.   14._____
    B. It is altogether too fine a day for us to stay indoors.
    C. However much you dislike him, you should treat him fairly.
    D. The judges were already there when the contestants arrived.
    E. The boy's mother reported that he was alright again after the accident.

15. A. Ham and eggs is a substantial breakfast.   15._____
    B. By the end of the week the pond had frozen.
    C. I should appreciate any assistance you could offer me.
    D. Being that tomorrow is Sunday, we expect to close early.
    E. If he were to win the medal, I for one would be disturbed.

16. A. Give the letter to whoever comes for it.   16._____
    B. He feels bad, but his sister is the one who looks sicker.
    C. He had an unbelievable large capacity for hard physical work.
    D. Earth has nothing more beautiful to offer than the autumn colors of this
       section of the country.
    E. Happily we all have hopes that the future will soon bring forth fruits of a
       lasting peace.

17. A. This kind of apples is my favorite.   17._____
    B. Either of the players is capable of performing ably.
    C. Though trying my best to be calm, the choice was not an easy one for me.
    D. The nearest star is not several light years away; it is only 93,000,000 miles
       away.
    E. There were two things I still wished to do—to see the Lincoln Memorial and
       to climb up the Washington Monument.

18. A. It is I who is to blame.   18._____
    B. That dress looks very good on Jane.
    C. People often take my brother to be me.
    D. I could but think she had deceived me.
    E. He himself told us that the story was true,

19. A. They all went but Mabel and me.   19._____
    B. Has he ever swum across the river?
    C. We have a dozen other suggestions besides these.
    D. The Jones's are going to visit their friends in Chicago.
    E. The ideal that Arthur and his knights were in quest of was a better world
       order.

20. A. Would I were able to be there with you!   20._____
    B. Whomever he desires to see should be admitted.
    C. It is not for such as we to follow fashion blindly.
    D. His causing the confusion seemed to affect him not at all.
    E. Please notify all those whom you think should have this information.

21. A. She was not only competent but also friendly in nature.
    B. Not only must we visualize the play we are reading; we must actually hear it.
    C. The firm was not only acquiring a bad reputation but also indulging in illegal practices.
    D. The bank was not only uncooperative but also was indifferent to new business offered them.
    E. I know that a conscious effort was made not only to guard the material but also to keep it from being used.

    21.____

22. A. How old shall you be on your next birthday?
    B. I am sure that he has been here and did what was expected of him.
    C. Near to the bank of the river, stood, secluded and still, the house of the hermit.
    D. Because of its efficacy in treating many ailments, penicillin has become an important addition to the druggist's stock.
    E. ROBINSON CRUSOE, which is a fairy tale to the child, is a work of social philosophy to the mature thinker.

    22.____

23. A. We had no sooner started than it rained.
    B. The fact that the prisoner is a minor will be taken into consideration.
    C. Many parents think more of their older children than of their younger ones.
    D. The boy laid a book, a knife and a fishing line on the table.
    E. John is the tallest of any boy in his class.

    23.____

24. A. Although we have been friend for many years, I must admit that May is most inconsiderate.
    B. He is not able to run, not even to walk.
    C. You will bear this pain as you have so many greater ones.
    D. The harder the work, the more studious she became.
    E. Too many "and's" in a sentence produce an immature style.

    24.____

25. A. It would be preferable to have you submit questions after, not before, the lecture.
    B. Plan your work; then work your plan.
    C. At last John met his brother, who had been waiting two hours for him.
    D. Should one penalize ones self for not trying?
    E. There are other considerations besides this one.

    25.____

KEY (CORRECT ANSWERS)

1. C
2. D
3. A
4. B
5. E

6. C
7. A
8. A
9. E
10. E

11. E
12. D
13. B
14. E
15. D

16. C
17. C
18. A
19. D
20. E

21. D
22. B
23. E
24. C
25. D

TEST 2

DIRECTIONS: The following questions are designed to test your knowledge of grammar, sentence structure, correct usage, and punctuation. In each group, there is one sentence that contains an error. Select the letter of the INCORRECT sentence. *PRINT THE LETTER OF THE CORRECT ANSWER IN THE SPACE AT THE RIGHT.*

1.
   A. "Halt!" cried the sentry, "Who goes there?"
   B. "It is in talk alone," said Robert Louis Stevenson, "that we can learn our period and ourselves."
   C. The world will long remember the "culture" of the Nazis.
   D. When duty says, "You must," the youth replies, "I can."
   E. Who said, "Give me liberty or give me death?"

   1.____

2.
   A. Why are you so quiet, Martha?
   B. Edward Jones, a banker who lives near us, expects to retire very soon.
   C. I picked up the solid-gold chain.
   D. Any boy, who refuses to tell the truth, will be punished.
   E. Yes, honey tastes sweet.

   2.____

3.
   A. I knew it to be him by the style of his clothes.
   B. No one saw him doing it.
   C. Her going away is a loss to the community.
   D. Mary objected to her being there.
   E. Illness prevented him graduating in June.

   3.____

4.
   A. Being tired, I stretched out on a grassy knoll.
   B. While we were rowing on the lake, a sudden squall almost capsized the boat.
   C. Entering the room, a strange mark on the floor attracted my attention.
   D. Mounting the curb, the empty car crossed the sidewalk and came to rest against a building.
   E. Sitting down, they watched him demonstrate his skill.

   4.____

5.
   A. The coming of peace effected a change in her way of life.
   B. Spain is as weak, if not weaker than, she was in 1900.
   C. In regard to that, I am not certain what my attitude will be.
   D. That unfortunate family faces the problem of adjusting itself to a new way of life.
   E. Fred Eastman states in his essay that one of the joys of reading lies in discovering courage.

   5.____

6.
   A. Not one in a thousand readers take the matter seriously.
   B. Let it lie there.
   C. You are not as tall as he.
   D. The people began to realize how much she had done.
   E. He was able partially to accomplish his purpose.

   6.____

7. A. In the case of members who are absent, a special letter will be sent.
    B. The visitors were all ready to see it.
    C. I like Burns's poem "To a Mountain Daisy."
    D. John told William that he was sure he had seen it.
    E. Both men are Yale alumni.

8. A. The audience took their seats promptly.
    B. Each boy and girl must finish his examination this morning.
    C. Every person turned their eyes toward the door.
    D. Everyone has his own opinion.
    E. The club nominated its officers by secret ballot.

9. A. I can do that more easily than you.
    B. This kind of weather is more healthful.
    C. Pick out the really important points.
    D. Because of his aggressive nature, he only plays the hardest games.
    E. He pleaded with me to let him go.

10. A. It is I who am mistaken.
    B. Is it John or Susie who stand at the head of the class?
    C. He is one of those who always do their lessons.
    D. He is a man on whom I can depend in time of trouble.
    E. Had he known who it was, he would have come.

11. A. Somebody has forgotten his umbrella.
    B. Please let Joe and me use the car.
    C. We thought the author to be he.
    D. Whoever they send will be welcome.
    E. They thought the intruders were we.

12. A. If I had known that you were coming, I should have met you.
    B. All the girls but her were at the game.
    C. I expected to have heard the concert before the present time.
    D. Walter would not have said it if he had thought it would make her unhappy.
    E. I have always believed that cork is the best material for insulation.

13. A. Their contributions amounted to the no insignificant sum of ten thousand dollars.
    B. None of them was there.
    C. Ten dollars is the amount I agreed to pay.
    D. Fewer than one hundred persons assembled.
    E. Exactly what many others have done and are doing, Frank did.

14. A. Neither Jane or her sister has arrived.
    B. Either Richard or his brother is going to drive.
    C. Refilling storage batteries is the work of the youngest employee.
    D. Helen has to lie still for two weeks.
    E. Mother lay down for an hour yesterday.

15. A. He is not the man whom you saw entering the house.
    B. He asked why I wouldn't come.
    C. This is the cow whose horns are the longest.
    D. Helen, this is a man I met on the train one day last February.
    E. He greeted every foreign representative which came to the conference.

16. A. You, but not I, are invited.
    B. Guy's technique of service and return is masterly.
    C. Please pass me one of the books that are lying on the table.
    D. Mathematics is my most difficult subject.
    E. Unable to agree on a plan of organization, the class has departed in several directions.

17. A. He spoke to Gertrude and to me of the seriousness of the occasion.
    B. They seem to have decided to invite everyone except you and I.
    C. Your attitude is insulting to me who am your friend.
    D. He wished to know who our representative was.
    E. You may tell whomsoever you wish.

18. A. My favorite studies were Latin and science.
    B. The committee made its report.
    C. To get your work done promptly is better than leaving it until the last minute.
    D. That's what he would do if he were governor.
    E. He said that his chosen colors were red and blue.

19. A. Punish whoever disobeys orders.
    B. Come here, Henry; and sit with me.
    C. Has either of them his notebook?
    D. He talked as if he meant it.
    E. You did well; therefore you should be rewarded.

20. A. Many of us students were called to work.
    B. He shot the albatross with a crossbow.
    C. A house that is set on a hill is conspicuous.
    D. The wooden beams had raised slowly about a foot and then had settled back into place.
    E. Whom do you want to go with you?

21. A. He does not drive as he should.
    B. I can't hardly wait for the holidays.
    C. I like it less well than last week's.
    D. You were troubled by his coming.
    E. I don't know but that you are correct.

22. A. He was angry at both of us, her and me.
    B. When one enters the town, they see big crowds.
    C. They laid the tools on the ground every night.
    D. He is the only one of my friends who has written.
    E. He asked for a raise in wages.

23. A. None came with his excuse.
    B. Walking down the street, a house comes into view.
    C. "Never!" shouted the boy.
    D. Both are masters of their subject.
    E. His advice was to drive slowly.

    23._____

24. A. There is both beef and lamb on the market.
    B. Either beans or beets are enough with potatoes.
    C. Where does your mother buy bananas?
    D. Dinners at the new restaurant are excellent.
    E. Each was rewarded according to his deeds.

    24._____

25. A. Accordingly, we must prepare the food.
    B. The work, moreover, must be done today.
    C. Nevertheless, we must first have dinner.
    D. I always chose the most liveliest of the ponies.
    E. At six o'clock tomorrow the job will have been completed,

    25._____

KEY (CORRECT ANSWERS)

1.	E		11.	C
2.	D		12.	C
3.	E		13.	A
4.	C		14.	A
5.	B		15.	E
6.	A		16.	E
7.	C		17.	B
8.	C		18.	C
9.	D		19.	B
10.	B		20.	D

21.	B
22.	B
23.	B
24.	A
25.	D

TEST 3

DIRECTIONS: In each group of five sentences below, one or more sentences contain an error in usage. Choose the lettered answer which indicates ALL the sentences containing errors in usage. *PRINT THE LETTER OF THE CORRECT ANSWER IN THE SPACE AT THE RIGHT.*

1. I. Shortly after the terms of the contract for the new road transpired, an aroused constituency showed its disapproval by voting the senator out of office.
    II. Neither father nor sons work for a living but spend their days in drinking and gambling at the pub.
    III. Like his Italian predecessor, Boccaccio, whose DECAMERON was used as a model, a company of people of various occupations and stations in life, brought together for a pilgrimage, are called upon to relate stories to help relieve the tedium of their journey,
    IV. Sarah hurried into the kitchen and after a half hour emerged with a nauseous brew which she called coffee.
    V. It was to the major that the people applied for redress and by his armed guards that they were driven away.
    The CORRECT answer is:
    A. I   B. III   C. I, II, III   D. IV, III   E. II, III

1.____

2. I. As we approached the castle, which was illuminated suddenly by the full moon breaking through the clouds, we described a rider coming to meet us.
    II. The reason for his loss of interest in boxing, as far as I can see, was due to the pressure of his work and the distance of the local "Y" from his home.
    III. Accompanied by a handsome member of the British legation, Elsie was about to enter the luxuriously furnished salon to meet the countess.
    IV. In spite of all of John's gifts and attentions, little Rosalie, upon being asked to make a choice, said she liked me better than him.
    V. The scar of the clearing for the power line extended for a hundred miles over the mountains, and the great poles with fifty feet between each carried cable from Niagara to Albany.
    The CORRECT answer is:
    A. II, III   B. I, IV, III   C. I, II, IV, III
    D. II, V   E. III, V

2.____

3. I. The high wind had blown the roofs of several houses; the water supply had been contaminated by the floods; transportation to the business center had ground to a half; but the mayor said there was no reason for alarm!
    II. Because there is a need to soften tragic or painful news, we resort to such euphuisms for the simple "to die" as "to pass away," "to go to a better world," or "to join the great majority."
    III. Hardly had the salient on the western shore of the river been obliterated than one on the eastern bank crossed on a pontoon bridge and in boats of all sorts.
    IV. The distinction between the man who gives in a spirit of charity and him who gives for social recognition is often to be seen in the nature of the gift.
    V. After a few months in office, the new superintendent effected many changes, not all of them for the good, in the administration of the plant.

3.____

The CORRECT answer is:
A. II, III   B. II, III, IV   C. III, IV   D. I, II, V   E. I, II, III

4. I. The defendants published an advertisement and notice giving information, directly and indirectly, stating where, how, and when, and by what means and what purports to be the said book can be purchased.
    II. In common with most Eskimos of her time, she had long spells of silence; and nature, while endowing her with immense sagacity, had thrust on her a compelling reticence.
    III. The entire report was read in less than half an hour to the full committee, giving no time for comment or question, and offered for vote.
    IV. Students going through this course almost always find themselves becoming critical of their own writing.
    V. In his report of 1968, Mr. Jones states that his chief problem is the rapid turnover of personnel which has prevailed to the moment of writing.
    The CORRECT answer is:
    A. I, IV   B. II, III   C. III, IV, V   D. I, IV, V   E. I, III

4.____

5. I. The material was destroyed after it had served our purposes, and after portions of it had been excluded and portions included in our report.
    II. We checked our results very carefully, too carefully perhaps, for we spent several hours on our task.
    III. We should keep constantly in mind the fact that writing has no purpose save to meet the needs of the reader.
    IV. Not even discussed in October, when Lathrop flew in from the Coast, the problem of expense was settled at the June meeting.
    V. Whether our facts were right or not, it was not necessary for you to rebuke him in such a discourteous manner.
    The CORRECT answer is:
    A. I only   B. I, IV   C. II, III   D. V only   E. I, V

5.____

6. I. At first the novel was interesting and liked by members of the class; but later the long reading assignments dampened the pupils' enthusiasm.
    II. Donnie had no love or confidence in his mother, who, when abandoned by her husband, put the boy in an orphanage and seldom went to visit him.
    III. Built during the Civil War, the house has a delicate air, supported as it is by iron columns and rimmed by an iron railing.
    IV. Recently a newspaper editor from the South returned from an eight-week trip through the Caribbean and made a number of recommendations on what we should do to counter the lack of accurate information about the United States.
    V. The need is to be candid about our problems, to be informed on what we are going about them, and to resolve them as expeditiously as possible.
    The CORRECT answer is:
    A. I, II   B. II, III   C. III, IV   D. I, V   E. I, III

6.____

7. I. "Man is flying too fast for a world that is round," he said. "Soon he will catch up with himself in a great rear-end collision."
    II. After the raid on the club, each of the men suspected of accepting racetrack bets, along with the owner of the club, were held for questioning at police headquarters.
    III. It seems to me that at the opening performance of the play the audience were of different opinions about its merit and about its chances for a long run.
    IV. Oak from the forests of Vermont and steel from the mills of Pittsburgh are the material of this magnificent modern structure.
    V. The machine is subjected to severe strains which it must withstand and at the same time work easily and rapidly.
    The CORRECT answer is:
    A. I, II   B. II, III   C. IV, V   D. I, V   E. II, V

8. I. We don't have to worry about cutting down on expenses; money is no object in this venture.
    II. And now, my dear, let you and I tell our guests of the plans we have for the future.
    III. For all his errors of the past, no one can or has said that he did not turn out on this occasion a perfectpiece of work.
    IV. Hercule Poirot, when looking for a suspect in the murder case never thought of its being me.
    V. During the interpellation the minister refused to answer any questions concerning his predecessor's conduct of the war.
    The CORRECT answer is:
    A. I, III   B. I, IV, V   C. II, III, IV   D. III, IV   E. II, III

9. I. John Steinbeck received the Nobel Prize only a few years ago for his work of the thirties, work, which now, according to some critics, has lost its timeliness and which never had timelessness.
    II. Respect is shown the flag by no matter when it is displayed, whether it be in the window of a private home or on the pole of a public building.
    III. When dinner was over we strolled through the garden and exclaimed at the beauty of the red gladioluses, the pride of the Jenkinses' gardener.
    IV. Mrs. Cosgrove's gift of $100,000 to the hospitals is only the latest of the many acts of generosity by which she has before now benefited her fellow men.
    V. Am I repeating your question exactly when I say, "How many of you are willing to join me in my attempt to rid America of the traitors who are threatening its freedom"?
    The CORRECT answer is:
    A. I, II, III, IV   B. II, IV   C. II, III, IV
    D. I, IV, V   E. I, II, IV

10. I. Slashing the original 73 projects to 20 with little loss of subject matter in the consolidated schedule, a stalemate was avoided and the work of the Council speeded up.

II. I was particularly struck by the unselfishness of the American school children, many of whom willingly donating their allowances, because they felt that they should help the refugees.
III. As a result of Henry VIII's defiance of the Church of Rome, the ecclesiastical principle of government was substituted by the national.
IV. I wish you had invited me to the concert, for I should have liked particularly to hear Piatigorsky.
V. John will be in the best possible position for getting the most out of his vacation and of making business contacts in new markets.
The CORRECT answer is:
   A. I, II, III, IV   B. I, II, III, V   C. I, II, III
   D. III, IV, V   E. I, II, III, IV, V

11.
I. They took him to be me despite ever so many differences in our appearance and despite his addiction to loquacity.
II. They may have more money, they may have more possessions, but they are not any happier than us, as we and they all know.
III. Either Betty or Bob must have thought the teacher's remarks were addressed to him.
IV. There was present at today's conference—and at next week's conference the same group is expected—representatives of many foreign countries, including Italy, France, England, and Germany.
V. The most important criteria in judging the performance of a pianist is not virtuosity but maturity of interpretation.
The CORRECT answer is:
   A. I, IV   B. II, III, V   C. II, IV, V   D. I, III   E. I, IV, V

12.
I. Thoroughly exhausted after we had swum for six hours, we lay breathless on the sand and oblivious of anything but our utter fatigue.
II. The jury seems in violent disagreement about the culpability of the defendant; such shouting as we hear from the jury room is most unusual among these halls.
III. The difference between the class' average grades for the first week and those for the eighth week, on alternate forms of the same test, were quite insignificant, indicating, we thought, that instruction had been ineffective.
IV. Each tree and each bush give forth a flaming hue such as we have not seen for many seasons in these climes.
V. We met a man whom we thought we had met many years since, when we lived in South Africa.
The CORRECT answer is:
   A. III, IV, V   B. I, II, V   C. III, IV   D. I, II   E. I, III, IV

13.
I. That old friend, whom I met again last night after a lapse of many a year, stands head and shoulders above any person I have ever known.
II. This is one of the finest pictures which have ever been put on canvas, bringing out rare qualities of tone-color, mature interpretation, and virtuosity in execution.
III. Which of them would you prefer to have working for you, considering the inordinate physical and mental demands of the work, him or his brother?

IV. Throughout Saturday and Sunday, the townsfolk took scarcely any notice of the absence of Jed Gorman, believing him to be off on a drunken spree; but on Monday a body was discovered in the river obviously that of the missing handyman.
V. Things being so pleasant as they were, we could not fathom the reason for John leaving so soon after he had started what we considered an excellent job with unlimited opportunities.

The CORRECT answer is:
A. I, V   B. II, III, V   C. II, III   D. II, IV, V   E. I, IV, V

14.
I. He is unfailingly polite not only to his superiors and his colleagues but even to those who are in subordinate positions, and, in general, to whoever else he thinks is deserving of kindly consideration.
II. Without more ado, he took the books off the radiator, where they had lain quite neglected for several days and where their bindings were beginning to grow loose.
III. We can still include a discussion of the lunchroom situation among the topics, for the agenda have not yet been printed and will not be for another hour or two.
IV. We knew who would be at the party and who would take us home, but we didn't know who to expect to meet us at the station upon our arrival.
V. Despite his protestations, we know that the true reason why he was suffering such obvious anguish and failing to do his work was because of marital trouble.

The CORRECT answer is:
A. I, III, IV   B. II, III, V   C. I, IV, V   D. I, II   E. IV, V

15.
I. A difficult stretch of bad road in addition to a long detour which caused a series of minor motor mishaps, have much delayed our visitor's arrival and have created an awkward situation for us all.
II. To make the campaign effective, there is posted in every building, in full view of all entrants, one notice of the location of the shelter, and a second notice intended to boost morale and win cooperation.
III. One day while leading sheep in the desert and musing upon his people's future, the angel of the Lord appeared to Moses.
IV. Though he plead with the tongue of an angel, he will not ever alter her cold eyes nor trouble her calm fount of speech.
V. Despite continuous and well-advised and well-directed efforts by each of us, neither he nor I am able to improve the situation.

The CORRECT answer is:
A. I, V   B. III, IV, V   C. I, II, III   D. II, III, IV   E. I, III

16.
I. Though business has been brisk of late, this kind of appliances have not sold well at all, despite our continuous and concentrated efforts.
II. The return trip was a desperate one, with time of the essence; and partly blinded by the unexpected snowstorm, the trip was doubly hazardous.
III. I started on my journey by foot through forest and mountain, after a last warning to be careful about snake bites by my parents—a warning I knew I must heed on that dangerous terrain.

IV. That he was losing to a better man, a man who had worked diligently and a man of impeccable virtue, was a consideration of but small import to him.
V. The precarious state of affairs was aggravated by a new hazard, notwithstanding all our cautions to avoid any change in the situation.
The CORRECT answer is:
   A. I, III, V   B. II, IV   C. IV, V   D. I, II, III   E. II, III

17. I. Who's responsible for the feeding of his cat and its young, I'd like to know, we or they? If we, let's feed them.
    II. The books that had lain on the desk for many weeks were laid in the bookcase, where they lay until picked up by the messenger from the second-handbook shop.
    III. You say I merit the award for competence in my duties; but he deserves an award as well as I, for he is as good, without doubt, or even better than I.
    IV. The Joneses' car was more luxurious than, but not necessarily as expensive as, the Browns'.
    V. Slowly they tiptoed into the living room hoping not to be heard, but we were fully aware of it being they.
    The CORRECT answer is:
       A. II, IV   B. I, III, IV   C. I, V   D. I, II, V   E. III, V

18. I. I shall lay the rug in the sun, where it has laid many times before; and I shall lie in the sun, too, as always I have lain at leisure while the rug has been drying.
    II. Though he knew a great deal about printing machinery, he thought, mistakenly, that the new machine could be made to cast type as well as setting it up.
    III. Knowledge in several major fields with sympathy for varied points of view make him an excellent choice for student adviser.
    IV. You will find the girls' equipment in the teachers' lounge where the boy's father left it at Professor Wills's suggestion.
    V. I know that the Burnses have worked for the mill for generations, and that the Smiths have but recently removed from town, but does either of the Norton boys work here?
    The CORRECT answer is:
       A. I, II, III   B. II, III, IV   C. I, IV, V   D. III, V   E. I, II, IV

19. I. I can put two and two together as quick as most mean; but understanding how he, a slow-witted dolt, could achieve so notable a victory over his opponent is one of the things that puzzle and, forevermore, will puzzle me.
    II. Besides my two brothers, my sister, and I, there are a cousin and my father's nephew living at home with us,
    III. He has lived in the Reno for many years; previously he lived in Chicago for a short space, after he had come from Los Angeles.
    IV. Researchers have been baffled for a long time by this statistic, for it contradicts many of their most highly cherished hypotheses.
    V. So intense was the heat near the furnace that all the men at work could not carry on; consequently, production came to a halt,

The CORRECT answer is:
A. I, II, IV   B. III, V   C. I, III, IV   D. I, II, V   E. II, V

20. I. If we can escape from our desks for a brief interval, let's you, Henry, and I put in an appearance at the party.
    II. If you persevere in your ambitions, you are likely to achieve at least a modicum of success; if you malinger, you are liable to court failure.
    III. You may find conditions here congenial, but since I neither like he work nor the salary, it is to no avail for you to attempt to persuade me to stay.
    IV. He has never deigned to take a drink with us, his office colleagues, though we know him now for over fifteen years; and he takes an occasional drink, we know, at home and at his golf club,
    V. Though the results of your investigation are at variance with the hypothesis we advanced, I believe you have interpreted these data in the only ways that have scientific validity.
    The CORRECT answer is:
    A. I, II, IV   B. I, II   C. IV, V   D. II, III, V   E. I, III, IV

21. I. He can't hardly hear anything unless the room is completely quiet.
    II. His attitude seemed perfectly alright to me.
    III. One can't be too careful, can one?
    IV. He is one of those people who believe in the perfectability of man.
    V. His uneasiness is reflected in his unwillingness to compromise on even the smallest point.
    The CORRECT answer is:
    A. II, III, V   B. I, III   C. I, IV, V   D. I, II, IV   E. III, IV

22. I. "Have you found what you were looking for?" he asked.
    II. "I have never," she insisted, "Seen such careless disregard for the rights of others."
    III. "I found this ticket on the step," he said. "Did you lose it?"
    IV. "In one way I'd like to enter the contest," said Anne; "in another way I'm not too eager."
    V. "Did he say, "I'm coming?"
    The CORRECT answer is:
    A. I, III, IV   B. II, V   C. III, V   D. II, IV   E. I, II, IV

23. I. Were I the owner of the dog, I'd keep him muzzled.
    II. In the tennis match Don was paired with Bill; Ed, with Al.
    III. He was given an excellent trade-in allowance on his old car.
    IV. Why doesn't this window raise?
    V. The prow of the vessel had almost completely sank by the time the rescuers arrived on the scene.
    The CORRECT answer is:
    A. I, II, V   B. I, IV, V   C. I, II, III   D. II, V   E. IV, V

24. I. Turning the pages rapidly, his glance fell upon a peculiarly worded advertisement.
    II. Turning the pages rapidly, his eyes noticed a peculiarly worded advertisement.
    III. Turning the pages rapidly, he noticed a peculiarly worded advertisement.
    IV. Turning the pages rapidly made him more attentive to the unusual.
    V. Turning the pages rapidly does not guarantee rapid comprehension.
    The CORRECT answer is:
    A. III, IV, V   B. I, II, IV   C. III, V   D. I, II   E. I, II, III

25. I. They told us how they had suffered.
    II. It is interesting (a) to the student, (b) to the parent, and (c) to the teacher.
    III. There were blue, green and red banners.
    IV. "Will you help", he asked?
    V. In addition to reproducibility, an attitude scale must meet various other requirements characteristic of scale analysis procedures.
    The CORRECT answer is:
    A. I, II   B. II, III   C. I only   D. IV only   E. IV, V

KEY (CORRECT ANSWERS)

1. C
2. D
3. A
4. E
5. A

6. A
7. E
8. A
9. B
10. B

11. C
12. C
13. D
14. E
15. C

16. D
17. C
18. A
19. E
20. F

21. D
22. B
23. E
24. D
25. D

PREPARING WRITTEN MATERIAL
EXAMINATION SECTION
TEST 1

DIRECTIONS: Each question or incomplete statement is followed by several suggested answers or completions. Select the one that BEST answers the question or completes the statement. *PRINT THE LETTER OF THE CORRECT ANSWER IN THE SPACE AT THE RIGHT.*

Questions 1-4.

DIRECTIONS: Questions 1 through 4 each consist of a sentence which may or may not be an example of good English. The underlined parts of each sentence may be correct or incorrect. Examine each sentence, considering grammar, punctuation, spelling, and capitalization. If the English usage in the underlined parts of the sentence given is better than any of the changes in the underlined words suggested in options B, C, or D, choose option A. If the changes in the underlined words suggested in options B, C, or D would make the sentence correct, choose the correct option. Do not choose an option that will change the meaning of the sentence.

1. This <u>Fall</u>, the office will be closed on <u>Columbus Day</u>, <u>October</u> 9th. 1.____
   A. Correct as is
   B. fall...Columbus Day; October
   C. Fall...columbus day, October
   D. fall...Columbus Day – October

2. There <u>weren't no</u> paper in the supply closet. 2.____
   A. Correct as is
   B. weren't any
   C. wasn't any
   D. wasn't no

3. The <u>alphabet, or A to Z sequence are</u> the basis of most filing systems. 3.____
   A. Correct as is
   B. alphabet, or A to Z sequence, is
   C. alphabet, or A to Z sequence, are
   D. alphabet, or A too Z sequence, is

4. The Office Aide checked the <u>register and finding</u> the date of the meeting. 4.____
   A. Correct as is
   B. regaster and finding
   C. register and found
   D. regaster and found

Questions 5-10.

DIRECTIONS: Questions 5 through 10 consist of sentences which contain examples of correct or incorrect English usage. Examine each sentence with reference to grammar, spelling, punctuation, and capitalization. Chooses one of the following options that would be BEST for correct English usage:

A. The sentence is correct
B. There is one mistake
C. There are two mistakes
D. There are three mistakes

5. Mrs. Fitzgerald came to the 59th Precinct to retreive her property which were stolen earlier in the week. 5.____

6. The two officer's responded to the call, only to find that the perpatrator and the victim have left the scene. 6.____

7. Mr. Coleman called the 61st Precinct to report that, upon arriving at his store, he discovered that there was a large hole in the wall and that three boxes of radios were missing. 7.____

8. The Administrative Leiutenant of the 62nd Precinct held a meeting which was attended by all the civilians, assigned to the Precinct. 8.____

9. Three days after the robbery occurred the detective apprahended two suspects and recovered the stolen items. 9.____

10. The Community Affairs Officer of the 64th Precinct is the liaison between the Precinct and the community; he works closely with various community organizations, and elected officials, 10.____

Questions 11-18.

DIRECTIONS: Questions 11 through 18 are to be answered on the basis of the following paragraph, which contains some deliberate errors in spelling and/or grammar and/or punctuation. Each line of the paragraph is preceded by a number. There are 9 lines and 9 numbers.

Line No.	Paragraph Line
1	The protection of life and proporty are, one of
2	the oldest and most important functions of a city.
3	New York City has it's own full-time police Agency.
4	The police Department has the power an it shall
5	be there duty to preserve the Public piece,
6	prevent crime detect and arrest offenders, supress
7	riots, protect the rites of persons and property, etc.
8	The maintainance of sound relations with the community they
9	serve is an important function of law enforcement officers

11. How many errors are contained in line one? 11.____

12. How many errors are contained in line two? 12.____

13. How many errors are contained in line three? 13.____

14. How many errors are contained in line four? 14.____

15. How many errors are contained in line five? 15.____

16. How many errors are contained in line six? 16.____

17. How many errors are contained in line seven? 17.____

18. How many errors are contained in line eight? 18.____

19. In the sentence, *The candidate wants to file his application for preference* 19.____
    before it is too late, the word *before* is used as a(n)
    A. preposition   B. subordinating conjunction
    C. pronoun   D. adverb

20. The one of the following sentences which is grammatically PREFERABLE to 20.____
    the others is:
    A. Our engineers will go over your blueprints so that you may have no problems in construction.
    B. For a long time he had been arguing that we, not he, are to blame for the confusion.
    C. I worked on this automobile for two hours and still cannot find out what is wrong with it.
    D. Accustomed to all kinds of hardships, fatigue seldom bothers veteran policemen.

KEY (CORRECT ANSWERS)

1.	A	11.	C
2.	C	12.	D
3.	B	13.	C
4.	C	14.	B
5.	C	15.	C
6.	D	16.	B
7.	A	17.	A
8.	C	18.	A
9.	C	19.	B
10.	B	20.	A

TEST 2

DIRECTIONS: Each question or incomplete statement is followed by several suggested answers or completions. Select the one that BEST answers the question or completes the statement. *PRINT THE LETTER OF THE CORRECT ANSWER IN THE SPACE AT THE RIGHT.*

1. The plural of
   A. turkey is turkies
   B. cargo is cargoes
   C. bankruptcy is bankruptcys
   D. son-in-law is son-in-laws

   1.____

2. The abbreviation *viz.* means MOST NEARLY
   A. namely
   B. for example
   C. the following
   D. see

   2.____

3. In the sentence, *A man in a light-grey suit waited thirty-five minutes in the ante-room for the all-important document,* the word IMPROPERLY hyphenated is
   A. light-grey
   B. thirty-five
   C. ante-room
   D. all-important

   3.____

4. The MOST accurate of the following sentences is:
   A. The commissioner, as well as his deputy and various bureau heads, were present.
   B. A new organization of employers and employees have been formed.
   C. One or the other of these men have been selected.
   D. The number of pages in the book is enough to discourage a reader.

   4.____

5. The MOST accurate of the following sentences is:
   A. Between you and me, I think he is the better man.
   B. He was believed to be me.
   C. Is it us that you wish to see?
   D. The winners are him and her.

   5.____

Questions 6-13.

DIRECTIONS: The sentences numbered 6 through 13 deal with some phase of police activity. They may be classified most appropriately under one of the following four categories.

   A. Faulty because of incorrect grammar
   B. Faulty because of incorrect punctuation
   C. Faulty because of incorrect use of a word
   D. Correct

Examine each sentence carefully. Then, in the space at the right, print the capital letter preceding the option which is the BEST of the four suggested above. All incorrect sentences contain only one type of error. Consider a sentence correct if it contains none of the types of errors mentioned, even though there may be other correct ways of expressing the same thought.

6. The Department Medal of Honor is awarded to a member of the Police Force   6._____
who distinguishes himself inconspicuously in the line of police duty by the
performance of an act of gallantry.

7. Members of the Detective Division are charged with the prevention of crime,   7._____
the detection and arrest of criminals and the recovery of lost or stolen property,

8. Detectives are selected from the uniformed patrol forces after they have   8._____
indicated by conduct, aptitude and performance that they are qualified for the
more intricate duties of a detective.

9. The patrolman, pursuing his assailant, exchanged shots with the gunman and   9._____
immortally wounded him as he fled into a nearby building.

10. The members of the Traffic Division has to enforce the Vehicle and Traffic Law,   10._____
the Traffic Regulations and ordinances relating to vehicular and pedestrian
traffic.

11. After firing a shot at the gunman, the crowd dispersed from the patrolman's line   11._____
of fire.

12. The efficiency of the Missing Persons Bureau is maintained with a maximum   12._____
of public personnel due to the specialized training given to its members.

13. Records of persons arrested for violations of Vehicle and Traffic Regulations   13._____
are transmitted upon request to precincts, courts and other authorized agencies.

14. Following are two sentences which may or may not be written in correct English: 14._____
   I. Two clients assaulted the officer.
   II. The van is illegally parked.
Which one of the following statements is CORRECT?
   A. Only Sentence I is written in correct English.
   B. Only Sentence II is written in correct English.
   C. Sentences I and II are both written in correct English.
   D. Neither Sentence I nor Sentence II is written in correct English.

15. Following are two sentences which may or may not be written in correct English: 15._____
   I. Security Officer Rollo escorted the visitor to the patrolroom.
   II. Two entry were made in the facility logbook.
Which one of the following statements is CORRECT?
   A. Only Sentence I is written in correct English.
   B. Only Sentence II is written in correct English.
   C. Sentences I and II are both written in correct English.
   D. Neither Sentence I nor Sentence II is written in correct English.

16. Following are two sentences which may or may not be written in correct English:
    I. Officer McElroy putted out a small fire in the wastepaper basket.
    II. Special Officer Janssen told the visitor where he could obtained a pass.
    Which one of the following statements is CORRECT?
    A. Only Sentence I is written in correct English.
    B. Only Sentence II is written in correct English.
    C. Sentences I and II are both written in correct English.
    D. Neither Sentence I nor Sentence II is written in correct English.

16.____

17. Following are two sentences which may or may not be written in correct English:
    I. Security Officer Warren observed a broken window while he was on his post in Hallway C.
    II. The worker reported that two typewriters had been stolen from the office,
    Which one of the following statements is CORRECT?
    A. Only Sentence I is written in correct English.
    B. Only Sentence II is written in correct English.
    C. Sentences I and II are both written in correct English.
    D. Neither Sentence I nor Sentence II is written in correct English,

17.____

18. Following are two sentences which may or may not be written in correct English:
    I. Special Officer Cleveland was attempting to calm an emotionally disturbed visitor.
    II. The visitor did not stop crying and calling for his wife.
    Which one of the following statements is CORRECT?
    A. Only Sentence I is written in correct English.
    B. Only Sentence II is written in correct English.
    C. Sentences I and II are both written in correct English.
    D. Neither Sentence I nor Sentence II is written in correct English.

18.____

19. Following are two sentences that may or may not be written in correct English:
    I. While on patrol, I observes a vagrant loitering near the drug dispensary.
    II. I escorted the vagrant out of the building and off the premises.
    Which one of the following statements is CORRECT?
    A. Only Sentence I is written in correct English.
    B. Only Sentence II is written in correct English.
    C. Sentences I and II are both written in correct English.
    D. Neither Sentence I nor Sentence II is written in correct English.

19.____

20. Following are two sentences which may or may not be written in correct English:
    I. At 4:00 P.M., Sergeant Raymond told me to evacuate the waiting area immediately due to a bomb threat.
    II. Some of the clients did not want to leave the building.
    Which one of the following statements is CORRECT?
    A. Only Sentence I is written in correct English.
    B. Only Sentence II is written in correct English.
    C. Sentences I and II are both written in correct English.
    D. Neither Sentence I nor Sentence II is written in correct English.

20.____

KEY (CORRECT ANSWERS)

1.	B	11.	A
2.	A	12.	C
3.	C	13.	D
4.	D	14.	C
5.	A	15.	A
6.	C	16.	D
7.	B	17.	A
8.	D	18.	A
9.	C	19.	B
10.	A	20.	C

PHILOSOPHY, PRINCIPLES, PRACTICES, AND TECHNICS OF SUPERVISION, ADMINISTRATION, MANAGEMENT, AND ORGANIZATION

TABLE OF CONTENTS

	Page
MEANING OF SUPERVISION	1
THE OLD AND THE NEW SUPERVISION	1
THE EIGHT (8) BASIC PRINCIPLES OF THE NEW SUPERVISION	1
I. Principle of Responsibility	1
II. Principle of Authority	2
III. Principle of Self-Growth	2
IV. Principle of Individual Worth	2
V. Principle of Creative Leadership	2
VI. Principle of Success and Failure	2
VII. Principle of Science	3
VIII. Principle of Cooperation	3
WHAT IS ADMINISTRATION?	3
I. Practices Commonly Classed as "Supervisory"	3
II. Practices Commonly Classed as "Administrative"	3
III. Practices Commonly Classed as Both "Supervisory" and "Administrative"	4
RESPONSIBILITIES OF THE SUPERVISOR	4
COMPETENCIES OF THE SUPERVISOR	4
THE PROFESSIONAL SUPERVISOR-EMPLOYEE RELATIONSHIP	4
MINI-TEXT IN SUPERVISION, ADMINISTRATION, MANAGEMENT, AND ORGANIZATION	5
I. Brief Highlights	5
A. Levels of Management	6
B. What the Supervisor Must Learn	6
C. A Definition of Supervision	6
D. Elements of the Team Concept	6
E. Principles of Organization	6
F. The Four Important Parts of Every Job	7
G. Principles of Delegation	7
H. Principles of Effective Communications	7
I. Principles of Work Improvement	7
J. Areas of Job Improvement	7
K. Seven Key Points in Making Improvements	8

	L.	Corrective Techniques for Job Improvement	8
	M.	A Planning Checklist	8
	N.	Five Characteristics of Good Directions	9
	O.	Types of Directions	9
	P.	Controls	9
	Q.	Orienting the New Employee	9
	R.	Checklist for Orienting New Employees	9
	S.	Principles of Learning	10
	T.	Causes of Poor Performance	10
	U.	Four Major Steps in On-the-Job Instructions	10
	V.	Employees Want Five Things	10
	W.	Some Don'ts in Regard to Praise	11
	X.	How to Gain Your Workers' Confidence	11
	Y.	Sources of Employee Problems	11
	Z.	The Supervisor's Key to Discipline	11
	AA.	Five Important Processes of Management	12
	BB.	When the Supervisor Fails to Plan	12
	CC.	Fourteen General Principles of Management	12
	DD.	Change	12
II.	Brief Topical Summaries		13
	A.	Who/What is the Supervisor?	13
	B.	The Sociology of Work	13
	C.	Principles and Practices of Supervision	14
	D.	Dynamic Leadership	14
	E.	Processes for Solving Problems	15
	F.	Training for Results	15
	G.	Health, Safety, and Accident Prevention	16
	H.	Equal Employment Opportunity	16
	I.	Improving Communications	16
	J.	Self-Development	17
	K.	Teaching and Training	17
		1. The Teaching Process	17
		a. Preparation	17
		b. Presentation	18
		c. Summary	18
		d. Application	18
		e. Evaluation	18
		2. Teaching Methods	18
		a. Lecture	18
		b. Discussion	18
		c. Demonstration	19
		d. Performance	19
		e. Which Method to Use	19

PHILOSOPHY, PRINCIPLES, PRACTICES, AND TECHNICS
OF
SUPERVISION, ADMINISTRATION, MANAGEMENT, AND ORGANIZATION

MEANING OF SUPERVISION

The extension of the democratic philosophy has been accompanied by an extension in the scope of supervision. Modern leaders and supervisors no longer think of supervision in the narrow sense of being confined chiefly to visiting employees, supplying materials, or rating the staff. They regard supervision as being intimately related to all the concerned agencies of society, they speak of the supervisor's function in terms of "growth," rather than the "improvement" of employees.

This modern concept of supervision may be defined as follows: Supervision is leadership and the development of leadership within groups which are cooperatively engaged in inspection, research, training, guidance, and evaluation.

THE OLD AND THE NEW SUPERVISION

TRADITIONAL
1. Inspection
2. Focused on the employee
3. Visitation
4. Random and haphazard
5. Imposed and authoritarian
6. One person usually

MODERN
1. Study and analysis
2. Focused on aims, materials, methods, supervisors, employees, environment
3. Demonstrations, intervisitation, workshops, directed reading, bulletins, etc.
4. Definitely organized and planned (scientific)
5. Cooperative and democratic
6. Many persons involved (creative)

THE EIGHT (8) BASIC PRINCIPLES OF THE NEW SUPERVISION

I. Principle of Responsibility
   Authority to act and responsibility for acting must be joined.
   A. If you give responsibility, give authority.
   B. Define employee duties clearly.
   C. Protect employees from criticism by others.
   D. Recognize the rights as well as obligations of employees.
   E. Achieve the aims of a democratic society insofar as it is possible within the area of your work.
   F. Establish a situation favorable to training and learning.
   G. Accept ultimate responsibility for everything done in your section, unit, office, division, department.
   H. Good administration and good supervision are inseparable.

II. Principle of Authority
The success of the supervisor is measured by the extent to which the power of authority is not used.
   A. Exercise simplicity and informality in supervision
   B. Use the simplest machinery of supervision
   C. If it is good for the organization as a whole, it is probably justified.
   D. Seldom be arbitrary or authoritative.
   E. Do not base your work on the power of position or of personality.
   F. Permit and encourage the free expression of opinions.

III. Principle of Self-Growth
The success of the supervisor is measured by the extent to which, and the speed with which, he is no longer needed.
   A. Base criticism on principles, not on specifics.
   B. Point out higher activities to employees.
   C. Train for self-thinking by employees to meet new situations.
   D. Stimulate initiative, self-reliance, and individual responsibility
   E. Concentrate on stimulating the growth of employees rather than on removing defects.

IV. Principle of Individual Worth
Respect for the individual is a paramount consideration in supervision.
   A. Be human and sympathetic in dealing with employees.
   B. Don't nag about things to be done.
   C. Recognize the individual differences among employees and seek opportunities to permit best expression of each personality.

V. Principle of Creative Leadership
The best supervision is that which is not apparent to the employee.
   A. Stimulate, don't drive employees to creative action.
   B. Emphasize doing good things.
   C. Encourage employees to do what they do best.
   D. Do not be too greatly concerned with details of subject or method.
   E. Do not be concerned exclusively with immediate problems and activities.
   F. Reveal higher activities and make them both desired and maximally possible.
   G. Determine procedures in the light of each situation but see that these are derived from a sound basic philosophy.
   H. Aid, inspire, and lead so as to liberate the creative spirit latent in all good employees.

VI. Principle of Success and Failure
There are no unsuccessful employees, only unsuccessful supervisors who have failed to give proper leadership.
   A. Adapt suggestions to the capacities, attitudes, and prejudices of employees.
   B. Be gradual, be progressive, be persistent.
   C. Help the employee find the general principle; have the employee apply his own problem to the general principle.
   D. Give adequate appreciation for good work and honest effort.
   E. Anticipate employee difficulties and help to prevent them.
   F. Encourage employees to do the desirable things they will do anyway.
   G. Judge your supervision by the results it secures.

VII. Principle of Science
Successful supervision is scientific, objective, and experimental. It is based on facts, not on prejudices.
   A. Be cumulative in results.
   B. Never divorce your suggestions from the goals of training.
   C. Don't be impatient of results.
   D. Keep all matters on a professional, not a personal, level.
   E. Do not be concerned exclusively with immediate problems and activities.
   F. Use objective means of determining achievement and rating where possible.

VIII. Principle of Cooperation
Supervision is a cooperative enterprise between supervisor and employee.
   A. Begin with conditions as they are.
   B. Ask opinions of all involved when formulating policies.
   C. Organization is as good as its weakest link.
   D. Let employees help to determine policies and department programs.
   E. Be approachable and accessible—physically and mentally.
   F. Develop pleasant social relationships.

WHAT IS ADMINISTRATION

Administration is concerned with providing the environment, the material facilities, and the operational procedures that will promote the maximum growth and development of supervisors and employees. (Organization is an aspect and a concomitant of administration.)

There is no sharp line of demarcation between supervision and administration; these functions are intimately interrelated and, often, overlapping. They are complementary activities.

I. Practices Commonly Classed as "Supervisory"
   A. Conducting employees' conferences
   B. Visiting sections, units, offices, divisions, departments
   C. Arranging for demonstrations
   D. Examining plans
   E. Suggesting professional reading
   F. Interpreting bulletins
   G. Recommending in-service training courses
   H. Encouraging experimentation
   I. Appraising employee morale
   J. Providing for intervisitation

II. Practices Commonly Classified as "Administrative"
   A. Management of the office
   B. Arrangement of schedules for extra duties
   C. Assignment of rooms or areas
   D. Distribution of supplies
   E. Keeping records and reports
   F. Care of audio-visual materials
   G. Keeping inventory records
   H. Checking record cards and books

I. Programming special activities
J. Checking on the attendance and punctuality of employees

III. Practices Commonly Classified as Both "Supervisory" and "Administrative"
A. Program construction
B. Testing or evaluating outcomes
C. Personnel accounting
D. Ordering instructional materials

RESPONSIBILITIES OF THE SUPERVISOR

A person employed in a supervisory capacity must constantly be able to improve his own efficiency and ability. He represent the employer to the employees and only continuous self-examination can make him a capable supervisor.

Leadership and training are the supervisor's responsibility. An efficient working unit is one in which the employees work with the supervisor. It is his job to bring out the best in his employees. He must always be relaxed, courteous, and calm in his association with his employees. Their feelings are important, and a harsh attitude does not develop the most efficient employees.

COMPETENCES OF THE SUPERVISOR

I. Complete knowledge of the duties and responsibilities of his position.
II. To be able to organize a job, plan ahead, and carry through.
III. To have self-confidence and initiative.
IV. To be able to handle the unexpected situation and make quick decisions.
V. To be able to properly train subordinates in the positions they are best suited for.
VI. To be able to keep good human relations among his subordinates.
VII. To be able to keep good human relations between his subordinates and himself and to earn their respect and trust.

THE PROFESSIONAL SUPERVISOR-EMPLOYEE RELATIONSHIP

There are two kinds of efficiency: one kind is only apparent and is produced in organizations through the exercise of mere discipline; this is but a simulation of the second, or true, efficiency which springs from spontaneous cooperation. If you are a manager, no matter how great or small your responsibility, it is your job, in the final analysis, to create and develop this involuntary cooperation among the people whom you supervise. For, no matter how powerful a combination of money, machines, and materials a company may have, this is a dead and sterile thing without a team of willing, thinking, and articulate people to guide it.

The following 21 points are presented as indicative of the exemplary basic relationship that should exist between supervisor and employee:

1. Each person wants to be liked and respected by his fellow employee and wants to be treated with consideration and respect by his superior.
2. The most competent employee will make an error. However, in a unit where good relations exist between the supervisor and his employees, tenseness and fear do not exist. Thus, errors are not hidden or covered up, and the efficiency of a unit is not impaired.

3. Subordinates resent rules, regulations, or orders that are unreasonable or unexplained.
4. Subordinates are quick to resent unfairness, harshness, injustices, and favoritism.
5. An employee will accept responsibility if he knows that he will be complimented for a job well done, and not too harshly chastised for failure; that his supervisor will check the cause of the failure, and, if it was the supervisor's fault, he will assume the blame therefore. If it was the employee's fault, his supervisor will explain the correct method or means of handling the responsibility.
6. An employee wants to receive credit for a suggestion he has made, that is used. If a suggestion cannot be used, the employee is entitled to an explanation. The supervisor should not say "no" and close the subject.
7. Fear and worry slow up a worker's ability. Poor working environment can impair his physical and mental health. A good supervisor avoids forceful methods, threats, and arguments to get a job done.
8. A forceful supervisor is able to train his employees individually and as a team, and is able to motivate them in the proper channels.
9. A mature supervisor is able to properly evaluate his subordinates and to keep them happy and satisfied.
10. A sensitive supervisor will never patronize his subordinates.
11. A worthy supervisor will respect his employees' confidences.
12. Definite and clear-cut responsibilities should be assigned to each executive.
13. Responsibility should always be coupled with corresponding authority.
14. No change should be made in the scope or responsibilities of a position without a definite understanding to that effect on the part of all persons concerned.
15. No executive or employee, occupying a single position in the organization, should be subject to definite orders from more than one source.
16. Orders should never be given to subordinates over the head of a responsible executive. Rather than do this, the officer in question should be supplanted.
17. Criticisms of subordinates should, whoever possible, be made privately, and in no case should a subordinate be criticized in the presence of executives or employees of equal or lower rank.
18. No dispute or difference between executives or employees as to authority or responsibilities should be considered too trivial for prompt and careful adjudication.
19. Promotions, wage changes, and disciplinary action should always be approved by the executive immediately superior to the one directly responsible.
20. No executive or employee should ever be required, or expected, to be at the same time an assistant to, and critic of, another.
21. Any executive whose work is subject to regular inspection should, wherever practicable, be given the assistance and facilities necessary to enable him to maintain an independent check of the quality of his work.

MINI-TEXT IN SUPERVISION, ADMINISTRATION, MANAGEMENT, AND ORGANIZATION

I. Brief Highlights

Listed concisely and sequentially are major headings and important data in the field for quick recall and review.

A. Levels of Management
Any organization of some size has several levels of management. In terms of a ladder, the levels are:

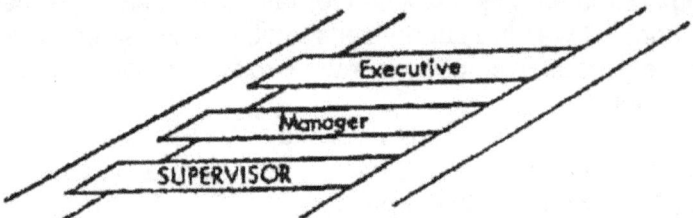

The first level is very important because it is the beginning point of management leadership.

B. What the Supervisor Must Learn
A supervisor must learn to:
1. Deal with people and their differences
2. Get the job done through people
3. Recognize the problems when they exist
4. Overcome obstacles to good performance
5. Evaluate the performance of people
6. Check his own performance in terms of accomplishment

C. A Definition of Supervisor
The term supervisor means any individual having authority, in the interests of the employer, to hire, transfer, suspend, lay-off, recall, promote, discharge, assign, reward, or discipline other employees or responsibility to direct them, or to adjust their grievances, or effectively to recommend such action, if, in connection with the foregoing, exercise of such authority is not of a merely routine or clerical nature but requires the use of independent judgment.

D. Elements of the Team Concept
What is involved in teamwork? The component parts are:
1. Members
2. A leader
3. Goals
4. Plans
5. Cooperation
6. Spirit

E. Principles of Organization
1. A team member must know what his job is.
2. Be sure that the nature and scope of a job are understood.
3. Authority and responsibility should be carefully spelled out.
4. A supervisor should be permitted to make the maximum number of decisions affecting his employees.
5. Employees should report to only one supervisor.
6. A supervisor should direct only as many employees as he can handle effectively.
7. An organization plan should be flexible.

8. Inspection and performance of work should be separate.
9. Organizational problems should receive immediate attention.
10. Assign work in line with ability and experience.

F. The Four Important Parts of Every Job
1. Inherent in every job is the *accountability* for results.
2. A second set of factors in every job is *responsibilities*.
3. Along with duties and responsibilities one must have the *authority* to act within certain limits without obtaining permission to proceed.
4. No job exists in a vacuum. The supervisor is surrounded by key *relationships*.

G. Principles of Delegation
Where work is delegated for the first time, the supervisor should think in terms of these questions:
1. Who is best qualified to do this?
2. Can an employee improve his abilities by doing this?
3. How long should an employee spend on this?
4. Are there any special problems for which he will need guidance?
5. How broad a delegation can I make?

H. Principles of Effective Communications
1. Determine the media.
2. To whom directed?
3. Identification and source authority.
4. Is communication understood?

I. Principles of Work Improvement
1. Most people usually do only the work which is assigned to them.
2. Workers are likely to fit assigned work into the time available to perform it.
3. A good workload usually stimulates output.
4. People usually do their best work when they know that results will be reviewed or inspected.
5. Employees usually feel that someone else is responsible for conditions of work, workplace layout, job methods, type of tools/equipment, and other such factors.
6. Employees are usually defensive about their job security.
7. Employees have natural resistance to change.
8. Employees can support or destroy a supervisor.
9. A supervisor usually earns the respect of his people through his personal example of diligence and efficiency.

J. Areas of Job Improvement
The areas of job improvement are quite numerous, but the most common ones which a supervisor can identify and utilize are:
1. Departmental layout
2. Flow of work
3. Workplace layout
4. Utilization of manpower
5. Work methods
6. Materials handling

7. Utilization
8. Motion economy

K. Seven Key Points in Making Improvements
1. Select the job to be improved
2. Study how it is being done now
3. Question the present method
4. Determine actions to be taken
5. Chart proposed method
6. Get approval and apply
7. Solicit worker participation

L. Corrective Techniques of Job Improvement
Specific Problems
1. Size of workload
2. Inability to meet schedules
3. Strain and fatigue
4. Improper use of men and skills
5. Waste, poor quality, unsafe conditions
6. Bottleneck conditions that hinder output
7. Poor utilization of equipment and machine
8. Efficiency and productivity of labor

General Improvement
1. Departmental layout
2. Flow of work
3. Work plan layout
4. Utilization of manpower
5. Work methods
6. Materials handling
7. Utilization of equipment
8. Motion economy

Corrective Techniques
1. Study with scale model
2. Flow chart study
3. Motion analysis
4. Comparison of units produced to standard allowance
5. Methods analysis
6. Flow chart and equipment study
7. Down time vs. running time
8. Motion analysis

M. A Planning Checklist
1. Objectives
2. Controls
3. Delegations
4. Communications
5. Resources
6. Manpower

7. Equipment
8. Supplies and materials
9. Utilization of time
10. Safety
11. Money
12. Work
13. Timing of improvements

N. Five Characteristics of Good Directions
In order to get results, directions must be:
1. Possible of accomplishment
2. Agreeable with worker interests
3. Related to mission
4. Planned and complete
5. Unmistakably clear

O. Types of Directions
1. Demands or direct orders
2. Requests
3. Suggestion or implication
4. volunteering

P. Controls
A typical listing of the overall areas in which the supervisor should establish controls might be:
1. Manpower
2. Materials
3. Quality of work
4. Quantity of work
5. Time
6. Space
7. Money
8. Methods

Q. Orienting the New Employee
1. Prepare for him
2. Welcome the new employee
3. Orientation for the job
4. Follow-up

R. Checklist for Orienting New Employees   Yes   No
1. Do you appreciate the feelings of new employees when they first report for work? ___ ___
2. Are you aware of the fact that the new employee must make a big adjustment to his job? ___ ___
3. Have you given him good reasons for liking the job and the organization? ___ ___
4. Have you prepared for his first day on the job? ___ ___
5. Did you welcome him cordially and make him feel needed? ___ ___

		Yes	No

6. Did you establish rapport with him so that he feels free to talk and discuss matters with you? ___ ___
7. Did you explain his job to him and his relationship to you? ___ ___
8. Does he know that his work will be evaluated periodically on a basis that is fair and objective? ___ ___
9. Did you introduce him to his fellow workers in such a way that they are likely to accept him? ___ ___
10. Does he know what employee benefits he will receive? ___ ___
11. Does he understand the importance of being on the job and what to do if he must leave his duty station? ___ ___
12. Has he been impressed with the importance of accident prevention and safe practice? ___ ___
13. Does he generally know his way around the department? ___ ___
14. Is he under the guidance of a sponsor who will teach the right way of doing things? ___ ___
15. Do you plan to follow-up so that he will continue to adjust successfully to his job? ___ ___

S. Principles of Learning
   1. Motivation
   2. Demonstration or explanation
   3. Practice

T. Causes of Poor Performance
   1. Improper training for job
   2. Wrong tools
   3. Inadequate directions
   4. Lack of supervisory follow-up
   5. Poor communications
   6. Lack of standards of performance
   7. Wrong work habits
   8. Low morale
   9. Other

U. Four Major Steps in On-The-Job Instruction
   1. Prepare the worker
   2. Present the operation
   3. Tryout performance
   4. Follow-up

V. Employees Want Five Things
   1. Security
   2. Opportunity
   3. Recognition
   4. Inclusion
   5. Expression

W. Some Don'ts in Regard to Praise
1. Don't praise a person for something he hasn't done.
2. Don't praise a person unless you can be sincere.
3. Don't be sparing in praise just because your superior withholds it from you.
4. Don't let too much time elapse between good performance and recognition of it

X. How to Gain Your Workers' Confidence
Methods of developing confidence include such things as:
1. Knowing the interests, habits, hobbies of employees
2. Admitting your own inadequacies
3. Sharing and telling of confidence in others
4. Supporting people when they are in trouble
5. Delegating matters that can be well handled
6. Being frank and straightforward about problems and working conditions
7. Encouraging others to bring their problems to you
8. Taking action on problems which impede worker progress

Y. Sources of Employee Problems
On-the-job causes might be such things as:
1. A feeling that favoritism is exercised in assignments
2. Assignment of overtime
3. An undue amount of supervision
4. Changing methods or systems
5. Stealing of ideas or trade secrets
6. Lack of interest in job
7. Threat of reduction in force
8. Ignorance or lack of communications
9. Poor equipment
10. Lack of knowing how supervisor feels toward employee
11. Shift assignments

Off-the-job problems might have to do with:
1. Health
2. Finances
3. Housing
4. Family

Z. The Supervisor's Key to Discipline
There are several key points about discipline which the supervisor should keep in mind:
1. Job discipline is one of the disciplines of life and is directed by the supervisor.
2. It is more important to correct an employee fault than to fix blame for it.
3. Employee performance is affected by problems both on the job and off.
4. Sudden or abrupt changes in behavior can be indications of important employee problems.
5. Problems should be dealt with as soon as possible after they are identified.
6. The attitude of the supervisor may have more to do with solving problems than the techniques of problem solving.
7. Correction of employee behavior should be resorted to only after the supervisor is sure that training or counseling will not be helpful.

8. Be sure to document your disciplinary actions.
9. Make sure that you are disciplining on the basis of facts rather than personal feelings.
10. Take each disciplinary step in order, being careful not to make snap judgments, or decisions based on impatience.

AA. Five Important Processes of Management
1. Planning
2. Organizing
3. Scheduling
4. Controlling
5. Motivating

BB. When the Supervisor Fails to Plan
1. Supervisor creates impression of not knowing his job
2. May lead to excessive overtime
3. Job runs itself—supervisor lacks control
4. Deadlines and appointments missed
5. Parts of the work go undone
6. Work interrupted by emergencies
7. Sets a bad example
8. Uneven workload creates peaks and valleys
9. Too much time on minor details at expense of more important tasks

CC. Fourteen General Principles of Management
1. Division of work
2. Authority and responsibility
3. Discipline
4. Unity of command
5. Unity of direction
6. Subordination of individual interest to general interest
7. Remuneration of personnel
8. Centralization
9. Scalar chain
10. Order
11. Equity
12. Stability of tenure of personnel
13. Initiative
14. Esprit de corps

DD. Change

Bringing about change is perhaps attempted more often, and yet less well understood, than anything else the supervisor does. How do people generally react to change? (People tend to resist change that is imposed upon them by other individuals or circumstances.

Change is characteristic of every situation. It is a part of every real endeavor where the efforts of people are concerned.

1. Why do people resist change?
   People may resist change because of:
   a. Fear of the unknown
   b. Implied criticism
   c. Unpleasant experiences in the past
   d. Fear of loss of status
   e. Threat to the ego
   f. Fear of loss of economic stability

2. How can we best overcome the resistance to change?
   In initiating change, take these steps:
   a. Get ready to sell
   b. Identify sources of help
   c. Anticipate objections
   d. Sell benefits
   e. Listen in depth
   f. Follow up

II. Brief Topical Summaries

   A. Who/What is the Supervisor?
      1. The supervisor is often called the "highest level employee and the lowest level manager."
      2. A supervisor is a member of both management and the work group. He acts as a bridge between the two.
      3. Most problems in supervision are in the area of human relations, or people problems.
      4. Employees expect: Respect, opportunity to learn and to advance, and a sense of belonging, and so forth.
      5. Supervisors are responsible for directing people and organizing work. Planning is of paramount importance.
      6. A position description is a set of duties and responsibilities inherent to a given position.
      7. It is important to keep the position description up-to-date and to provide each employee with his own copy.

   B. The Sociology of Work
      1. People are alike in many ways; however, each individual is unique.
      2. The supervisor is challenged in getting to know employee differences. Acquiring skills in evaluating individuals is an asset.
      3. Maintaining meaningful working relationships in the organization is of great importance.
      4. The supervisor has an obligation to help individuals to develop to their fullest potential.
      5. Job rotation on a planned basis helps to build versatility and to maintain interest and enthusiasm in work groups.
      6. Cross training (job rotation) provides backup skills.

7. The supervisor can help reduce tension by maintaining a sense of humor, providing guidance to employees, and by making reasonable and timely decisions. Employees respond favorably to working under reasonably predictable circumstances.
8. Change is characteristic of all managerial behavior. The supervisor must adjust to changes in procedures, new methods, technological changes, and to a number of new and sometimes challenging situations.
9. To overcome the natural tendency for people to resist change, the supervisor should become more skillful in initiating change.

C. Principles and Practices of Supervision
1. Employees should be required to answer to only one superior.
2. A supervisor can effectively direct only a limited number of employees, depending upon the complexity, variety, and proximity of the jobs involved.
3. The organizational chart presents the organization in graphic form. It reflects lines of authority and responsibility as well as interrelationships of units within the organization.
4. Distribution of work can be improved through an analysis using the "Work Distribution Chart."
5. The "Work Distribution Chart" reflects the division of work within a unit in understandable form.
6. When related tasks are given to an employee, he has a better chance of increasing his skills through training.
7. The individual who is given the responsibility for tasks must also be given the appropriate authority to insure adequate results.
8. The supervisor should delegate repetitive, routine work. Preparation of recurring reports, maintaining leave and attendance records are some examples.
9. Good discipline is essential to good task performance. Discipline is reflected in the actions of employees on the job in the absence of supervision.
10. Disciplinary action may have to be taken when the positive aspects of discipline have failed. Reprimand, warning, and suspension are examples of disciplinary action.
11. If a situation calls for a reprimand, be sure it is deserved and remember it is to be done in private.

D. Dynamic Leadership
1. A style is a personal method or manner of exerting influence.
2. Authoritarian leaders often see themselves as the source of power and authority.
3. The democratic leader often perceives the group as the source of authority and power.
4. Supervisors tend to do better when using the pattern of leadership that is most natural for them.
5. Social scientists suggest that the effective supervisor use the leadership style that best fits the problem or circumstances involved.
6. All four styles—telling, selling, consulting, joining—have their place. Using one does not preclude using the other at another time.

7. The theory X point of view assumes that the average person dislikes work, will avoid it whenever possible, and must be coerced to achieve organizational objectives.
8. The theory Y point of view assumes that the average person considers work to be a natural as play, and, when the individual is committed, he requires little supervision or direction to accomplish desired objectives.
9. The leader's basic assumptions concerning human behavior and human nature affect his actions, decisions, and other managerial practices.
10. Dissatisfaction among employees is often present, but difficult to isolate. The supervisor should seek to weaken dissatisfaction by keeping promises, being sincere and considerate, keeping employees informed, and so forth.
11. Constructive suggestions should be encouraged during the natural progress of the work.

E. Processes for Solving Problems
1. People find their daily tasks more meaningful and satisfying when they can improve them.
2. The causes of problems, or the key factors, are often hidden in the background. Ability to solve problems often involves the ability to isolate them from their backgrounds. There is some substance to the cliché that some persons "can't see the forest for the trees."
3. New procedures are often developed from old ones. Problems should be broken down into manageable parts. New ideas can be adapted from old one.
4. People think differently in problem-solving situations. Using a logical, patterned approach is often useful. One approach found to be useful includes these steps:
   a. Define the problem
   b. Establish objectives
   c. Get the facts
   d. Weigh and decide
   e. Take action
   f. Evaluate action

F. Training for Results
1. Participants respond best when they feel training is important to them.
2. The supervisor has responsibility for the training and development of those who report to him.
3. When training is delegated to others, great care must be exercised to insure the trainer has knowledge, aptitude, and interest for his work as a trainer.
4. Training (learning) of some type goes on continually. The most successful supervisor makes certain the learning contributes in a productive manner to operational goals.
5. New employees are particularly susceptible to training. Older employees facing new job situations require specific training, as well as having need for development and growth opportunities.
6. Training needs require continuous monitoring.
7. The training officer of an agency is a professional with a responsibility to assist supervisors in solving training problems.

8. Many of the self-development steps important to the supervisor's own growth are equally important to the development of peers and subordinates. Knowledge of these is important when the supervisor consults with others on development and growth opportunities.

G. Health, Safety, and Accident Prevention
 1. Management-minded supervisors take appropriate measures to assist employees in maintaining health and in assuring safe practices in the work environment.
 2. Effective safety training and practices help to avoid injury and accidents.
 3. Safety should be a management goal. All infractions of safety which are observed should be corrected without exception.
 4. Employees' safety attitude, training and instruction, provision of safe tools and equipment, supervision, and leadership are considered highly important factors which contribute to safety and which can be influenced directly by supervisors.
 5. When accidents do occur, they should be investigated promptly for very important reasons, including the fact that information which is gained can be used to prevent accidents in the future.

H. Equal Employment Opportunity
 1. The supervisor should endeavor to treat all employees fairly, without regard to religion, race, sex, or national origin.
 2. Groups tend to reflect the attitude of the leader. Prejudice can be detected even in very subtle form. Supervisors must strive to create a feeling of mutual respect and confidence in every employee.
 3. Complete utilization of all human resources is a national goal. Equitable consideration should be accorded women in the work force, minority-group members, the physically and mentally handicapped, and the older employee. The important question is: "Who can do the job?"
 4. Training opportunities, recognition for performance, overtime assignments, promotional opportunities, and all other personnel actions are to be handled on an equitable basis.

I. Improving Communications
 1. Communications is achieving understanding between the sender and the receiver of a message. It also means sharing information—the creation of understanding.
 2. Communication is basic to all human activity. Words are means of conveying meanings; however, real meanings are in people.
 3. There are very practical differences in the effectiveness of one-way, impersonal, and two-way communications. Words spoken face-to-face are better understood. Telephone conversations are effective, but lack the rapport of person-to-person exchanges. The whole person communicates.
 4. Cooperation and communication in an organization go hand in hand. When there is a mutual respect between people, spelling out rules and procedures for communicating is unnecessary.
 5. There are several barriers to effective communications. These include failure to listen with respect and understanding, lack of skill in feedback, and misinterpreting the meanings of words used by the speaker. It is also common

practice to listen to what we want to hear, and tune out things we do not want to hear.
6. Communication is management's chief problem. The supervisor should accept the challenge to communicate more effectively and to improve interagency and intra-agency communications.
7. The supervisor may often plan for and conduct meetings. The planning phase is critical and may determine the success or the failure of a meeting.
8. Speaking before groups usually requires extra effort. Stage fright may never disappear completely, but it can be controlled.

J. Self-Development
1. Every employee is responsible for his own self-development.
2. Toastmaster and toastmistress clubs offer opportunities to improve skills in oral communications.
3. Planning for one's own self-development is of vital importance. Supervisors know their own strengths and limitations better than anyone else.
4. Many opportunities are open to aid the supervisor in his developmental efforts, including job assignments; training opportunities, both governmental and non-governmental—to include universities and professional conferences and seminars.
5. Programmed instruction offers a means of studying at one's own rate.
6. Where difficulties may arise from a supervisor's being away from his work for training, he may participate in televised home study or correspondence courses to meet his self-development needs.

K. Teaching and Training
1. The Teaching Process
Teaching is encouraging and guiding the learning activities of students toward established goals. In most cases this process consists of five steps: preparation, presentation, summarization, evaluation, and application.

   a. Preparation
   Preparation is two-fold in nature; that of the supervisor and the employee. Preparation by the supervisor is absolutely essential to success. He must know what, when, where, how, and whom he will teach. Some of the factors that should be considered are:
   1) The objectives
   2) The materials needed
   3) The methods to be used
   4) Employee participation
   5) Employee interest
   6) Training aids
   7) Evaluation
   8) Summarization

   Employee preparation consists in preparing the employee to receive the material. Probably the most important single factor in the preparation of the employee is arousing and maintaining his interest. He must know the objectives of the training, why he is there, how the material can be used, and its importance to him.

b. Presentation
In presentation, have a carefully designed plan and follow it. The plan should be accurate and complete, yet flexible enough to meet situations as they arise. The method of presentation will be determined by the particular situation and objectives.

c. Summary
A summary should be made at the end of every training unit and program. In addition, there may be internal summaries depending on the nature of the material being taught. The important thing is that the trainee must always be able to understand how each part of the new material relates to the whole.

d. Application
The supervisor must arrange work so the employee will be given a chance to apply new knowledge or skills while the material is still clear in his mind and interest is high. The trainee does not really know whether he has learned the material until he has been given a chance to apply it. If the material is not applied, it loses most of its value.

e. Evaluation
The purpose of all training is to promote learning. To determine whether the training has been a success or failure, the supervisor must evaluate this learning.
In the broadest sense, evaluation includes all the devices, methods, skills, and techniques used by the supervisor to keep himself and the employees informed as to their progress toward the objectives they are pursuing. The extent to which the employee has mastered the knowledge, skills, and abilities, or changed his attitudes, as determined by the program objectives, is the extent to which instruction has succeeded or failed.
Evaluation should not be confined to the end of the lesson, day, or program but should be used continuously. We shall note later the way this relates to the rest of the teaching process.

2. Teaching Methods
A teaching method is a pattern of identifiable student and instructor activity used in presenting training material.
All supervisors are faced with the problem of deciding which method should be used at a given time.

a. Lecture
The lecture is direct oral presentation of material by the supervisor. The present trend is to place less emphasis on the trainer's activity and more on that of the trainee.

b. Discussion
Teaching by discussion or conference involves using questions and other techniques to arouse interest and focus attention upon certain areas, and by doing so creating a learning situation. This can be one of the most

valuable methods because it gives the employees an opportunity to express their ideas and pool their knowledge.

    c. Demonstration
The demonstration is used to teach how something works or how to do something. It can be used to show a principle or what the results of a series of actions will be. A well-staged demonstration is particularly effective because it shows proper methods of performance in a realistic manner.

    d. Performance
Performance is one of the most fundamental of all learning techniques or teaching methods. The trainee may be able to tell how a specific operation should be performed but he cannot be sure he knows how to perform the operation until he has done so.
As with all methods, there are certain advantages and disadvantages to each method.

    e. Which Method to Use
Moreover, there are other methods and techniques of teaching. It is difficult to use any method without other methods entering into it. In any learning situation, a combination of methods is usually more effective than any one method alone.

Finally, evaluation must be integrated into the other aspects of the teaching-learning process.

It must be used in the motivation of the trainees; it must be used to assist in developing understanding during the training; and it must be related to employee application of the results of training.

This is distinctly the role of the supervisor.